The System Reform of the Economic and Monetary Union (2010-2022)

STUDIES IN EUROPEAN INTEGRATION, STATE AND SOCIETY

Edited by Zdzisław Mach and Bożena Gierat-Bieroń

VOLUME 14

Janusz Józef Węc

The System Reform of the Economic and Monetary Union (2010-2022)

Dynamics-Successes-Failures

PETER LANG
Lausanne - Berlin - Bruxelles - Chennai - New York - Oxford

Bibliografische Information der Deutschen Nationalbibliothek
Die Deutsche Nationalbibliothek verzeichnet diese Publikation in der Deutschen Nationalbibliografie; detaillierte bibliografische Daten sind im Internet über http://dnb.d-nb.de.

Library of Congress Cataloging-in-Publication Data
A CIP catalog record for this book has been applied for at the Library of Congress.

This publication was financially supported by the Faculty of International and Political Studies of the Jagiellonian University in Kraków.

This publication has been peer reviewed by
Piotr Stanek, Krakow University of Economics

Translated by Dariusz Sielski

ISSN 2193-2352
ISBN 978-3-631-89619-8 (Print)
E-ISBN 978-3-631-90268-4 (E-PDF)
E-ISBN 978-3-631-90269-1 (E-PUB)
DOI 10.3726/b20858

Published by Peter Lang GmbH, Berlin, Deutschland

info@peterlang.com - www.peterlang.com

This publication has been peer reviewed.

I dedicate this book to my wife Edyta

Contents

List of important abbreviations 11

Introductory remarks 13

Chapter I: The euro area debt crisis in 2010–2018. The origin, dynamics and resolution instruments 21

1. The crisis relevance of the shortcomings of EU primary and secondary law 21
2. Direct causes of the crisis 30
3. The anti-crisis activity of the German and French governments as a cause of the deepening of the crisis 37
4. The European Union's main tools for fighting the crisis 46
    - 4.1. Financial assistance programmes for the indebted economies 46
    - 4.2. Recovery programmes in the Member States experiencing the crisis 49
        - 4.2.1. Greece 49
        - 4.2.2. Ireland 51
        - 4.2.3. Cyprus 53
        - 4.2.4. Spain 54
        - 4.2.5. Portugal 55
        - 4.2.6. Italy 56
    - 4.3. The Eurosystem programmes as tools for boosting economic growth in the euro area 56
5. Taking stock of the implementation of the financial assistance and recovery programmes and of the Eurosystem projects 64
6. The economic consequences of the crisis 67

Chapter II: The first stage of the system reform of the Economic and Monetary Union in 2010–2015 77

1. Strengthening economic and budgetary governance in the Economic and Monetary Union (2010–2012/13) ... 77
   1.1. The European Semester ... 77
   1.2. The Euro Plus Pact ... 81
   1.3. New crisis management tools reinforcing the financial stability of the euro area ... 82
   1.4. From the 'six-pack' to the 'two-pack' ... 92
   1.5. New tools for the supervision of financial markets in the European Union ... 99
   1.6. The Fiscal Compact ... 101
2. Herman Van Rompuy's report approved on 14 December 2012. The system reforms proposed ... 108
3. The implementation of the assumptions of Van Rompuy's report in 2012/13–2015 ... 112
4. The legitimacy of system changes to the Economic and Monetary Union in 2010–2015 ... 125

Chapter III: The second stage of the reform of the Economic and Monetary Union in 2015–2022 ... 141

1. The Five Presidents' Report of 22 June 2015. The system reforms proposed ... 141
   1.1. The Financial Union ... 144
      1.1.1. The Banking Union ... 144
      1.1.2. The Capital Markets Union ... 145
   1.2. The Fiscal Union ... 146
      1.2.1. The system of fiscal councils in the euro area ... 147
      1.2.2. The fiscal stabilisation function ... 147
   1.3. The Economic Union ... 148
      1.3.1. A euro area system of Competitiveness Authorities ... 149
      1.3.2. Improving and strengthening the Macroeconomic Imbalance Procedure ... 149
      1.3.3. Employment and social performance ... 150
      1.3.4. A stronger coordination of economic policies ... 150

1.4. Legitimacy 151
1.4.1. The European Parliament and the national parliaments 151
1.4.2. The Eurogroup 153
1.4.3. Consolidating the external representation of the euro area 153
1.4.4. Integrating intergovernmental solutions into EU law and the harmonisation of national laws 153
1.4.5. A European Fiscal Board and a euro area treasury 154

2. The implementation of the assumptions of the Five Presidents' Report in 2015–2017. The European Council decisions and the legislative initiatives by the European Commission 155

3. The implementation of the assumptions of the Five Presidents' Report in 2017–2022. Divergent views of the European Commission and of the euro area Member States 163
3.1. The initiatives by the European Commission 163
3.1.1. The White Paper of 1 March 2017 163
3.1.2. The Reflection Paper on the deepening of the Economic and Monetary Union of 31 May 2017 165
3.1.3. Jean-Claude Juncker's address of 13 September 2017 170
3.1.4. The legislative package of 6 December 2017 171
3.1.4.1. The European Monetary Fund 176
3.1.4.2. The European Minister of Economy and Finance 179
3.1.4.3. The Stabilisation Function 180
3.2. The euro area Member States' positions towards the proposals from the European Commission 186
3.2.1. France's Initiative for Europe of 26 September 2017 186
3.2.2. The euro area Member States' positions on the proposed establishment of a European Deposit Insurance Scheme 187
3.2.3. The stance of the Euro Summit and of the Eurogroup on the European Commission's 'roadmap' 191

Conclusions 211

List of Tables, Charts and Figures 219

Bibliography 221

1. Documents 221
2. Monographs 238
3. Publications in Scientific Periodicals and Volumes 242
4. Internet Publications 251

Name Index 255

List of important abbreviations

ABSPP	Asset-backed Securities Purchase Programme
AGS	Annual Growth Survey
AMR	Alert Mechanism Report
APP	Asset Purchase Programme
ASGS	Annual Sustainable Growth Survey
BRRD	Bank Recovery and Resolution Directive
CB	Common Backstop
CBPP3	Covered Bond Purchase Programme
CEECs	Central and Eastern Europe Countries
CMDI	Crisis Management and Deposit Insurance
CRD	Capital Requirements Directive
CRR	Capital Requirements Regulation
CSPP	Corporate Sector Purchase Programme
DGSD	Deposit Guarantee Schemes Directive
DIF	Deposit Insurance Fund
EBA	European Banking Authority
ECB	European Central Bank
EDIS	European Deposit Insurance Scheme
EFSF	European Financial Stability Facility
EFSM	European Financial Stabilisation Mechanism
EIB	European Investment Bank
EIOPA	European Insurance and Occupational Pensions Authority
EMF	European Monetary Fund
EMU	Economic and Monetary Union
ERM	Exchange Rate Mechanism
ESFS	European System of Financial Supervision

ESIF	European Structural and Investment Funds
ESM	European Stability Mechanism
ESMA	European Securities and Markets Authority
ESRB	European Systemic Risk Board
EU	European Union
FRG	Federal Republic of Germany
GDP	Gross Domestic Product
ICMs	Interparliamentary Committee Meetings
IMF	International Monetary Fund
MIP	Macroeconomic Imbalance Procedure
NCAs	national supervisory authorities
OECD	Organisation for Economic Co-operation and Development
PASOK	Panelinio Sosialistiko Kinima
PSPP	Public Sector Purchase Programme
QE	Guantitative Easing
RRF	Recovery and Resilience Facility
SCDP	Common Security and Defence Policy
SRB	Single Resolution Board
SRF	Single Resolution Fund
SRM	Single Resolution Mechanism
SRSS	Structural Reform Support Service
SSM	Single Supervisory Mechanism
TEU	Treaty on the European Union
TFEU	Treaty on the Functioning of the European Union
UK	United Kingdom

Introductory remarks

The monograph has two research objectives. The main objective is to present the dynamics of the system reform of the Economic and Monetary Union (EMU) in the period 2010–2022. The other is to take stock of the reform and to highlight its successes and failures. In this context, the monograph puts forward two research hypotheses. The first hypothesis assumes that the shortcomings in EU primary and secondary law regarding the Economic and Monetary Union and the course of the euro area debt crisis were two main reasons for reforming the EMU, whereby the crisis in question actually forced the European Union and the euro area countries to implement the reform. The second hypothesis is based on the assumption that the implementation of the system reform encountered many difficulties and obstacles arising from the negative attitude of the governments of some euro area Member States to the execution of selected projects, but also from the accumulation of various severe crises that the European Union faced during the reform, in particular the euro area debt crisis (2010–2018), the migration crisis (2015–2016 and again from 2022), the pandemic crisis (2020–2022) and the geopolitical crisis following Russia's aggression against Ukraine (2022).

Further, the monograph asks the following six research questions. Firstly, has the euro area debt crisis been fully overcome? Secondly, will the system reform of the EMU system, in particular the planned creation of a Fiscal Union, allow to strengthen the competitiveness of the euro area economies weakened by the crisis (Greece, Italy, Cyprus, Spain and Portugal)? Thirdly, what role was played in the further course of the system reform by Council Regulation (EU) 2020/2094 of 14 December 2020 on debt mutualisation as the basis for the functioning of the European Union Recovery Instrument (Next Generation EU)[1] whose funds were intended for the resolution of the economic and social implications of the pandemic crisis? Fourthly, to what degree have disputes among the Member States of the Economic and Monetary Union about the limits of financial solidarity determined the direction of system changes? Fifthly, what were the main successes of the system reform of the Economic and Monetary Union? Sixthly and lastly, which system changes failed and why?

1 Council Regulation (EU) 2020/2094 of 14 December 2020 establishing a European Union Recovery Instrument to support the recovery in the aftermath of the COVID-19 crisis, Official Journal of the European Union, L 433I, 22.12.2020, pp. 23–27.

The monograph addresses the system reform of the Economic and Monetary Union, including the euro area (also called the 'Eurozone' or 'eurozone') as its component. The reform initiated in 2010 aimed to strengthen the euro area by establishing within the EMU three new structures, previously not provided for in the Treaties: a Financial Union, a Fiscal Union and a genuine Economic Union. According to various authors, the euro area only functioned without structural problems until the outbreak of a major financial and banking crisis in the world[2]. Its consequences in the European Union, or the euro area debt crisis, speeded up efforts to reform the Economic and Monetary Union. Therefore, on the one hand, the title of the monograph is determined by the scope of system changes, not limited to the euro area but covering the whole Economic and Monetary Union. On the other hand, virtually all fundamental source documents of

2 J. Czekaj, Kryzys strefy euro. Przyczyny, skutki, drogi wyjścia [The euro area crisis. The causes, consequences, ways out], 'Zarządzanie Publiczne' 2012, no. 3, pp. 5–26. W.M. Orłowski, Stabilność finansowa Unii Europejskiej: czy potrzebne są kolejne reformy? [The financial stability of the European Union: are further reforms necessary?], 'Studia BAS' 2021, no. 3. M. Rosińska-Bukowska, Kryzys w strefie euro – wybrane aspekty makro- i mikroekonomiczne [The crisis in the euro area – selected macro- and microeconomic aspects], 'Acta Universitatis Lodziensis'. Folia Oeconomica 2012, no. 273, p. 350. J. Frankel, Causes of Eurozone Crises, [in:] The Eurozone Crisis: A Consensus View of the Causes and a Few Possible Solutions, R. Baldwin and F. Giavazzi (eds.), London 2015, pp. 109–120. T. Beck and J.-L. Peydró, Five Years of Crisis (Resolution) – Some Lessons, [in:] Eurozone Crisis, op. cit., pp. 63–71. P. De Grauwe, Design Failures of the Eurozone, [in:] Eurozone Crisis, op. cit., pp. 99–108. T. Kunstein, W. Wessels, Die Europäische Union in der Währungskrise. Eckdaten und Schlüsselentscheidungen, 'Integration' 2011, H. 4, pp. 308–322. M. Pietrzykowski, Polska na drodze do reformowanej strefy euro [Poland on the way towards the euro area under reform], Poznań 2014, pp. 44–58. J. Koleśnik, Europejska unia bankowa – nowy wymiar ryzyka systemowego [The European banking union – a new dimension of systemic risk], 'Problemy Zarządzania' 2013, no. 2, pp. 101–103. A. Jurkowska-Zeidler, Fundamentalne zmiany regulacji i nadzoru jednolitego rynku finansowego Unii Europejskiej w ramach Unii Bankowej [The fundamental changes to the regulations applicable to and supervision of the single financial market of the European Union within the Banking Union], 'Gdańskie Studia Prawnicze' 2015, Vol. XXXIII, pp. 189–192. R. Poliński, Strefa euro. Kryzys i reformy [The euro area. The crisis and reforms], 2017, www.pte.pl/, pp. 7–23 [accessed: 22 December 2019]. Idem, Problemy strefy euro [The euro area issues], Nowy Dwór Mazowiecki-Warszawa 2017, pp. 89–92. Narodowy Bank Polski. Kryzys w strefie euro. Przyczyny, przebieg i perspektywy jego rozwiązania [National Bank of Poland. The crisis in the euro area. The causes, course and prospects for resolving it], Warszawa 2013, pp. 6–27.

the European Union institutions and the EU Member States' governments, responsible for implementing the reform, concerned the Economic and Monetary Union as a whole rather than the euro area only[3].

The time span of the study is defined by two turning points: on the one hand, the year 2010, marking the beginning of the euro area debt crisis and the starting point for reforming the EMU system; on the other hand, the year 2022, as a significant moment of the reform due to making important political decisions for the planned Financial Union (such as abandoning the idea of establishing a European Deposit Insurance Scheme and moving towards strengthening the common crisis management framework for banks and reinforcing national deposit guarantee schemes). The above-mentioned research objectives determine the structure of the monograph. It is composed of three chapters. Chapter I discusses the shortcomings of the European Union's primary and secondary law and the course of the euro area debt crisis as the two main reasons for reforming the Economic and Monetary Union. Chapter II addresses the implementation of the system reform in 2010–2015, including initiatives aimed at strengthening economic and budgetary governance in the Economic and Monetary Union (2010–2012) and – as those measures proved to be insufficient – executing a comprehensive system reform with a view to establishing in the European Union, in addition to the full Monetary Union existing from 1 January 2002, the following three new structures: a Financial Union, a Fiscal Union and a genuine Economic Union (2012–2015). Chapter III analyses the process of comprehensively reforming the Economic and Monetary Union between 2015 and 2022. The period in question witnessed very important orientation decisions, significantly narrowing the scope of previous system reform plans. Due to disputes among the Member States about the limits of financial solidarity, the idea of creating a European Deposit Insurance Scheme was abandoned and the work on developing a stabilisation function for the euro area was discontinued. The pandemic thwarted two draft regulations intended as important components of the legislative package defining the Multiannual Financial Framework for 2021–2027, i.e. a proposal for a regulation establishing the budgetary instrument for convergence and competitiveness (a separate budget line for the euro area) and a draft reform support programme for 2021–2027.

---

3 For instance, the reform of the Economic and Monetary Union was expressly addressed by the various sources referred to in this monograph: the EU's legal acts, intergovernmental agreements of the EMU Member States, policy papers and information documents by the EU institutions.

The sources used in the monograph include the treaties and international agreements, in particular acts of primary law and intergovernmental agreements; Euro Summit documents, such as statements and leaders' agendas; documents by the Council of the European Union and the European Parliament, i.e. the EU's legislative and non-legislative acts; political conclusions and press releases of the Council of the European Union; the European Council documents – decisions, conclusions, reports, press releases and statements; the European Commission documents – legislative proposals, communications, white papers, state of the Union addresses and reflection papers; Eurogroup documents – Eurogroup statements and statements by the Eurogroup President; statistical documents by Eurostat, the Polish Central Statistical Office (GUS), the National Bank of Poland, assistance programmes under the European Financial Stability Facility, the European Financial Stabilisation Mechanism and the European Stability Mechanism; as well as documents from the EU's Legislative Observatory.

The existing studies of the European Union's system conducted in Poland have been significantly enhanced by the following collaborative publications and textbooks edited by Jan Barcz: *Zasady ustrojowe Unii Europejskiej, Warszawa 2010; Ustrój Unii Europejskiej*, Volumes 1 and 2, Warszawa 2009; *Prawo Unii Europejskiej. Zagadnienia systemowe*, Warszawa 2006; *Prawo Unii Europejskiej. Prawo materialne i polityki*, Warszawa 2006; as well as a book published in the *Skrypty Becka* series, edited by Waltraud Hakenberg and Igor B. Nestoruk, *Prawo europejskie*, Warszawa 2012[4]. As regards foreign literature, the contributions worth highlighting include the fundamental works by Walter Frenz, *Handbuch Europarecht*, Bd. 1–6, Berlin – Heidelberg 2012, and by Thomas Oppermann, *Europarecht. Ein Studienbuch*, München 2009[5]. Noteworthy collaborative studies by foreign authors comprise those edited by Armin von Bogdandy and Jürgen Bast, *Principles of European Constitutional Law*, Oxford 2010; by Andreas Marchetti and Claire Demesmay, *Der Vertrag von Lissabon. Analyse und Bewertung*, Baden-Baden 2010; by Koen Lenaerts, Piet Van Nuffel and Robert Bray, *Constitutional Law of the European Union*, London 2009;

---

4 *Zasady ustrojowe Unii Europejskiej [The constitutional principles of the European Union]*, J. Barcz (ed.), Warszawa 2010. Ustrój Unii Europejskiej [The system of the European Union], J. Barcz (ed.), Vol. 1–2, Warszawa 2009. Prawo Unii Europejskiej. Zagadnienia systemowe [European Union law. System issues], J. Barcz (ed.), Warszawa 2006. Prawo Unii Europejskiej. Prawo materialne i polityki [European Union law. Substantive law and policies], J. Barcz (ed.), Warszawa 2006. W. Hakenberg, I. B. Nestoruk, Prawo europejskie [European law], Warszawa 2012.

5 W. Frenz, *Handbuch Europarecht*, Bd. 1–6, Berlin–Heidelberg 2012. T. Oppermann, *Europarecht. Ein Studienbuch,* München 2009.

by Damian Chalmers and Adam Tomkins, *European Union Public Law*, Cambridge 2007; by Andreas Haratsch, Christian Koenig and Matthias Pechstein, *Europarecht*, Tübingen 2006; by Roland Bieber, Astrid Epiney and Marcel Haag, *Die Europäische Union. Europarecht und Politik*, Baden-Baden 2005[6].

The most important studies specifically addressing the system reform of the European Union include, again, monographs by Jan Barcz, for example: *Główne kierunki reformy ustrojowej post-lizbońskiej Unii Europejskiej*, Piaseczno 2015; *Unia Europejska na rozstajach. Traktat z Lizbony. Dynamika i główne kierunki reformy ustrojowej*, Warszawa 2010; and *Traktat z Lizbony. Wybrane aspekty prawne działań implementacyjnych*, Warszawa 2012. For the sake of completeness, it must be noted that this category of scholarly works also comprises the monograph by Janusz Józef Węc entitled *Traktat Lizboński. Polityczne aspekty reformy ustrojowej Unii Europejskiej w latach 2007–2015. Orzecznictwo sądów konstytucyjnych wybranych państw członkowskich UE oraz proces implementacji traktatu lizbońskiego*, Kraków 2016. Other noteworthy foreign studies include the monographs by Vanessa Hellmann, *Der Vertrag von Lissabon 2009. Vom Verfassungsvertrag zur Änderung der bestehenden Verträge – Einführung mit Synopse und Übersichten*, Berlin 2009; by Janusz Józef Węc, *Germany's Position on the System Reform of the European Union in 2002–2016*, Berlin-Bern-Bruxelles-New York-Oxford-Warszawa-Wien 2018; as well as the collaborative works edited by Thomas Christiansen and Christine Reh, *Constitutionalizing the European Union*, Basingstoke 2009; by Jan Wouters, Luc Verhey and Philippe Kiiver, *European Constitutionalism beyond Lisbon*, Antwerp 2009; and by Thomas Eilmansberger, Stefan Griller and Walter Obwexer (Hrsg.), *Rechtsfragen der Implementierung des Vertrages von Lissabon*, Wien – New York 2011[7].

---

6 *Principles of European Constitutional Law*, A. von Bogdandy, J. Bast (eds.), Oxford 2010. A. Marchetti, C. Demesmay, *Der Vertrag von Lissabon. Analyse und Bewertung*, Baden-Baden 2010. K. Lenaerts, P. Van Nuffel, R. Bray, *Constitutional Law of the European Union*, London 2009. D. Chalmers, A. Tomkins, *European Union Public Law*, Cambridge 2007. A. Haratsch, Ch. Koenig, M. Pechstein, *Europarecht*, Tübingen 2006. R. Bieber, A. Epiney, M. Haag, *Die Europäische Union. Europarecht und Politik*, Baden-Baden 2005. It is also worth mentioning the following works: *System ochrony prawnej w Unii Europejskiej [The legal protection system in the European Union]*, A. Wyrozumska (ed.), Warszawa 2010. *50 years of the European treaties: looking back and thinking forward*, M. Dougan, S. Currie (eds.), Oxford 2009. *The European Union: Origins – Structure – Acquis*, W. Góralski, Sz. Kardaś (eds.), Warszawa 2008. *Unia Europejska od Traktatów Rzymskich do Traktatu Lizbońskiego [The European Union from the Treaties of Rome to the Treaty of Lisbon]*, T. Wasilewski (ed.), Toruń 2008.

7 J. Barcz, Główne kierunki reformy ustrojowej post-lizbońskiej Unii Europejskiej [The main directions of the system reform of the post-Lisbon European Union],

In addition to the above-mentioned publications addressing the system of the European Union and the system reform of the EU, there are rather numerous studies, especially contributory works, on the euro area debt crisis or the system of the Economic and Monetary Union. In this context, it is worth emphasising two foreign collaborative works, edited by Richard Baldwin and Francesco Giavazzi, *The Eurozone Crisis: A Consensus View of the Causes and a Few Possible Solutions*, London 2015; and by Thorsten Beck, *Banking Union for Europe. Risks and Challenges*, London 2012; as well as the contributory study by Agnès Bénassy-Quéré and Xavier Ragot, *Which Fiscal Union for the euro area?*, 'Bruegel Policy Contribution', February 2016[8]. The Polish literature encompasses particularly valuable monographs by Artur Nowak-Far on the Economic and Monetary Union, *Finanse Unii Europejskiej: aspekty instytucjonalne i prawne*, Warszawa 2010, *Pakt Stabilności i Wzrostu. Funkcje, działanie i przyszłość*, Warszawa 2007, *Unia Gospodarcza i Walutowa w Europie*, Warszawa 2001[9], as well as a critical analysis of the functioning of

Piaseczno 2015. Idem, *Unia Europejska na rozstajach. Traktat z Lizbony. Dynamika i główne kierunki reformy ustrojowej [The European Union at a crossroads. The Treaty of Lisbon. The dynamics and main directions of the system reform]*, Warszawa 2010. V. Hellmann, Der Vertrag von Lissabon 2009. Vom Verfassungsvertrag zur Änderung der bestehenden Verträge – Einführung mit Synopse und Übersichten, Berlin 2009. Th. Christiansen, Ch. Reh, Constitutionalizing the European Union, Basingstoke 2009. J. Wouters, L. Verhey, P. Kiiver, *European Constitutionalism beyond Lisbon*, Antwerp 2009. Traktat z Lizbony. Główne reformy ustrojowe Unii Europejskiej [The Treaty of Lisbon. The main system reforms of the European Union], J. Barcz (ed.), Warszawa 2008. J.J. Węc, Traktat Lizboński. Polityczne aspekty reformy ustrojowej Unii Europejskiej w latach 2007–2015. Orzecznictwo sądów konstytucyjnych wybranych państw członkowskich UE oraz proces implementacji traktatu lizbońskiego [The political aspects of the system reform of the European Union in 2007–2015. The case-law of the constitutional courts of selected Member States of the EU and the implementation of the Lisbon Treaty], Kraków 2016. T. Eilmansberger, S. Griller, W. Obwexer (Hrsg.), Rechtsfragen der Implementierung des Vertrages von Lissabon, Wien – New York 2011. J.J. Węc, Germany's Position on the System Reform of the European Union in 2002–2016, Berlin–Bern–Bruxelles–New York–Oxford–Warszawa–Wien 2018.

8 The Eurozone Crisis: A Consensus View of the Causes and a Few Possible Solutions, R. Baldwin, F. Giavazzi (eds.), London 2015. Banking Union for Europe. Risks and Challenges, T. Beck (ed.), London 2012. A. Bénassy-Quéré, X. Ragot, Which Fiscal Union for the euro area?, 'Bruegel Policy Contribution', February 2016.

9 A. Nowak-Far, Finanse Unii Europejskiej: aspekty instytucjonalne i prawne [The European Union's finance: the institutional and legal aspects], Warszawa 2010. Idem, Pakt Stabilności i Wzrostu. Funkcje, działanie i przyszłość [The Stability and Growth Pact.

the EMU and the euro area by Stefan Kawalec and Ernest Pytlarczyk, *Paradoks euro. Jak wyjść z pułapki wspólnej waluty?* Warszawa 2016[10]. The following monographs are worthy of notice as well: Krystyna Gawlikowska-Hueckel and Anna Zielińska-Głębocka, *Integracja europejska. Od jednolitego rynku do unii walutowej*, Warszawa 2007; Leokadia Oręziak, *Euro. Nowy pieniądz*, Warszawa 2004; Witold M. Orłowski, *Optymalna ścieżka do euro*, Warszawa 2004[11]. Among contributory works, further studies by Artur Nowak-Far deserve to be mentioned: *Narzędzia Unii Europejskiej w przeciwdziałaniu skutkom światowego kryzysu finansowego*, [in:] *Unia Europejska wobec kryzysu ekonomicznego*, J. Osiński (ed.), Warszawa 2009; and *Funkcjonowanie rynku wewnętrznego Unii Europejskiej – wyzwania dla Polski*, [in:] *Polska w Unii Europejskiej. Nowe wyzwania*, J. Barcz, S. Domaradzki, R. Kuligowski, M. Szewczyk, E. Szklarczyk-Amati (eds.), Warszawa 2018[12]. The above-mentioned publications are predominantly legal or economic analyses. However, in the existing body of scholarly works, whether by Polish or foreign authors, there was no monograph showing the system reform of the Economic and Monetary Union from the point of view of individual Member States' governments and of the Economic Union's institutions and bodies. Such expectations are met by this monograph.

The functions, functioning and future], Warszawa 2007. Idem, Unia Gospodarcza i Walutowa w Europie [The Economic and Monetary Union in Europe], Warszawa 2001.

10 S. Kawalec, E. Pytlarczyk, Paradoks euro. Jak wyjść z pułapki wspólnej waluty [The paradox of the euro. How to escape the trap of the common currency], Warszawa 2016.

11 K. Gawlikowska-Hueckel, A. Zielińska-Głębocka, Integracja europejska. Od jednolitego rynku do unii walutowej [European integration. From the single market to Monetary Union], Warszawa 2007. L. Oręziak, Euro. Nowy pieniądz [The new currency], Warszawa 2004. W. M. Orłowski, Optymalna ścieżka do euro [The optimal path towards the euro], Warszawa 2004.

12 Cf. also A. Nowak-Far, Funkcjonowanie rynku wewnętrznego Unii Europejskiej – wyzwania dla Polski [The functioning of the internal market of the European Union – the challenges facing Poland], [in:] Polska w Unii Europejskiej. Nowe wyzwania [Poland in the European Union. New challenges], J. Barcz, S. Domaradzki, R. Kuligowski, M. Szewczyk, E. Szklarczyk-Amati (eds.), Warszawa 2018, pp. 115–125. Idem, Narzędzia Unii Europejskiej w przeciwdziałaniu skutkom światowego kryzysu finansowego [The European Union's tools for mitigating the consequences of the global financial crisis], [in:] Unia Europejska wobec kryzysu ekonomicznego [The European Union in the face of the economic crisis], J. Osiński (ed.), Warszawa 2009.

Chapter I: The euro area debt crisis in 2010–2018. The origin, dynamics and resolution instruments

1. The crisis relevance of the shortcomings of EU primary and secondary law

On 30 September 1991 in Brussels, as the Foreign Ministers of the 12 Member States of the European Communities, participating in the intergovernmental conferences held in 1990–1991 and aimed at the preparation and development of the Maastricht Treaty, rejected, by a majority of seven to five votes, the Dutch proposal for establishing a uniform international organisation, called a Political Union, the decision appeared to be extremely relevant to the further course of European integration. Those voting against the proposal included the delegations of France, Germany, Luxembourg, the United Kingdom, Denmark, Greece and Portugal. The Foreign Ministers of the Netherlands, Belgium, Italy, Spain and Ireland voted in favour of the Political Union proposal[13]. Ultimately, it was

---

13 The factor to 'tip the balance' during the intergovernmental conference was the position taken by the government of the reunified German state, having initially supported the creation of a Political Union and then changing its mind. Consenting to the establishment of the European Union, it withdrew from the idea of *iunctim*, i.e. simultaneously establishing a Political Union and an Economic and Monetary Union as a 'prototype' of a subsequent 'European federal state', advocated in 1989–1991, cf. J.J. Węc, Spór o kształt ustrojowy Wspólnot Europejskich i Unii Europejskiej w latach 1950–2010. Między ideą ponadnarodowości a współpracą międzyrządową. Analiza politologiczna [The dispute over the constitutional status of the European Communities and the European Union in 1950–2010. Between the idea of supranationality and international cooperation], Kraków 2012, pp. 201–208. The German government decided to shift away from the idea of a Political Union and towards that of a European Union not only due to strong objections from half of the Member States; in addition, following German unification in 1990, one of the main axioms of the FRG's European policy, pursued from the time of Chancellor Konrad Adenauer and based on the assumption that obtaining other Member States' agreement to unification would be much easier within a European federation, became obsolete, cf. J.J. Węc, CDU/CSU wobec polityki niemieckiej Republiki Federalnej Niemiec [CDU/CSU and the policies pursued by the Federal Republic of Germany], Kraków 2000, pp. 89–94.

decided to establish, in place of the planned Political Union, a European Union as a non-uniform international organisation composed of three pillars and two legal orders, whereby the first pillar would be governed by Community law and the second and third pillars would be based on public international law. The European Union was intended as a *sui generis* international organisation, devoid of legal personality, characterised by significant incoherence. The decision made by the above-mentioned seven Member States also implied that the Economic and Monetary Union would have no mechanism to protect it against tensions between monetary and fiscal policies, thus no guarantee of stable functioning.

Signed on 7 February 1992 by the Foreign and Finance Ministers of the 12 Member States of the European Communities, the Treaty of Maastricht did stipulate the establishment of an independent European Central Bank, but the supervision of the financial sector was left to the central banks of the Member States of the Monetary Union, whereas the surveillance of fiscal policies – to the governments of those States. No common resolution mechanisms were agreed for credit institutions, including banks. The signatories to the Treaty focused on the issues of budget deficit and public debt, without establishing any system for monitoring private sector finance (e.g. the stability of the banking sector and debt), or fiscal policy control tools. Although the convergence criteria introduced under the Treaty (ex Article 109j(1) TEC – Article 140(1) TFEU) could be basically effective when used at the stage of qualification for Economic and Monetary Union[14], they were insufficient for monitoring a Member State's fiscal

---

14 The Maastricht Treaty set out the following convergence criteria: (1) price stability, determined on the basis of an inflation rate not exceeding by more than 1.5 percentage points that of the three best performing Member States in terms of price stability; (2) the sustainability of the government financial position, apparent from having achieved an annual government deficit and government debt not exceeding 3% of GDP and 60% of GDP respectively; (3) participation in the Exchange Rate Mechanism (ERM) for at least two years and the observance of the normal fluctuation margins provided for by the European Monetary System, without devaluing against the currency of any other Member State; (4) having achieved an average long-term interest rate not exceeding by more than 2 percentage points that of the three best performing Member States in terms of price stability. For more on the subject, cf. J.J. Węc, Polityczno-prawne aspekty procesu konstytuowania oraz reformy Unii Gospodarczej i Walutowej. Od planu Wernera do traktatu konstytucyjnego (1970–2004) [The political and legal aspects of the proces of constituting and reforming the Economic and Monetary Union. From the Werner Plan to the Constitutional Treaty], 'Politeja' 2009, no. 12, p. 195. Cf. also: Globalizacja i regionalizacja w gospodarce światowej [Globalisation and regionalisation

policy after that Member State's joining the EMU; in particular, there was no system of automatic and effective penalties for failure to comply with the fiscal policy rules[15].

The Treaty provided for no common fiscal or economic policies, but it did establish certain instruments limiting the competences of the Member States in that regard, i.e. a procedure for avoiding excessive deficits (ex Article 104c(1) to (14) TEC – Article 126(1) to (14) TFEU) and a procedure for multilateral surveillance (ex Article 103(1) to (5) TEC – Article 121(1) to (6) TFEU). Whereas the excessive deficit procedure was intended for monitoring fiscal policies, the multilateral surveillance procedure aimed to ensure the coordination and harmonisation of the economic policies of the Member States[16]. In the excessive deficit procedure, new powers were conferred on the European Commission, i.e. control of the Member States' general government deficits and public debt levels. The multilateral surveillance procedure engaged more entities and had a broader scope, but the relevant powers of the European Commission were weaker than in the excessive deficit procedure[17]. In contrast, the Treaty conferred significant new powers in the multilateral surveillance procedure on the Council of the European Union. The institution was responsible for ensuring closer coordination

in the world economy], R. Orłowska, K. Żołądkiewicz (eds.), Warszawa 2012, pp. 211–216.

15 For more on the subject, cf. W.M. Orłowski, Stabilność finansowa Unii Europejskiej [The financial stability of the European Union], op. cit., pp. 9–10. M. Koczor, Proces wzmacniania Unii Gospodarczej i Walutowej w kontekście kryzysu w strefie euro [The process of strengthening the Economic and Monetary Union in the context of the euro area crisis], 'Politeja' 2015, no. 5, p. 233. L. Oręziak, Finanse publiczne w krajach strefy euro – skuteczność mechanizmów dyscyplinujących politykę budżetową [Public finances of the euro area countries – the effectiveness of mechanisms aimed to discipline fiscal policy], [in:] Euro – ekonomia i polityka [The euro – economics and politics], D. Rosati (ed.), Warszawa 2009, pp. 48–49.

16 Convergence in the European Union is the process of reducing economic, institutional or structural differences between the Member States. Economic convergence means narrowing development gaps, institutional convergence is measured by the economic freedom index and the regulatory system assessment index, whereas structural convergence is the process of economies becoming more similar in terms of production structure and developing the same sectors in industry and business services, cf. M. Klucznik, K. Marczewski, An EU of convergence or divisions? The European economy 30 years after the Treaty of Maastricht, Polish Economic Institute, Warsaw 2022, pp. 10–28.

17 For more on the subject, cf. W. Nicoll, T.C. Salmon, Zrozumieć Unię Europejską, translated by S. Barkowski, Warszawa 2002, pp. 329–330.

of economic policies and sustained convergence of the economic performances of the Member States. Therefore, the Council of the European Union, based on reports submitted by the European Commission, monitored economic developments in each of the Member States and in the EU as well as the consistency of economic policies with the broad guidelines adopted by the Council, acting on recommendations from the Commission[18].

The Treaty of Maastricht also laid down two other rules, intended to function as incentives for the Member States to pursue responsible fiscal policies[19]. The first rule was introduced under provisions prohibiting the European Central Bank and the central banks of the Member States from granting 'overdraft facilities or any other type of credit facility' to the European Union's institutions or bodies, central governments, regional, local or other public authorities, other bodies governed by public law, or public undertakings of Member States, but also from purchasing directly from them by the European Central Bank or national central banks of 'debt instruments' (ex Article 104(1) TEC – Article 123(1) TFEU). The national central banks should pursue their monetary policies based on purchasing debt instruments in the secondary market rather than directly from the issuers. The second rule was adopted as provisions prohibiting the European Union and the Member States from being liable for or assume the commitments of central governments, regional, local or other public authorities, other bodies governed by public law, or public undertakings of any (or another) Member State (ex Article 104b(1) TEC – Article 125(1) TFEU).

As already mentioned before, the convergence criteria were insufficient for monitoring a Member State's fiscal policy after that Member State's joining the Economic and Monetary Union; therefore, as early as the European Council meeting in Madrid in December 1995, the German government proposed to lay down provisions reinforcing the supranational surveillance of the Member States' fiscal policies, referred to as the Stability Pact. Initially, some of the Member States, especially France, objected to the proposal, but finally a compromise solution was reached. On 16–17 June 1997, the Amsterdam European Council adopted two documents: (1) the Resolution on growth and employment; and (2) the Resolution on the Stability and Growth Pact. Whereas the former, dated 16 June, regarded combating unemployment and promoting employment as a primary goal of the European Union, the latter, adopted on the following day, contained binding political guidance on implementing the Stability and Growth

18 For more on the subject, cf. J.J.Węc, Polityczno-prawne aspekty..., op. cit., pp. 196–197.
19 M. Koczor, op. cit., p. 233.

Pact in a strict and timely manner. Those were followed by two legislative acts of the Council of 7 July 1997: (1) Council Regulation (EC) No 1466/97 on the strengthening of the surveillance of budgetary positions and the surveillance and coordination of economic policies; and (2) Council Regulation (EC) No 1467/97 of 7 July 1997 on speeding up and clarifying the implementation of the excessive deficit procedure. Regulations (1) and (2) entered into force on 1 July 1998 and 1 January 1999 respectively[20].

Together with the above-mentioned Resolution of the European Council of 17 June 1997, the two Regulations formed the Stability and Growth Pact[21]. The first Regulation constituted the legal basis for measures aimed to prevent, at an early stage, the occurrence of excessive public finance (general government) deficits in the Member States and to promote the surveillance and coordination of economic policies[22]. It was therefore called the preventive arm of the Stability and Growth Pact. The Regulation imposed on the EMU Member States an obligation to submit to the Council of the European Union and to the European Commission, on an annual basis, stability programmes (participating Member States) and convergence programmes (non-participating Member States). The objective was to ensure budgetary discipline through the surveillance and coordination of fiscal policies in the euro area and in the EMU as a whole. Such programmes represented part of multilateral surveillance by the Council of the European Union and the European Commission and included medium-term public debt and budget deficit forecasts for at least the following three years, information on economic policy instruments aimed to achieve the programme objectives as well as the main assumptions about expected economic developments and macroeconomic variables, e.g. GDP, inflation, investment expenditure and employment. The Council of the European Union was also entitled to invite or recommend the EMU Member States to adjust such stability programmes and convergence programmes submitted by them (Article 5(2) and Article 9(2) of

20 For more on the subject, cf. J.J.Węc, Polityczno-prawne aspekty..., op. cit., pp. 197–201.

21 Council Regulation (EC) No 1466/97 of 7 July 1997 on the strengthening of the surveillance of budgetary positions and the surveillance and coordination of economic policies, Official Journal of the European Union, L 209, 2.8.1997, pp. 1–5. Council Regulation (EC) No 1467/97 of 7 July 1997 on speeding up and clarifying the implementation of the excessive deficit procedure, Official Journal of the European Union, L 209, 2.8.1997, pp. 6–11. Resolution of the European Council on the Stability and Growth Pact, Amsterdam, 17 June 1997, Official Journal of the European Union, C 236, 2.8.1997, pp. 1–2.

22 J.J. Węc, Polityczno-prawne aspekty..., op. cit., pp. 197–202, 208.

the Regulation)[23]. The second Regulation aimed to initiate an excessive deficit procedure where preventive measures appeared to be no longer sufficient. It was not applied until an excessive budget deficit had actually occurred[24]. Therefore, it was referred to as the corrective arm of the Stability and Growth Pact. In contrast to the Maastricht Treaty, the second Regulation laid down specific provisions on the excessive deficit procedure, setting out time frames for its subsequent steps and stipulating that where the Council of the European Union should decide to impose a sanction, it would be a non-interest-bearing deposit comprising fixed and variable components. The fixed component would be equal to 0.2% of the GDP of the Member State concerned. However, it could be increased by 0.1% of GDP – i.e. the variable component – if the Member State should exceed the reference value of 3% of GDP (the convergence criterion). On the one hand, the deposit amount could not exceed 0.5% of GDP. Such a deposit should be lodged with the European Commission and would be, 'as a rule', transformed by the Council of the European Union into a fine where, after two years following the relevant decision requiring such a deposit from the Member State concerned, the excessive budget deficit had not been, 'in the Council's view', corrected. Interest on such deposits and fines would be treated as 'other revenue' and 'distributed' among the euro area Member States not running excessive deficits. However, if the Member State concerned should manage to reduce its deficit below 3% of GDP, the relevant deposit would be reimbursed to it[25].

In 2005, under pressure from Germany and France, struggling with serious budgetary difficulties, the Stability and Growth Pact was reformed by the following two amending legislative acts: (1) Council Regulation (EC) No 1055/2005 of 27 June 2005 amending Regulation (EC) No 1466/97 on the strengthening of the surveillance of budgetary positions and the surveillance and coordination of economic policies; and (2) Council Regulation (EC) No 1056/2005 of 27 June 2005 amending Regulation (EC) No 1467/97 on speeding up and clarifying the

23 Council Regulation (EC) No 1466/97, op. cit. pp. 3–5.

24 Council Regulation (EC) No 1467/97, op. cit. pp. 6–11.

25 Ibidem, pp. 8–11. For an interpretation of the provisions of the Stability and Growth Pact, cf. E. Latoszek, K. Sacharski, Instrumenty zarządzania kryzysem w obszarze polityki budżetowej w unii gospodarczej i walutowej [The crisis management instruments for budgetary policies in the Economic and Monetary Union], 'Studia Europejskie' 2013, no. 3, pp. 90–92. M. Misiak, Pakt Stabilności i Wzrostu w dobie kryzysu fiskalnego w Unii Europejskiej [The Stability and Growth Pact in the days of the fiscal crisis in the European Union], 'Acta Universitatis Lodziensis' 2010, Folia Oeconomica 238, pp. 138–140.

implementation of the excessive deficit procedure[26]. But the amendments did not consist in making the Stability and Growth Pact more restrictive; instead, surprisingly, its fiscal rules were relaxed[27]. Such a solution offered an opportunity for virtually unlimited justification of excessive deficits in certain Member States, thus infringing the principle of equal treatment of other Member States. The essence of the amendment was removing the requirement of a close to balance or in surplus budgetary position towards setting budgetary objectives separately for particular Member States, taking into account their economic and fiscal situations, in particular GDP growth rates and debt levels[28]. The relaxation of the original fiscal rules of 1997, at the request of Germany and France, led to a legal crisis in the EMU since the already initiated excessive deficit procedures against Germany and France were unlawfully held in abeyance, as subsequently demonstrated by the Court of Justice in its judgment in Case C-27/04 *Commission* v *Council*[29].

It must be emphasised that the Stability and Growth Pact, in both its original version of 1997 and the amended version of 2005, proved to be completely ineffective. As a matter of fact, the Council of the European Union never actually imposed any sanctions for repeated infringements of the adopted fiscal rules by individual Member States participating in the euro area[30]. The global financial and economic crisis spreading across the European Union in 2010 exposed more weaknesses of the surveillance of fiscal policies and of the coordination of economic policies in the Economic and Monetary Union. The main failure was the ineffectiveness of the preventive arm of the Stability and Growth Pact[31].

---

26 Council Regulation (EC) No 1055/2005 of 27 June 2005 amending Regulation (EC) No 1466/97 on the strengthening of the surveillance of budgetary positions and the surveillance and coordination of economic policies, Official Journal of the European Union, L 174, 7.7.2005, pp. 1–4. Council Regulation (EC) No 1056/2005 of 27 June 2005 amending Regulation (EC) No 1467/97 on speeding up and clarifying the implementation of the excessive deficit procedure, Official Journal of the European Union, L 174, 7.7.2005, pp. 5–9.

27 E. Latoszek, K. Sacharski, op. cit., p. 92. L. Oręziak, Reforma Paktu Stabilności i Wzrostu i jej potencjalne konsekwencje [The reform of the Stability and Growth Pact and its potential consequences], 'Bank i Kredyt', July 2005.

28 R. Poliński, Strefa euro, op. cit., pp. 10–11.

29 For more on the subject, cf. A. Nowak-Far, Pakt Stabilności i Wzrostu, op. cit., pp. 73–82.

30 R. Poliński, Strefa euro, op. cit., p. 11.

31 M. Misiak, op. cit., p. 142.

The amending treaties – the Treaty of Amsterdam of 2 October 1997 and the Treaty of Nice of 26 February 2001 – basically confirmed the system solutions codified in the Maastricht Treaty, without interfering with the Member States' powers regarding financial, fiscal or economic policies. Material changes in the functioning of the Economic and Monetary Union were not introduced until the Treaty of Lisbon of 13 December 2007. It slightly revised the EU's monetary and economic policies. Monetary policy became an area of exclusive competence of the European Union (Article 3(1) TFEU). The coordination of economic policies was included in a separate category of competence division between the European Union and the Member States (Article 5(1) TFEU), with specific provisions stipulated by the Treaty for the euro area Member States. The euro was recognised as the currency of the Economic and Monetary Union (Article 3(4) TEU) as well as one of the symbols of the Union (Declaration 52). Price stability was included in the catalogue of the objectives of the European Union (Article 3(3) TEU) and regarded as a condition for achieving other economic objectives. The Treaty imposed on the euro area Member States new obligations concerning compliance with budgetary discipline and the principles of conducting their economic policies: they became obliged to strengthen the coordination and surveillance of their budgetary discipline and to set out economic policy guidelines compatible with those adopted for the whole of the European Union. Furthermore, the Treaty reinforced the significance of the Stability and Growth Pact, giving it the role of an important tool to raise growth potential and to secure 'sound budgetary positions' of the European Union and of the Member States (Declaration 30)[32]. On the other hand, however, the principles of conducting economic policies should continue to be based on balanced budgets and budgetary discipline. No provisions were laid down to strengthen links

32 Treaty of Lisbon amending the Treaty on European Union and the Treaty establishing the European Community, signed at Lisbon, 13 December 2007 (consolidated versions), Official Journal of the European Union, C 202, 7.6.2016, pp. 17–18 (Articles 3 and 4 TEU), 51–52 (Articles 3 to 5 TFEU). Declaration on Article 126 of the Treaty on the Functioning of the European Union (Declaration 30), [in:] Treaty of Lisbon, op. cit., pp. 347–348. Declaration by the Kingdom of Belgium, the Republic of Bulgaria, the Federal Republic of Germany, the Hellenic Republic, the Kingdom of Spain, the Italian Republic, the Republic of Cyprus, the Republic of Lithuania, the Grand-Duchy of Luxembourg, the Republic of Hungary, the Republic of Malta, the Republic of Austria, the Portuguese Republic, Romania, the Republic of Slovenia and the Slovak Republic on the symbols of the European Union (Declaration 52), [in:] Treaty of Lisbon, p. 355.

between economic policy guidelines and fiscal policy recommendations[33]. Institutional changes included reinforcing the positions of the European Central Bank (ECB), the Eurosystem and the Eurogroup (referred to as the 'Euro Group' in the Treaty). Thus, for the first time, the ECB became the Union's institution (Article 13(1) TEU), the Eurosystem, composed of the ECB and the national central banks of the euro area Member States, acquired Treaty status (Article 282(1) TFEU), whereas the Eurogroup, in addition to its Treaty status, was conferred new powers and obtained a new function of a president elected for two and a half years (Article 137 TFEU and Protocol No 14)[34].

But the changes introduced to the system of the Economic and Monetary Union in 1997–2007 were so inconsistent that they failed to remedy its major weakness: the enormous and still growing macroeconomic imbalances between the North and the South of the euro area, which contributed as a serious cause of the euro area debt crisis, in addition to the global financial and economic crisis that peaked in 2008–2009. Those imbalances were mostly reflected in the existence of strong current account deficits in the countries of the South, particularly in Greece and Spain, whereas those of the North, primarily Germany, the Netherlands, Austria and Finland, increased their current account surpluses. Those developments, in turn, resulted in major and uncontrolled capital flows, basically through the banking sector, from the North to the South, which further deteriorated the debt situation of the latter. But the system structure of the Economic and Monetary Union adopted in the Union Treaties, characterised by the absence of three structures – a Financial Union, a Fiscal Union and a genuine Economic Union – to accompany the establishment of the Monetary Union (cf. Figure 1), did not allow an adequate response to the rising imbalances[35]. Therefore, the euro area only functioned without significant turbulence until the first major financial and banking crisis in the world.

---

33 I. Linder, M. Stubits, A Constitutional Treaty for an Enlarged Union. Are there Fundamental Changes for EMU?, 'Proceedings of OeNB Workshops', 5 November 2004, no. 4, p. 22. A. Nowak-Far, Pakt Stabilności i Wzrostu. Funkcje, działanie i przyszłość [The Stability and Growth Pact. The functions, functioning and future], Warszawa 2007. Cf. also: A. Nowak-Far, Unia Gospodarcza i Walutowa w Europie [The Economic and Monetary Union in Europe], Warszawa 2001.

34 For more on the subject, cf. J.J. Węc, Traktat Lizboński, op. cit., pp. 204–207.

35 Cf. W.M. Orłowski, Stabilność finansowa Unii Europejskiej, op. cit., pp. 11–12.

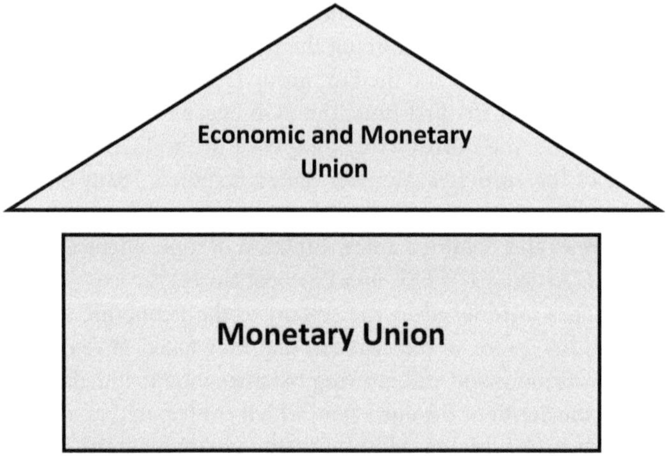

Figure 1: Organisational structure of the Economic and Monetary Union before the euro area debt crisis
Source: prepared by the author.

2. Direct causes of the crisis

The outbreak of the financial and economic crisis in the USA in mid-2008, spreading worldwide in the following years, directly affected the functioning of the euro area and led to a sovereign debt crisis in the EMU. Economists differ in their opinions on the factors contributing to the euro area debt crisis. According to some experts, it was fundamentally caused by the global financial and economic crisis. But most authors additionally point to the above-mentioned deep economic imbalances existing as early as 1997–2007, i.e. high public debt and budget deficit levels, widening differences in economic competitiveness between the euro area Member States. Other causes indicated by scholars include the poor ability of the euro area Member States to manage and absorb economic shocks ('asymmetric shocks')[36], the ineffectiveness of institutional and market

36 An economic shock is a sudden event in the economy affecting the main macroeconomic variables (e.g. employment and inflation). In terms of demand and supply, there are two basic types of shock: (1) a demand shock, resulting from sudden changes in demand (such as a surge in demand in a country due to economic reforms); and (2) a supply shock, arising from sharp fluctuations in supply (e.g. a plunge in food supply

mechanisms forcing governments to conduct sustainable fiscal policies, the lack of sufficient supervision of the financial sector, the absence of crisis management mechanisms and quick financial support for the most vulnerable economies as well as the European Central Bank's policy prioritising the maintenance of low inflation rates, with adverse effects on economic growth[37]. It is argued that the euro area debt crisis was mainly caused by the structural and systemic weaknesses of the Economic and Monetary Union and of the euro area itself. The global financial and economic crisis is seen as only one of the many reasons, a 'spark' for the eurozone crisis, exposing the existing weaknesses of the system[38].

Even more radical opinions are formulated by supporters of the optimum currency area theory, created by the Canadian economist Robert Mundell in 1961. According to the theory in question, further developed by other economists from the US (Peter Kenen) and Canada (Ronald I. McKinnon), an optimum currency area established by a group of countries should meet the following conditions: (1) the countries of such an area should have a similar business cycle and be resilient to asymmetric shocks; (2) inside such an optimum currency area, there can be no 'significant' barriers to the movement of capital or labour; (3)

---

in the aftermath of a natural disaster). Depending on the strength and directions of the relationships concerned, it can be a symmetric shock, of a similar nature in several countries (e.g. soaring oil prices affect a number of countries in like manner), or an asymmetric shock, having varying effects on different countries (e.g. rising oil prices have an unfavourable impact on importers, at the same time being advantageous to exporters), cf. B. Ślusarczyk, S. Ślusarczyk, Podstawy mikro- i makroekonomii [The basics of micro- and macroeconomics], Lublin 2011, pp. 398–400. S. Marciniak, Makro- i mikroekonomia. Podstawowe problemy współczesności [Macro- and microeconomics. The main problems of modern times], Warszawa 2013, pp. 481–492.

37 Narodowy Bank Polski. Kryzys w strefie euro. Przyczyny, przebieg i perspektywy jego rozwiązania [National Bank of Poland. The euro area crisis. The causes, course and prospects for resolving it], Warszawa 2013, p. 6.

38 For more on the subject, cf. J. Czekaj, op. cit., pp. 5–26. M. Rosińska-Bukowska, op. cit., p. 350. J. Frankel, op. cit., pp. 109–120. T. Beck, J.-L. Peydró, op. cit., pp. 63–71. P. De Grauwe, op. cit., pp. 99–108. T. Kunstein, W. Wessels, op. cit, pp. 308–322. M. Pietrzykowski, op. cit., pp. 44–58. J. Koleśnik, op. cit., pp. 101–103. A. Jurkowska-Zeidler, Fundamentalne zmiany, op. cit., pp. 189–192. R. Poliński, Strefa euro, op. cit., pp. 7–23. Idem, Problemy strefy euro, op. cit., pp. 89–92. Cf. also: J.J. Węc, Germany's Position, op. cit., pp. 40–41. M. Götz, Kryzys i przyszłość strefy euro [The euro area crisis and future], Warszawa 2012. M. Gruszczyński, Kryzysy walutowe, bankowe i zadłużeniowe w gospodarce światowej [The currency, banking and debt crises in the world economy], Warszawa 2013.

such an optimum currency area should have a centralised (unified) fiscal policy and a system facilitating the redistribution of funds with a view to supporting countries (regions) experiencing economic difficulties[39]. Relying on Mundell's theory, as early as the 1990s, some US economists warned about economic effects of the introduction of the euro in the European Communities/European Union. They argued that the euro area would fail to meet the requirements of an optimum currency area for the following four reasons: (1) the lack of a common budget of an adequate size; (2) cultural and language barriers hindering the movement of labour; (3) weaker – as compared to states in the USA – synchronisation of business cycles between the euro area Member States; (4) restrictions on the movement of capital[40].

The first symptoms of the global financial and economic crisis appeared as early as the second half of 2007, as a collapse in the US sub-prime mortgage market. It turned out that many mortgages had become non-performing loans as the borrowers were individuals with low creditworthiness. As a breakthrough event, the fourth largest bank in the USA, Lehman Brothers, went bankrupt in September 2008. The bubble burst in the US sub-prime mortgage and other credit markets triggered the global financial and banking crisis. Since the world's financial markets are strongly interrelated, tensions in the US banking system quickly spread to other continents, including Europe. In the wake of the collapse of Lehman Brothers, many European banks started to experience serious problems, pushing them to the verge of bankruptcy. In such a situation, it appeared to be necessary to either bail them out or buy them out from public funds. As early as 2007–2008, the phenomenon affected Irish, UK, German, Benelux banks and French investment funds. All those institutions had previously invested their

39 R. Mundell, A Theory of Optimum Currency Areas, 'The American Economic Review' 1961, no. 4, pp. 657–665. Cf. also K. Beck, Why business cycles diverge? Structural evidence from the European Union, 'Journal of Economic Dynamics and Control', December 2021, Vol. 133, pp. 1–19. K. Beck, M. Grodzicki, Konwergencja realna i synchronizacja cykli koniunkturalnych w Unii Europejskiej. Wymiar strukturalny [Real convergence and synchronisation of economic cycles in the European Union. The structural dimension], Warszawa 2014, pp. 125– 235. P. De Grauwe, Economics of Monetary Union, Oxford 2018. M. Gwóźdź-Lasoń, S. Miklaszewicz, K. Pujer, Unia Europejska i strefa euro. Doświadczenia i wyzwania ekonomiczne, techniczne, inżynieryjne [The European Union and the euro. Economic, technical and engineering experience and challenges], Warszawa 2017, pp. 20–26. A. Bień, Optymalny obszar walutowy. Teoria i praktyka [The optimum currency area. Theory and practice], Warszawa 1988.

40 For more on the subject, cf. S. Kawalec, E. Pytlarczyk, op. cit., pp. 26, 113–115.

assets in the US real estate market[41]. The highest bail-out or buy-out costs were incurred by Ireland. But the critical point in the euro area was primarily Greece's disclosure of the actual budget deficit (-15.1% of GDP) and public debt (126.7% of GDP) in 2009. Apparently, those indicators significantly exceeded the figures shown in official statistics. In the same year, public debt levels became alarming in other euro area countries, particularly in Italy (116.6% of GDP) and Portugal (87.8% of GDP). That, in turn, changed financial market sentiment towards both Greece and the euro area as a whole (cf. Table 1).

The European Union was hit by the financial and banking crisis in 2008, but at the turn of 2010/2011 it transformed into the euro area debt crisis[42]. Therefore, the turning points of the euro area debt crisis are as follows: the year 2010 as the onset of the crisis and the year 2018 as the date of the conclusion for Greece, i.e. the last euro area Member State affected by the crisis, of financial assistance programmes of the European Union and of the International Monetary Fund. The debt crisis hit six Member States – Greece, Ireland, Cyprus, Spain, Portugal and Italy. However, in the opinion of various economists, the crisis also had characteristics of a banking and economic crisis[43]. Not all elements of the crisis were

---

41 A. Neuhaus, Wie die Finanzkrise in Deutschland ankam, 'Handelsblatt', 29. Juli 2017, https://www. handelsblatt.com/finanzen/banken-versicherungen/de/, pp. 1–2 [accessed: 20 July 2022]. M. Rosińska-Bukowska, Kryzys w strefie euro – wybrane aspekty makro- i mikroekonomiczne [The euro area crisis – selected macro- and microeconomic aspects], 'Acta Universitatis Lodziensis' 2012, Folia Oeconomica 273, p. 348.

42 According to the European Commission, the euro area debt crisis started in 2010/2011, cf. European Commission. MEMO – Banking union: restoring financial stability in the Eurozone. Updated version of first memo published on 15/04/2014, Brussels, 9 March 2015, MEMO/14/294, p. 1. Narodowy Bank Polski. Kryzys w strefie euro, op. cit., p. 6. Cf. also: R. Poliński, Strefa euro, op. cit., p. 12. M. Rosińska-Bukowska, op. cit., pp. 345–346.

43 As, for example, in P. Kalka, Czy w strefie euro występuje jeszcze kryzys? [Is the euro area still in crisis?], 'Przegląd Zachodni' 2017, no. 2, p. 311. R. Poliński, Strefa euro, op. cit., pp. 6–8. E. M. Pluciński, Euroland: kryzys fiskalny czy fundamentalny. Wybrane aspekty z perspektywy paradygmatu ekonomii integracji oraz kryzysu globalnej gospodarki towarowo-pieniężnej [Euroland: a fiscal crisis or a fundamental crisis. Selected aspects from the perspective of the paradigm of integration economics and the crisis in the global merchandise and monetary economy], [in:] Globalizacja i regionalizacja w gospodarce światowej, Księga jubileuszowa Profesora Jana Rymarczyka [Globalisation and regionalisation in the world economy. Professor Jan Rymarczyk Anniversary Volume], B. Skulska, M. Domiter, W. Michalczyk (eds.), Wrocław 2012, pp. 111–125. K. Żukrowska, Globalne następstwa kryzysu – próba oceny i prognozy [The

identical in each of the affected euro area Member States, but all the countries experienced a public finance crisis, characterised by excessive public debt and budget deficit levels. In 2010, Greece's high public debt and budget deficit were accompanied by an economic downturn, poor competitiveness of the Greek economy and a significant share of the so-called 'bad loans' in total liabilities. According to Eurostat data, in the year in question, public debt in Greece was 147.5% of GDP, budget deficit reached -11.2% of GDP, whereas the economic growth rate was negative as well, having dropped to -5.5% (cf. Table 1).

Cyprus, Spain and Ireland also experienced a banking crisis. In the first country, it was mainly caused by unsuccessful Greek loan speculations[44], but also by a speculative bubble burst in the real estate market. Prior to the crisis, Cypriot banks not only extended risky loans to Greek businesses and consumers, but they also purchased very large quantities of Greek government bonds whose value subsequently plummeted during the crisis. In Spain and Ireland the crisis arose from bubble bursts in their respective real estate markets, i.e. phenomena resulting from too easily accessible loans and significant inflows of funds, in that case, from the European Union's regional policy funds. Consequently, the number of bad loans in Spain and Ireland rapidly increased, their banking systems suffered losses and bankruptcies, whereby economic development opportunities for the two countries diminished. Similarly to Cyprus, Spain and Ireland, Italy was hit by a banking crisis, following not only from a high level of bad loans, but also from the poor competitiveness of the Italian economy, considerable public debt and limited economic growth, persisting for years[45]. According to Eurostat data,

---

global implications of the crisis – an attempt at assessment and forecast], [in:] Wybrane aspekty z perspektywy paradygmatu ekonomii integracji oraz kryzysu globalnej gospodarki towarowo-pieniężnej, [in:] Globalizacja i regionalizacja w gospodarce światowej, Księga jubileuszowa Profesora Jana Rymarczyka, B. Skulska, M. Domiter, W. Michalczyk (eds.), Wrocław 2012, pp. 547–560. K. Starzyk, Załamanie międzynarodowej równowagi płatniczej jako przyczyna światowego kryzysu gospodarczego [The collapse of international payment equilibrium as a cause of the global economic crisis], [in:] Globalizacja i regionalizacja w gospodarce światowej, Księga jubileuszowa Profesora Jana Rymarczyka, B. Skulska, M. Domiter, W. Michalczyk (eds.), Wrocław 2012, pp. 537–546. T. Sporek, Rozwój strefy euro z perspektywy wybranych państw – wnioski i konsekwencje dla UE [The development of the euro area from the points of view of selected countries – the conclusions and consequences for the EU], 'Studia Europejskie' 2015, no. 2, pp. 61–87.

44 Narodowy Bank Polski. Kryzys w strefie euro, op. cit., p. 18.

45 Ibidem, pp. 18–19.

in all the countries in question except for Cyprus, the 2010 levels of public debt and budget deficit in relation to GDP failed to meet the convergence criteria codified in the Maastricht Treaty (cf. Table 1). Therefore, one must agree with the above-mentioned opinion of the European Commission that the eurozone crisis was first and foremost a debt crisis[46].

Table 1: Economic growth rates, budget deficit and public debt as a percentage of GDP in the Member States affected by the euro area debt crisis in 2009–2018

Country	Year	GDP growth/ contraction (in %)	Budget deficit/surplus (in % of GDP)	Public debt (in % of GDP)
Cyprus	2018	5.6	-4.4	98.1
	2017	5.7	1.7	92.6
	2016	6.6	0.1	102.6
	2015	3.4	-1.0	106.8
	2014	-1.8	-8.7	108.8
	2013	-6.6	-5.8	103.7
	2012	-3.4	-5.6	80.1
	2011	0.4	-5.7	65.8
	2010	2.3	-4.7	56.3
	2009	-2.0	-5.4	54.3
Greece	2018	1.7	1.0	186.4
	2017	1.1	0.7	179.5
	2016	-0.5	0.5	180.5
	2015	-0.2	-5.6	176.7
	2014	0.5	-3.6	180.3
	2013	-2.5	-13.2	178.2
	2012	-7.1	-8.9	162.0
	2011	-10.1	-10.3	175.2
	2010	-5.5	-11.2	147.5
	2009	-4.3	-15.1	126.7

46 For more on the development of the euro area debt crisis in 2010–2018, cf. J.J. Węc, Kryzys zadłużeniowy w strefie euro w latach 2010–2018. Geneza, dynamika oraz instrumenty jego przezwyciężenia [The euro area debt crisis in 2010–2018. The origin, dynamics and tools for overcoming it], 'Politeja' 2020, no. 3, pp. 29–52.

Country	Year	GDP growth/ contraction (in %)	Budget deficit/surplus (in % of GDP)	Public debt (in % of GDP)
Spain	2018	2.3	-2.5	100.4
	2017	3.0	-3.0	101.8
	2016	3.0	-4.3	102.7
	2015	3.8	-5.2	103.3
	2014	1.4	-5.9	105.1
	2013	-1.4	-7.0	100.5
	2012	-3.0	-10.7	90.0
	2011	-0.8	-9.7	69.9
	2010	0.2	-9.5	60.5
	2009	-3.8	-11.3	53.3
Ireland	2018	8.5	0.1	63.0
	2017	9.0	-0.3	67.6
	2016	2.0	-0.7	74.3
	2015	24.4	-1.9	76.7
	2014	8.6	-3.6	104.3
	2013	1.1	-6.2	119.9
	2012	0.0	-9.1	119.6
	2011	0.8	-12.8	110.5
	2010	1.7	-32.1	86.2
	2009*	-5.1	-13.8	61.5
Portugal	2018	2.8	-0.4	121.5
	2017	3.5	-3.0	126.1
	2016	2.0	-1.9	131.5
	2015	1.8	-4.4	131.2
	2014	0.8	-7.4	132.9
	2013	-0.9	-5.1	131.4
	2012	-4.1	-6.2	129.0
	2011	-1.7	-7.7	114.4
	2010	1.7	-11.4	100.2
	2009	-3.1	-9.9	87.8

Country	Year	GDP growth/ contraction (in %)	Budget deficit/surplus (in % of GDP)	Public debt (in % of GDP)
Italy	2018	0.9	-2.2	134.4
	2017	1.7	-2.4	134.2
	2016	1.3	-2.4	134.8
	2015	0.8	-2.6	135.3
	2014	0.0	-3.0	135.4
	2013	-1.8	-2.9	132.45
	2012	-3.0	-2.9	126.5
	2011	0.7	-3.6	119.7
	2010	1.7	-4.2	119.2
	2009	-5.3	-5.1	116.6

* Data for the Irish economy for 2008: GDP contraction: -4.5%; budget deficit: -7.0%; public debt: 42.40%.

Source: Eurostat. Real GDP growth rate – volume 2009–2018 (% change on previous period), Brussels 2021, https://ec.europa.eu/eurostat/en/, pp. 1–6 [accessed: 20 July 2022]. Eurostat. General government deficit/surplus 2009–2018 (% of GDP and million EUR), Brussels 2021, https://ec.europa.eu/eurostat/en/, pp. 1–6 [accessed: 20 July 2022]. Eurostat. Government finance and EDP statistics. General government gross debt 2009–2018, Brussels 2021, https://ec.europa.eu/eurostat/en, pp. 1–6 [accessed: 20 July 2022].

3. The anti-crisis activity of the German and French governments as a cause of the deepening of the crisis

The German and French governments had a significant influence on the dynamics of the euro area debt crisis. First and foremost, it is difficult not to appreciate the role of Germany's financial assistance, mostly in the form of loans, to combat the crisis. In 2010–2018, the overall support loans from the Federal Republic of Germany (FRG) for the indebted economies were EUR 105.64 billion, the highest amount among the euro area Member States (cf. Chapter I.4.4.)[47]. On the other hand, albeit paradoxically, the German and French governments had themselves contributed, whether indirectly or directly, to the exacerbation of the debt crisis. An indirect cause of the

47 Cf. EFSF-ESM. Überblick über die europäischen Finanzhilfen, hrsg. vom Bundesministerium der Finanzen. Stand 31. Dezember 2018, https://www.bundesfinanz ministerium.de/, pp. 2–17 [accessed: 2 July 2019]. Bundesministerium der Finanzen. Europäische Finanzhilfen im Überblick (Stand 31. Dezember 2018), Deutscher Gewährleistungsrahmen nach Stabilisierungsmechanismusgesetz, http://www.Bunde sfinanz ministerium/de, p. 4 [accessed: 2 July 2019].

crisis was the reckless manner of lending by German and French banks to real estate buyers in Ireland and Spain, consumers in Portugal and the Greek government. Nevertheless, rather than writing down their debts, as recommended by certain experts, such as the British economist Philippe Legrain[48], the German and French governments decided to grant loans to the indebted countries, shifting full responsibility for the crisis to their taxpayers. In that way, Germany and France directly contributed to the aggravation of the debt crisis. Moreover, the main method for fighting the crisis pushed by the German government, even contrary to the French government's doubts, became the policy of funding cuts. As it had no support in growth-friendly programmes, it could not boost economic growth and increase the competitiveness of the indebted economies; on the contrary, it also directly contributed to the deterioration of the crisis[49].

In the spring of 2010, Chancellor Merkel pushed through a proposal for establishing a European Financial Stability Facility (EFSF), with the aim of including it, together with financing from the International Monetary Fund, in rescue packages for Greece, Italy, Spain, Portugal and Ireland. Subsequently, contrary to the views of most of the European Union Member States' governments, she forced the countries affected by the crisis to take radical steps to reduce public debt[50]. The German government made its contribution to the rescue packages conditional on accepting those proposals. On 8–9 December 2011, under pressure from Germany and France, the European Council took a political decision to sign a fiscal compact, aimed at tightening fiscal discipline and sanctions for non-compliance. At the same time, Germany and France objected to proposals included in the Polish Presidency non-paper of 2 December 2011 on the establishment of a coherent and inclusive structure to guarantee maintaining cohesion between the European Union and the euro area following the introduction of economic and budgetary governance changes to the

48 Ph. Legrain, Euro-Zone Fiscal Colonialism, 'The New York Times', April 21, 2014, https://www.nytimes.com/2014/04/22/opinion/euro-zone-fiscal-colonialism.html, p. 1 [accessed: 20 July 2022].

49 For more on the subject, cf. J.J. Węc, Die politische Debatte zur zweiten Systemreform der Europäischen Union in Deutschland (2011–2012), 'Zeitschrift des Verbandes Polnischer Germanisten' 2014, H. 2, pp. 204–205. J.J. Węc, Germany's Position, op. cit., pp. 201–205. For more on the positions of the government, the parliamentary opposition and interest groups in the FRG regarding the euro area debt crisis, cf. E. Cziomer, Rola Niemiec w kryzysie strefy euro po 2009 r. [The role of Germany in the euro area debt crisis after 2009], Kraków 2013, pp. 70–110.

50 Cf. G. Müller-Brandeck-Bocquet, Deutschland – Europas einizige Führungsmacht?, 'Aus Politik und Zeitgeschichte' 2012, B 10, pp. 18–19.

latter[51]. From the very beginning of the debt crisis, the German government was also firmly opposed to proposals from the governments of the most indebted euro area Member States, supported by the European Commission and the European Parliament, with regard to conferring on the European Central Bank the power to purchase EU bonds and almost unlimited access of the EFSF, and subsequently also of the newly established European Stability Mechanism (ESM), to the ECB funds.

Such a method for combating the crisis met with strong criticism in the Southern euro area countries and even in Germany. In the Member States with the most indebted economies, especially in Greece, Germany and France were perceived as the main culprits of the debt crisis, caused by irresponsible lending policies of their banks. The German government was additionally condemned for imposing on those countries dramatic financial cuts, or even accused of facilitating Germany's increasing its competitive advantage over the Southern euro area countries and maintaining a significant current account surplus as a result of the very introduction of the euro[52]. Negative sentiment towards the FRG in the Southern countries was sometimes accompanied by very sharp criticism from certain German economists and opposition politicians of the policies pursued by the governments led by Gerhard Schröder (1998–2005) and Angela Merkel (2005–2021). As demonstrated by Heiner Flassbeck, a well-known German economist and former State Secretary in the German Federal Ministry of Finance (1998–1999), Germany's increasing current account surplus, especially in relations with the euro area Member States affected by the debt crisis, combined with very weak internal demand and a low investment rate in the FRG, led to economic imbalances throughout the euro area, thus the German government indirectly contributed to further aggravation of the crisis[53]. In his opinion, sluggish internal

51 J.J. Węc, Pierwsza polska prezydencja w Unii Europejskiej. Uwarunkowania – Procesy decyzyjne – Osiągnięcia i niepowodzenia [The first Polish Presidency in the European Union. Conditions – Decision-making – Successes and failures], Kraków 2012, pp. 128–129, 144–145.

52 For more on the subject, cf. S. Kawalec, E. Pytlarczyk, op. cit., pp. 161–162.

53 In the opinion of Flassbeck, due to 'German mercantilism', the Southern Member States began to lose their competitiveness in trade with non-euro area countries as well. Hence his appeal to Merkel's government along the following lines: The economy is a system of communicating vessels. A country undercutting its trading partners does harm to itself. Any country making its partners go bankrupt puts itself at risk of bankruptcy. This is Germany's case, cf. Heiner Flassbeck o tym, dlaczego uczciwość i pracowitość szkodzą [Heiner Flassbeck speaks of why honesty and diligence

demand primarily resulted from 'wage dumping' in Germany, caused by socially costly reforms of the German labour market and welfare system introduced by Schröder's government in 2003–2005 (the 'Hartz package')[54]. Those reforms formed part of the Agenda 2010, referring to the Lisbon Strategy adopted by the Lisbon European Council in 2000 and aimed, *inter alia*, to significantly improve the competitiveness of the EU economy by 2010.[55] According to Flassbeck, the Hartz reform package contributed to developments

---

do harm]. Interview by Żakowski with Flassbeck, 9 July 2013, https://www.polityka.pl/, p. 5 [accessed: 20 July 2022].

54 The term comes from the surname of the chairman of the German government committee for labour market reforms, Peter Hartz. The package was composed of four parts: Hartz I aimed at increasing labour market flexibility, establishing new forms of employment and promoting continuing vocational training by the German Federal Labour Agency; Hartz II introduced new types of low-paid (*Minijob*) and short-term (*Midijob*) employment and grants for unemployed persons to take up self-employment; Hartz III restructured the German Federal Labour Institution (*Bundesanstalt für Arbeit*), simultaneously changing its name to the Federal Labour Agency (*Bundesagentur für Arbeit*); Hartz IV significantly reduced social welfare benefits for the long-term unemployed. Although the package maintained previous 'temporary benefits', described in more detail below, but after the lapse of the period concerned unemployed persons could only receive lower social assistance benefits. Cf. T. Krebs, M. Scheffel, Reforma niemieckiego rynku pracy. Niepopularny sukces [The reform of the German labour market. An unpopular success], 24 September 2013 https://www.obserwatorfinansowy.pl/, pp. 1–2 [accessed: 20 July 2022]. For criticism of the Hartz reform package in the Polish literature, cf. M. Moszyński, Niedopasowania na niemieckim rynku pracy w świetle reform Hartza [Mismatches in the German labour market in the light of the Hartz reforms], [in:] Ekonomiczne problemy funkcjonowania współczesnego świata [Economic issues in the functioning of the modern world], D. Kopycińska (ed.), Szczecin 2009, pp. 154–165.

55 The tools for implementing the Lisbon Strategy included innovation (a knowledge-based economy), market liberalisation (in areas such as telecommunications, energy, transport and financial markets), entrepreneurship (facilities for taking up and pursuing economic activities) and social cohesion (building a new and active welfare state). Although the objectives of the Lisbon Strategy could not be achieved, some of them were subsequently included in the Europe 2020 strategy. For more on the subject, cf. Strategia Lizbońska. Droga do sukcesu zjednoczonej Europy [The Lisbon Strategy. Towards the success of a united Europe], Departament Analiz Ekonomicznych i Społecznych Urzędu Komitetu Integracji Europejskiej [2001], https://www.slaskie.pl/, pp. 4–5 [accessed: 20 July 2022]. J. Piotrowski, Strategia Lizbońska. Przyczyny niepowodzenia [The Lisbon Strategy. The causes of failure], Unia Europejska.pl, 2012, no. 1, pp. 39–50 [accessed: 20 July 2022].

such as growing competitiveness of the German economy accompanied by either declining (in 2005–2011) or stagnant wages (from 2012). Simultaneously, low internal demand resulted in further deterioration of the investment rate and increased public debt in Germany[56]. As pointed out by another well-known German economist, Hans-Werner Sinn, the introduction of the common currency led to a surge in capital flows from the North to the South of the euro area. The outflow of capital to the Southern countries contributed to the emergence of an inflationary credit bubble there in the following years, making them uncompetitive and susceptible to financial crises. In Germany, it drove down investment, resulting in economic malaise and rising unemployment, which to some extent forced Schröder's government to implement reforms[57].

On 4 June 2012, Germany's former Foreign Minister Joschka Fischer (1998–2005) published an article in 'Süddeutsche Zeitung' that sharply criticised the methods for fighting the euro area debt crisis used by Merkel's

56 According to Flassbeck, as Schröder reforms coincided with the FRG's joining the euro area, the German policy of frozen wages accompanied by rapid growth in labour productivity led to a rising surplus of production over wages and resulted in soaring competitiveness of the German economy. It worked as actual currency depreciation; in other euro area countries German products became cheaper in real terms. Previously, the euro area Member States agreed to keep an inflation rate of 2%. Germany breached that agreement from the beginning. On account of the freezing of wages, inflation in Germany was much lower, whereas it tended to exceed 2% in other countries. Therefore, German goods became more expensive at a slower pace than French or Italian products. As a result, the competitiveness gap between Germany and other euro area Member States increased to 25–30%, whereas Germany's trade surplus reached EUR 150 billion per year, or 6% of GDP, cf. Heiner Flassbeck, op. cit., pp. 1–2. Furthermore, Flassbeck openly criticised Schröder's economic policy, accusing him of dismantling the German social market economy model and returning to the neoclassical economics of Margaret Thatcher and Ronald Reagan, cf. ibidem, p. 2. For other critical opinions on Germany's policy towards the euro area debt crisis, cf. B. Zürcher, Exportweltmeister Deutschland mit Rückenwind, 27. März 2012, http://www.oekonomenstimme.org/de, pp. 1–2 [accessed: 20 July 2022]. K.G. Singer, Eurozone: Leistungsbilanz-Saldo auf Rekordhoch, http://www.time patternanalysis.de/, pp. 1–3 [accessed: 20 July 2022]. R. Berger, Czy zmieniać niemiecki model gospodarczy [Should the German economic model be changed], 'Rzeczpospolita', 28 January 2014, p. B11, http://www.rp.pl [accessed: 22 July 2022].

57 H.-W. Sinn, The Euro Trap. On Bursting Bubbles, Budgets, and Beliefs, Oxford 2017, passim.

government. He accused the German Federal Government of attempting to extinguish the 'fire' with kerosene instead of quenching it with water and of fanning the flames with the austerity policy forced by Merkel. Due to pursuing such a policy, within three years the euro area debt crisis turned into a genuine 'existential crisis', which put the euro area in jeopardy and even threatened the existence of the common market. Such developments could in turn lead to the outbreak of a global economic crisis on an unprecedented scale. To prevent the euro area from collapsing, Germany and France should persuade the Eurogroup to venture to build a Fiscal and Political Union. Germany needed to agree to the creation of a Fiscal Union, guaranteeing the survival of the euro area with its economic power and wealth, whereas France should accept the establishment of a Political Union, with common governance and common parliamentary scrutiny in the euro area. In order to avoid a depression in the euro area and to create conditions for economic growth, it would also be necessary to confer on the European Central Bank the power to purchase without limits bonds issued by the indebted euro area Member States, followed by the Europeanisation of debts via EU bonds and launching growth-friendly programmes[58].

It must be emphasised that Schröder's reforms were very successful in the sense that they led to an abrupt fall in unemployment (from 11% in 2005 to 7.5% in 2008 and to 5.5% in 2012). The success was mainly due to making the labour market more flexible by improving the job seeking process, deregulating the temporary agency work sector, creating flexible forms of employment with reduced taxes and insurance contributions as well as introducing dramatic changes to the unemployment benefit system, basically consisting in the elimination of benefits granted indefinitely[59]. As a consequence of the last modification, about 2.3 million unemployed persons lost their entitlements to long-term benefits, which resulted in a sharp fall in unemployment but

58 J. Fischer, Europa steht in Flammen, 'Süddeutsche Zeitung', 4. Juni 2012, http://www.sueddeutsche.de/, pp. 1–2 [accessed: 20 July 2022].

59 Before the reforms, there were three types of unemployment benefit in Germany: (1) temporary benefits (60% of the last salary), granted for 12 months to workers under 45 years of age or for 32 months to older workers; (2) benefits granted indefinitely (53% of the last salary) to workers having exercised their entitlements to temporary benefits in full; (3) social assistance benefits granted to unemployed persons not meeting the criteria for temporary benefits or for benefits granted for an indefinite period, depending on their wealth. For more on the subject, cf. S. Kawalec, E. Pytlarczyk, op. cit., pp. 82–89.

increased social discontent at the same time[60]. On the other hand, however, Schröder's reforms contributed to limiting the wage growth rate, although they did not imply, fortunately for German employees, their decline in nominal terms. Combined with the fact that other euro area Member States, as well as the Central and Eastern European countries, simultaneously experienced soaring wages, it considerably helped improve the competitiveness of the German economy relative to other euro area economies[61]. Enhanced competitiveness was reflected, *inter alia*, in a steadily increasing trade balance surplus, followed by a current account surplus of the FRG[62]. Although Germany's current account surplus in relations with euro area countries began to decline from 2010[63], it remained high in relations with the Member States most hit by the debt crisis (cf. Charts 1 and 2)[64].

The European Commission treated the persistence of a current account surplus in excess of 6% of GDP as a threat to the financial stability of the euro area Member States[65]. The opinion was also shared by the US Department of the Treasury, considering that the situation jeopardised financial stability on a regional or even global scale as a country with such a high current account surplus forced its trading partners to credit their imports and to run into permanent debts[66].

---

60 Ibidem, p. 86.

61 S. Kawalec, E. Pytlarczyk, op. cit., pp. 88–89.

62 K.G. Singer, op. cit., pp. 1–3. Statistisches Jahrbuch. Fakten zum deutschen Außenhandel 2013. Außenhandelsergebnisse im Jahre 2013, Statistisches Bundesamt, Berlin 2014, p. 1.

63 F. Hollenbeck, Germany's "Dangerous" Current Account Surplus, 20 November 2013, https://mises.org/library/germanys-dangerous-current-account-surplus [accessed: 20 July 2022].

64 Statistisches Jahrbuch. Fakten zum deutschen Außenhandel 2013, op. cit., p. 1.

65 S. Schulz, Kritik der EU-Kommission: Phantomstreit um Deutschlands Exporte, 5. März 2014, http://www.spiegel.de, pp. 1–2 [accessed: 20 July 2022]. R. Berger, op. cit., p. B11.

66 Ifo-Berechnung: Deutschland hat weltweit höchsten Exportüberschuss, Info, 2. February 2015, http://www.spiegel.de, p. 1 [accessed: 20 July 2022]. For more on the subject cf. J.J. Węc, Wpływ rządów Merkel na reformę ustrojową Unii Europejskiej i strefy euro [The influence of Merkel's government on the system reform of the European Union and the euro area], [in:] Interesy – Wartości – Kompromisy. Polityka zagraniczna Niemiec w erze Angeli Merkel [Interests – Values – Compromises. Germany's foreign policy in the era of Angela Merkel], K. Janoś, A. Kałabunowska, J. Kiwerska, T. Morozowski (eds.), Poznań 2022, pp. 31–35.

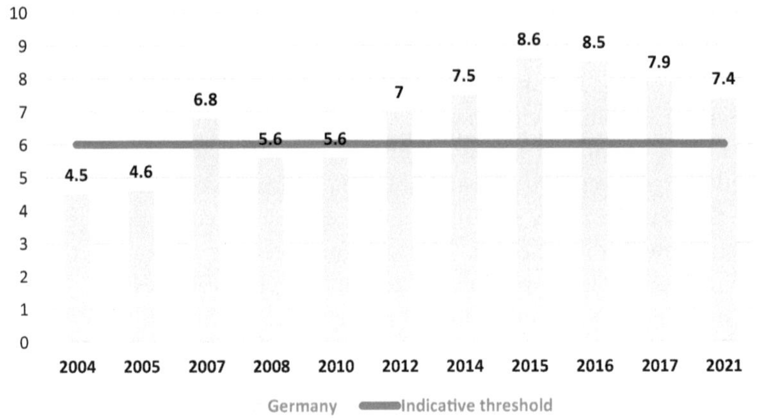

Chart 1: Germany's current account surplus in 2004–2021 (in % of GDP)

Source: prepared by the author on the basis of: J. Möbert, Deutschlands Leistungsbilanz: Das Ende der Kritik, https://www.dbresearch.de/, pp. 1–4 [accessed: 2 October 2022]. Saldo der Leistungsbilanz von Deutschland in Prozent des BIP in den Jahren 1991–2021, Institut der deutschen Wirtschaft Köln, https://www.deutschland inzahlen.de, pp. 1–2 [accessed: 2 October 2022].

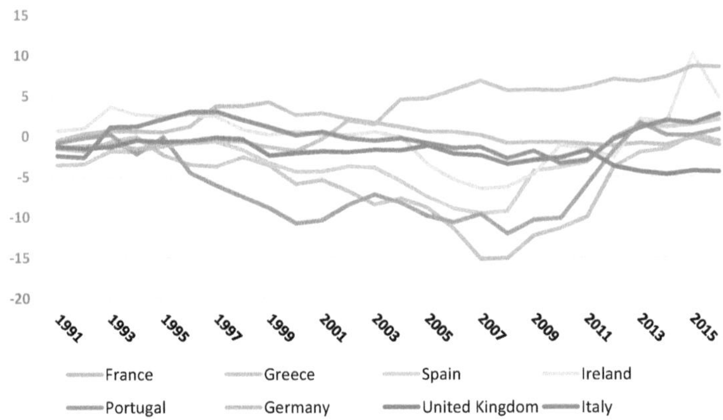

Chart 2: Current account balances of Germany, France, the United Kingdom, Italy, Ireland, Greece, Spain and Portugal in 1991–2015 (in % of GDP)

Source: prepared by the author on the basis of: Saldo der Leistungsbilanz von Deutschland, Frankreich, Großbritannien, Griechenland, Italien, Spanien, Portugal und Irland in Prozent des BIP in den Jahren 1991–2016, Institut der deutschen Wirtschaft Köln, https://www.deutschlandinzahlen.de, pp. 1–2 [accessed: 2 October 2022].

Although some euro area Member States, especially France and Italy, but also the European Commission, insisted that Germany take measures necessary to reduce the surplus, the German Federal Government maintained its unflinching stance. Opinions on the necessity for Germany to reduce the surplus were expressed by representatives of the International Monetary Fund and various economic experts as well[67].

It was not until 2013, when the European Commission started working on draft amendments to the Economic and Monetary Union aimed at overcoming the debt crisis in line with Herman Van Rompuy's report, that it also addressed the issue of the German current account surplus. On 5 March 2014, the Commission reprimanded the German Federal Government and simultaneously called upon it to take the necessary policy action to boost internal demand in Germany, arguing that the existing current account surplus would involve the risk of adverse effects on the functioning of the euro area as a whole[68]. Nevertheless, Germany's current account surplus not only persisted but even increased further to as much as 8.6% of GDP in 2015. The lion's share of the surplus was again an extremely favourable trade balance. From 2016, the surplus began to decline, to 7.9% of GDP in 2017 and to 7.4% of GDP in 2021. But it still remained above the indicative threshold allowed by the European Commission[69].

---

67 Eksperci: Model ekonomiczny Niemiec nie jest dobry dla całej strefy euro [Experts: the German economic model is not good for the whole euro area], PAP, 24 October 2014, interia.pl, p. 1 [accessed: 2 July 2019]. For a different view, but only concerning Germany's current account surplus until 2012, cf. D. Gros, M. Busse, The Macroeconomic Imbalance Procedure and Germany: When is a current account surplus an 'imbalance'? CEPS Policy Brief, 13 November 2013, no. 301, pp. 1–5, https://www.ceps.eu/ceps-publications/macroeconomic-imbalance-procedure-and-germany-when-current-account-surplus-imbalance/ [accessed: 10 January 2023].

68 S. Schulz, op. cit., pp. 1–2. Ifo-Berechnung, op. cit., p. 1. M. Matzke, Nagana dla prymusa. KE gani wysokie nadwyżki eksportowe Niemiec [The top performer reprimanded. The European Commission reproaches Germany for high export surpluses], http://www.dw.de, pp. 1–2 [accessed: 2 July 2019]. Cf. also: J.J. Węc, Relacje polsko-niemieckie w Unii Europejskiej i NATO na początku XXI w. Próba bilansu [Poland–Germany relations in the European Union and NATO at the beginning of the 21st century. An attempt at taking stock], 'Prace Komisji Środkowoeuropejskiej PAU', 2015, Vol. XXIII, pp. 130–134.

69 According to estimates for 2022, the current account surplus in Germany could drop to as low as 4% of GDP, as a result of a strong acceleration of inflation. It would be the lowest level since 2004; simultaneously, for the first time since 2010, the surplus would fall below the threshold of 6% of GDP, cf. J. Möbert, Deutschlands Leistungsbilanz: Das Ende der Kritik, https://www.dbresearch.de/, pp. 1–4 [accessed: 2 October 2022].

4. The European Union's main tools for fighting the crisis

In 2010–2018, the European Union basically concentrated on four main forms of combating the euro area debt crisis. Those were as follows: (1) financial assistance programmes for the indebted economies; (2) recovery programmes for the Member States experiencing the crisis; (3) the Eurosystem measures for overcoming the crisis; (4) the system reform of the Economic and Monetary Union[70].

4.1. Financial assistance programmes for the indebted economies

Early responses by the euro area Member States to the global crisis consisted in the introduction from 2009 of expansionary fiscal policies, i.e. increasing expenditure and cutting taxes, to spur economic growth and improve their labour market situations. At the same time, the European Central Bank began to reduce interest rates with a view to preventing investment and consumer demand from

70 Already in previous years, several other studies by the author addressed the system reform of the euro area and measures taken by the European Central Bank to combat the debt crisis, cf. J.J. Węc, Dynamika reformy ustrojowej strefy euro w latach 2012–2016 [The dynamics of the system reform of the euro area in 2012–2016], 'Politeja' 2016, no. 6, pp. 171–205. Idem, Podstawowe założenia, cele i zasady reformy ustrojowej strefy euro. Implikacje dla Polski [The main assumptions, objectives and principles of the system reform of the euro area. Implications for Poland], 'Krakowskie Studia Międzynarodowe' 2016, no. 1, pp. 107–129. Idem, Perspektywy zmian ustrojowych w Unii Europejskiej do 2025 r. Implikacje dla Polski [The prospects for system changes in the European Union by 2025. Implications for Poland], 'Przegląd Zachodni' 2018, no. 1, pp. 9–13, 21–22, 28–30. Idem, Unia Europejska na historycznym zakręcie. Bieżące wyzwania i scenariusze ich przezwyciężenia [The European Union at a historic turning point. Current challenges and scenarios of overcoming them], [in:] Integracja europejska – polska perspektywa [European integration – Poland's perspective], Z. Czachór, T.G. Grosse, W. Paruch (eds.), Warszawa 2018, pp. 175–177, 180–181, 187–196. Idem, Normatywna działalność Unii Europejskiej w walce z kryzysem zadłużeniowym strefy euro [The normative activities of the European Union in the fight against the euro area debt crisis], [in:] Integracja europejska. Główne obszary badawcze [European integration. The main research areas], K. Wojtaszczyk, J. Tymanowski, P. Stawarz (eds.), Warszawa 2015, pp. 163–176. Idem, Proces konstytuowania Unii Bankowej. Geneza, podstawy prawne, cele i zasady działania [The process of establishing the Banking Union. The origin, legal bases, objectives and principles of functioning], 'Rocznik Integracji Europejskiej' 2014, pp. 33–49. Idem, The European Union Debate on the Second Institutional Reform (2011–2012), 'Przegląd Zachodni' 2014, no. 1, pp. 7–30.

collapsing. But those initiatives further pushed up budget deficit and public debt levels in relation to GDP, particularly in Greece, Ireland, Spain, Portugal, Ireland and Italy (cf. Table 1). The first decisions on financial support for the indebted economies were made in 2010. In early May of the same year, the Finance Ministers of the euro area Member States, in agreement with the International Monetary Fund and the European Central Bank, reached an understanding on the first financial assistance programme for Greece, also referred to as the Greek Loan Facility. Under the programme, in 2010–2012, Greece received financial assistance of EUR 73.0 billion, of which bilateral loans from the European Union Member States represented EUR 52.9 billion and the International Monetary Fund assigned an amount of EUR 20.1 billion[71].

As the euro area debt crisis aggravated, apart from the short-term financial assistance to Greece, systemic action was also taken to cover other indebted euro area economies. Two new assistance instruments were established: the European Financial Stabilisation Mechanism (EFSM) under Council Regulation (EU) No 407/2010 of 11 May 2010[72] and the above-mentioned European Financial Stability Facility under the Decision of the 16 euro area Member States of 7 June of the same year[73]. Both instruments, of a temporary nature, were only established for three euro area Member States hit by the crisis, i.e. Greece, Portugal and Ireland, with loans extended in 2010–2013[74]. As the debt crisis began to affect other countries, a decision was made to also establish the above-mentioned European

71 European Stability Mechanism. EFSF-ESM, February 2019, https://www.esm.europa.eu/sites/default/files/efsfesmnewinvestorpresentationfebruary2019_0.pdf, p. 46 [accessed: 2 July 2019]. EFSF-ESM. Überblick über die europäischen Finanzhilfen, hrsg. vom Bundesministerium der Finanzen. Stand 31. Dezember 2018, https://www.bundesfinanzministerium.de/, p. 8 [accessed: 2 July 2019].

72 Council Regulation (EU) No 407/2010 of 11 May 2010 establishing a European financial stabilisation mechanism, Official Journal of the European Union, L 118, 12.5.2010, pp. 1–4.

73 Decision of the 16 euro area Member States, Luxembourg, 7 June 2010, https://www.consilium.europa.eu/, p. 1 [accessed: 20 July 2022].

74 According to the initial plan, the EFSM beneficiaries were supposed to only be Ireland and Portugal, whereas EFSF funds would be earmarked for Ireland, Portugal and Greece. In June 2015, however, Greece was also granted a short-term bridge loan amounting to EUR 7.16 billion from EFSM funds, cf. C. Alcidi, D. Gros, J.N. Ferrer, D. Rinaldi, The Instruments Providing Macro-Financial Support to EU Member States, CEPS. Research Report, 2017, no. 6, March 2017, https://www.ceps.eu/wp-content/uploads/2017/03/RRpt%20No%202017-06%20MacroFinSupport%20to%20MSs_0.pdf, p. 12 [accessed: 20 July 2022].

Stability Mechanism as a permanent crisis resolution tool for the euro area as a whole (cf. Chapter II.1.2 of this monograph).

Among the Member States benefiting from the financial assistance programmes under the European Financial Stabilisation Mechanism and the European Financial Stability Facility in 2010–2013, the highest amount of support, EUR 141.8 billion, was granted to Greece (EFSF)[75], followed by EUR 50.3 billion received by Portugal (including EUR 26 billion from the EFSF and EUR 24.3 billion from the EFSM)[76], whereas Ireland obtained EUR 40.2 billion (of which EUR 17.7 billion from the EFSF and EUR 22.5 billion from the EFSM)[77]. The beneficiaries of the European Stability Mechanism were Greece, Spain and Cyprus. That international organisation granted EUR 61.9 billion to Greece[78], Spain obtained EUR 41.3 billion, whereas Cyprus received EUR 6.3 billion[79] (cf. Infographic 1 and Table 2). The only Member State not to benefit from any

---

75 In 2012–2015, under the second financial assistance programme, Greece received a total of EUR 153.8 billion, of which EUR 141.8 billion came from the EFSF, whereas the International Monetary Fund (IMF) granted EUR 12 billion. The above-mentioned bridge loan of EUR 7.16 billion from the EFSM must also be added to the amount. It means that in the period in question Greece raised loans totalling EUR 160.96 billion, cf. European Stability Mechanism. EFSF-ESM, February 2019, https://www.esm.europa.eu/sites/default/files/efsfesmnewinvestorpresentation february2019_0.pdf, pp. 43, 46 [accessed: 20 July 2022]. C. Alcidi, D. Gros, J.N. Ferrer, D. Rinaldi, op. cit., p. 12. EFSF/ESM. Financial Assistance. Evaluation Report, Luxembourg 2017, https://www.esm.europa.eu/financial-assistance/evaluation-efsfesm-programmes, p. 38, [accessed: 20 July 2022]. Cf. also: EFSF-ESM. Überblick, op. cit., pp. 8–9.

76 Cf. C. Alcidi, D. Gros, J.N. Ferrer, D. Rinaldi, op. cit., p. 12. EFSF/ESM. Financial Assistance. Evaluation Report, op. cit., p. 38. EFSF-ESM. Überblick, op. cit., pp. 6–7. Additionally, Portugal received EUR 26.4 billion from the IMF. Cf. also: European Stability Mechanism. EFSF-ESM, op. cit., p. 45.

77 Furthermore, Ireland obtained EUR 22.5 billion from the IMF and EUR 4.8 billion in the form of bilateral loans from the United Kingdom (EUR 3.8 billion), Sweden (EUR 0.6 billion) and Denmark (EUR 0.4 billion). The Irish government also contributed an amount of EUR 17.5 billion from the Treasury and the National Pension Reserve Fund, cf. European Stability Mechanism. EFSF-ESM, op. cit., p. 44. Cf. also: EFSF-ESM. Überblick, op. cit., pp. 4–5.

78 The ESM loan simultaneously constituted the basis for the third financial assistance programme for Greece, implemented in 2015–2018, cf. EFSF-ESM. Überblick, op. cit., pp. 16–17.

79 Cyprus additionally obtained EUR 1.0 billion from the IMF, cf. European Stability Mechanism. EFSF-ESM, February 2019, op. cit., p. 49. Cf. also: EFSF-ESM. Überblick, op. cit., pp. 14–15.

external assistance was Italy. The Italian government decided to develop its own financial assistance programme, with appropriations of EUR 20 billion allocated to combating the crisis.

4.2. Recovery programmes in the Member States experiencing the crisis

4.2.1. Greece

The largest beneficiary of the financial assistance programmes of the European Union and of the International Monetary Fund, but simultaneously the Member State in need of implementing the deepest structural reforms in its economy was Greece. With the implementation in 2010–2018 of the three financial assistance programmes mentioned above, in negotiations with the Troika, i.e. the European Commission, the European Central Bank and the International Monetary Fund, the Greek government committed to launching a long-term recovery and austerity programme of reforms such as dramatically pushing down budget deficit below 3% of GDP by 2014; reducing public debt to 124% by 2020; raising consumer taxes; implementing structural reforms in areas such as the labour market; cutting salaries in the public sector and old-age pensions. In July 2011, at the request of the Greek government, the European Commission appointed a Task Force for Greece led by Horst Reichenbach. The objectives of the Task Force encompassed the coordination of technical assistance for the Greek authorities in the implementation of the recovery programme agreed with the European Union and the International Monetary Fund, but also the identification of legislative, regulatory and administrative measures allowing to better use the bilateral loans granted by the euro area Member States. The Task Force was composed of 60 experts from institutions such as the European Commission, the International Monetary Fund and Member States, working in both Athens and Brussels. In June 2015, the Task Force for Greece was replaced by the Structural Reform Support Service (SRSS), providing assistance to all the European Union Member States in the preparation, design and implementation of structural reforms, included in their measures for job creation and sustainable economic growth[80].

80 Financial assistance to euro area countries. Financial assistance to Greece, EFSF programme for Greece (expired 30 June 2015), https://www.esm.europa.eu/assistance/greece/efsf-programme-greece-expired, pp. 1–2 [accessed: 20 July 2022]. In collaboration with the competent services of the European Commission, the Structural Reform Support Service coordinated measures taken in the area of specialised technical support provided to the European Union Member States. Such support

In March 2012, the Finance Ministers of the euro area Member States approved the second financial assistance programme for Greece. Their governments and the International Monetary Fund assigned for that purpose unused amounts from the first assistance programme and decided to earmark an additional EUR 130 billion for 2012–2014. The period was subsequently extended to 30 June 2015. The euro area countries agreed that – in contrast to the first programme based on bilateral loans – the second financial assistance programme would be funded from the European Financial Stability Facility. Under the programme concerned, Greece would be granted loans for the total amount of EUR 164.5 billion, of which EUR 144.7 billion would come from the EFSF and EUR 19.8 billion – from the IMF. Ultimately, as mentioned before, the EFSF and IMF, but also the EFSM on a short-term basis, granted to the Greek government loans amounting to EUR 160.96 billion. However, as early as the spring of 2012, the uncertain political situation in Greece and the prospect of the first and, subsequently, second early parliamentary elections led to the outflow of capital and gave rise to doubts as to the ability of the Greek government to implement the recovery programme. The repeated election held on 17 June 2012 allowed the creation of a government coalition composed of three political parties: New Democracy, PASOK and Democratic Left. The new coalition government led by Antonis Samaras undertook to implement the economic adjustment programme agreed with the Troika. Soon afterwards, the Finance Ministers of the euro area Member States and the International Monetary Fund reached an understanding on a policy package aimed at reducing Greece's debt-to-GDP ratio to 124% by 2020. The package included measures such as lowering the interest rate and the guarantee fee costs paid by Greece on the loans granted to it, an extension of the

---

encompassed revenue administration, public finance management, measures for the rule of law, anti-corruption, anti-money-laundering and anti-fraud strategies, the investment climate, Energy Union efforts, climate policy, education, sectoral expertise, health care, labour market matters, funding and access to finance, the Capital Markets Union, immigration and border control. A Member State could request such support and no co-financing was needed. On 1 January 2020, the Structural Reform Support Service was transformed into the Directorate-General for Structural Reform Support (DG REFORM), cf. Structural Reform Support Service, https://ec.europa.eu/en/ pp. 1–2 [accessed: 20 July 2022]. Cf. also: M. Walkowski, Europa w kryzysie gospodarczym i finansowym: casus Grecji [Europe in economic and financial crisis: the case of Greece], [in:] Globalizacja i regionalizacja w gospodarce światowej, Księga jubileuszowa Profesora Jana Rymarczyka, B. Skulska, M. Domiter, W. Michalczyk (eds.), Wrocław 2012, pp. 573–590.

maturities of the bilateral and EFSF loans by 15 years and a deferral of interest payments of Greece on EFSF loans by 10 years[81].

Despite the still uncertain political situation in Greece, as reflected in two early parliamentary elections held in January and September 2015, but also due to the spectre of financial bankruptcy facing Greece again in July 2015, the new coalition government (Syriza–Independent Greeks) led by Prime Minister Alexis Tsipras made endeavours to implement the tax, pension and social security reform programme agreed with the European Union Member States and the International Monetary Fund in November 2011. It allowed Greece to obtain a short-term bridge loan of EUR 7.16 billion from the EFSM in June 2015 and subsequently an ESM loan of EUR 61.9 billion under the third financial assistance programme for 2015–2018. The condition for granting the above-mentioned loans was the Greek government's commitment to the completion and continuation of key economic reforms. In August 2018, Greece exited the third financial assistance programme, whereas the Greek government agreed to the Troika's monitoring the process of continuing economic reforms[82].

4.2.2. Ireland

As mentioned before, the fundamental cause of the banking crisis in Ireland was a real estate bubble burst. Since the state did not control banks' liabilities, mortgage debts exceeded half of Ireland's GDP in 2008[83]. It was an overwhelming burden on the Irish budget[84]. At the same time, the economy was experiencing a recession. In 2008, Ireland's GDP growth rate dropped to -4.5%, whereas budget deficit reached -7.0%. Only public debt remained in line with the Maastricht convergence criteria, at 42.40%. In 2009, Ireland's economic situation deteriorated further: GDP contracted at a rate of -5.1%, budget deficit fell to -13.8% of GDP and public debt exceeded the Maastricht convergence criterion, going up to 61.50% of GDP (cf. Table 1). Those development were accompanied by rising unemployment. In that situation, the Irish government requested help from the European Union and the International Monetary Fund. In 2011–2013, the European Union (the EFSM and the EFSF), the International Monetary Fund and

81 Financial assistance to euro area countries. Financial assistance to Greece, op. cit., pp. 2–9.

82 Ibidem, pp. 9–11.

83 Cf. M. Rosińska-Bukowska, op. cit., p. 352.

84 As mentioned before, for that reason Ireland had to pay the highest costs of aiding banks among the European Union Member States.

1st programme: May 2010 to March 2012 — Bilateral loans from EU Member States

2nd programme: March 2012 to June 2015 — Loans by EFSF*

3rd programme: August 2015 to August 2018 — Loans by ESM

Infographic 1. Financial assistance programmes of the European Union Member States for Greece in 2010–2018

* Plus the bridge loan of EUR 7.16 billion from the EFSM granted in June 2015

Source: prepared by the author on the basis of: Financial assistance to euro area countries. Financial assistance to Greece. Infographic – Financial assistance to Greece 2010–2018, https://www.consilium.europa.eu/en /infographics/financial-assistance-to-greece-2010-2018, pp. 1–2 [accessed: 20 July 2022]. J. Rymarczyk, Ratunek dla Grecji, [in:] Globalizacja i regionalizacja w gospodarce światowej, Księga jubileuszowa Profesora Jana Rymarczyka, B. Skulska, M. Domiter, W. Michalczyk (eds.), Wrocław 2012, pp. 591–603.

non-euro area countries (the United Kingdom, Sweden and Denmark) granted financial assistance to Ireland. In return, Ireland undertook to implement the necessary recovery reforms, including the strengthening and comprehensive overhaul of the banking sector; the correction of excessive deficit by 2015, through measures such as cutting expenditure on social assistance and pensions; reducing the minimum wage; increasing taxes; as well as growth-enhancing reforms, particularly in the labour market[85]. Having completed most of the above-mentioned reforms, Ireland exited the EFSM, EFSF and IMF programmes in December 2013[86].

4.2.3. Cyprus

Due to the banking crisis in Cyprus, in June 2012 the Cypriot government requested help from the European Union and the International Monetary Fund. As a result, the EU Member States granted Cyprus ESM loans totalling EUR 9 billion, whereas the International Monetary Fund promised financial assistance worth EUR 1 billion. Ultimately, Cyprus received ESM and IMF loans amounting to EUR 6.3 billion and EUR 1 billion respectively. In return, the Cypriot government undertook to modernise the country's economy. First of all, Cyprus restructured and recapitalised banks, improved financial regulations and financial supervision of banks and other credit institutions. On the other hand, the country reduced its budget deficit and balanced public debt. Furthermore, Cyprus implemented the necessary reforms in public administration, services and wage policy. As a consequence of the reforms, Cyprus restored investor confidence and could gradually return to the bond market. In March 2016, the Cypriot government exited the ESM programme[87], simultaneously agreeing to the Troika's monitoring of the repayment of financial liabilities and the implementation of the reforms, in particular efforts to reduce bad loans in accounts of Cypriot banks[88].

---

85 Financial assistance to euro area countries. Financial assistance to Ireland, https://economy-finance.ec.europa.eu/eu-financial-assistance/euro-area-countries/financial-assistance-ireland_en, pp. 1–2 [accessed: 20 July 2022]. Cf. also: M. Rosińska-Bukowska, op. cit., p. 352.

86 EFSF/ESM. Financial Assistance, op. cit., pp. 59, 63. However, the last disbursement from the EFSM to Ireland was made in March 2014.

87 EFSF/ESM. Financial Assistance, op. cit., pp. 59, 64.

88 Financial assistance to euro area countries. Financial assistance to Cyprus. ESM. How Cyprus modernised its economy, https://www.esm.europa.eu/assistance/cyprus/, pp. 1–2 [accessed: 20 July 2022].

4.2.4. Spain

As indicated before, the banking crisis in Spain, similarly to that experienced by Ireland, was mainly caused by a real estate bubble burst. The bubble was inflated by easy access to bank loans. In 1997–2008, house prices in Spain nearly tripled. When the crisis hit they plummeted; banks suffered huge losses as their clients were no longer able to repay their mortgage loans. Consequently, it substantially undermined banks' capacity to lend money or acquire capital. Another cause of the economic difficulties in Spain was a fall in employment by small and medium-sized enterprises, followed by a rise in unemployment, exceeding 20%, or even going up to 45% in the group of persons under 25 years of age[89]. Owing to the banking crisis and an upsurge in unemployment, in 2012 the Spanish economy as a whole experienced a major downturn (-3.0% of GDP), accompanied by high levels of budget deficit (-10.7% of GDP) and public debt (86.30% of GDP).

In order to overcome the crisis quickly, Spain requested financial assistance from the European Union as early as July 2012. The ESM granted Spain loans of up to EUR 100 billion, but eventually the Spanish government only used EUR 41.3 billion, allocating the funds to reforming the banking system. In accordance with bank resolution plans agreed with the European Commission and compatible with the State aid rules, Spain assigned an amount of around EUR 38.9 billion to bank recapitalisation, whereas approx. EUR 2.4 billion was used for capitalising a Spanish asset management company, Sareb[90]. The reform included both bank-specific conditionality and horizontal conditionality. The bank-specific conditionality comprised the segregation of impaired assets from the balance sheets of banks receiving public support and their transfer to an external asset management company (Sareb), the recapitalisation and restructuring of viable banks and an orderly resolution of non-viable banks as well as a comprehensive diagnostic with regard to the capital needs of individual banks. Horizontal conditionality comprised measures aimed at strengthening regulatory, supervisory and bank resolution frameworks, enhancing the bank governance structure as well as amending consumer protection legislation as regards the sale by banks of subordinated debt instruments. Spain completed the ESM programme in 2014, voluntarily commencing early loan repayment. The support enabled Spain to

89 M. Rosińska-Bukowska, op. cit., pp. 355–356.

90 ESM. European Stability Mechanism. Spain: a fast and effective programme, https://www.esm.europa.eu/assistance/spain, pp. 1–2 [accessed: 20 July 2022].

restructure its banking sector. The programme duration was 18 months, a much shorter period than those of the ESM and EFSF programmes agreed for other countries. Another difference between the ESM assistance package for Spain and those for other beneficiaries of the programme was the allocation of funds solely to the restructuring of banks[91].

4.2.5. Portugal

A public finance crisis, mainly caused by the levels of budget deficit (-11.4% of GDP) and public debt (100.20% of GDP) rising from 2010, forced the Portuguese government to seek external loans to remedy the situation. In April 2011, as the third country following in the footsteps of Greece and Ireland, Portugal requested financial assistance from the European Union and the International Monetary Fund. An economic adjustment programme, negotiated between the Portuguese government and representatives of the European Commission, the European Central Bank and the International Monetary Fund in May 2011, included a joint financing package for Portugal amounting to a total of EUR 78 billion, with equal contributions of EUR 26 billion from the EFSM, the EFSF and the IMF. Ultimately, however, between 2012 and 2014 Portugal used slightly lower loan amounts: EUR 24.3 billion from the EFSM, EUR 26 billion from the EFSF and EUR 26.5 billion from the IMF[92]. The economic adjustment programme encompassed structural reforms in the economy, aimed at boosting growth, creating jobs and improving the competitiveness of the Portuguese economy; gradually reducing public debt and considerably lowering budget deficit below 3% of GDP by 2014 by cutting social benefits and raising taxes; as well as recapitalising the financial sector through measures such as the privatisation of the energy corporation *Energias de Portugal*, the fuel company GALP, the airline TAP and the broadcaster RTP[93]. In May 2014, Portugal completed its three-year recovery programme which largely contributed to its limited economic growth (0.8% of

---

91 ESM. European Stability Mechanism. Spain: a fast and effective programme, op. cit., p. 2. Financial assistance to euro area countries. Financial assistance to Spain. Summary, https://www.esm.europa.eu/assistance/spain, pp. 1–2 [accessed: 20 July 2022]. EFSF/ESM. Financial Assistance, op. cit., pp. 59, 63.

92 Financial assistance to euro area countries. Financial assistance to Portugal. Post-Programme surveillance, https://www.esm.europa.eu/assistance/portugal, pp. 1–3 [accessed: 20 July 2022].

93 For more information on the Portuguese reprivatisation programme, cf. M. Rosińska-Bukowska, op. cit., pp. 352–353.

GDP), but with a rather significant level of budget deficit (-7.4% of GDP) and very high public debt (132.9% of GDP) (cf. Table 1)[94].

4.2.6. *Italy*

As mentioned before, the banking crisis in Italy, stemming from very high levels of bad loans in Italian banks, was accompanied by other serious economic difficulties such as the poor competitiveness of Italy's economy, substantial public debt and continuously low GDP growth rates. As the yield on Italian ten-year bonds reached the then record high of 5.77% in July 2011, the Italian government was provided assistance by the European Central Bank, buying out Italian debt instruments[95]. In 2012, the Italian economy experienced a slump (-3.0%), whereas public debt reached 126.50% of GDP, among the highest levels in the euro area (cf. Table 1). Nevertheless, as mentioned before, Italy was the only country not to use any external loans. At the initiative of the then Prime Minister and simultaneously a well-known economist, Mario Monti, a national financial assistance programme was developed, with anti-crisis funds of EUR 20 billion, in 2012. The programme involved structural reforms in the Italian economy, including measures such as enhancing labour market flexibility in order to increase labour productivity, cutting corporate taxes to stimulate economic growth as well as strengthening domestic industry and small enterprises, restructuring banks with a view to significantly reducing bad loans[96].

4.3. The Eurosystem programmes as tools for boosting economic growth in the euro area

The appointment of a well-known Italian economist and the head of the national central bank, Mario Draghi, as the President of the European Central Bank on 1 November 2011 was another turning point in the process of fighting the euro area debt crisis[97]. In his famous speech given in London on 12 July 2012, he said

94 EFSF/ESM. Financial Assistance, op. cit., pp. 59, 63. However, the last disbursement from the EFSM was made in November 2014.

95 M. Rosińska-Bukowska, op. cit., p. 354.

96 Ibidem, pp. 354–355.

97 The first measures aimed to overcome the crisis were taken by the ECB as early as 2010, at the initiative of the previous President Jean-Claude Trichet. On 14 May 2010, the ECB established a temporary securities markets programme (SMP). Under the programme, the European Central Bank and the national central banks of the euro area, according to their percentage shares in the key for subscription of the ECB's capital,

that within its mandate, 'the ECB is ready to do whatever it takes to preserve the euro. And believe me, it will be enough'[98]. Draghi was an unwavering supporter

could conduct outright interventions in the euro area public and private debt securities markets, cf. Decision of the European Central Bank of 14 May 2010 establishing a securities markets programme, Official Journal of the European Union, L 124, 20.5.2010, p. 8–9. The programme was implemented in 2010–2012 and cost a total of EUR 210 billion, cf. P. Kalka, op. cit., pp. 319–320. J. Janus. Zmiany struktury instytucjonalnej strefy euro a skuteczność polityki pieniężnej Europejskiego Banku Centralnego [Changes in the institutional structure of the euro area and the effectiveness of the monetary policy of the European Central Bank], [in:] Przyszły instytucjonalny kształt strefy euro [The future institutional shape of the euro area], A. Wojtyna (ed.), Warszawa 2015, p. 126. The subscribed capital of the ECB comes from the central banks of all the European Union Member States, whereby their percentage weightings depend on their respective shares in the total population and GDP of the Union. The weightings assigned to the NCBs are adjusted every five years and additionally after any change in the number of the EU Member States. The euro area NCBs pay up 100% of their subscriptions to the capital of the ECB, whereas the non-euro area NCBs contribute 3.75%, cf. European Central Bank. Eurosystem, Capital subscription, https://www.ecb.europa.eu/ecb/, pp. 1–3 [accessed: 27 September 2022]. According to the latest adjustment of 1 February 2020, following the withdrawal of the United Kingdom from the EU, the capital contributed by the EU Member States' central banks was EUR 10.82 billion, of which EUR 8.19 represented capital coming from the euro area NCBs. Since 1 February 2020, the highest contributions to the subscribed capital of the ECB have been those of Germany (26.36%), France (20.42%), Italy (16.98%) and Spain (11.92%). The eight non-euro area NCBs have contributed no subscribed capital, but they have covered part of the operating expenses of the ECB due to their membership of the European System of Central Banks, with the highest percentage shares paid by Poland (6.03%), Sweden (2.97%) and Romania (2.82%), cf. Decision (EU) 2020/138 of the European Central Bank of 22 January 2020 on the paying-up of the European Central Bank's capital by the national central banks of Member States whose currency is the euro and repealing Decision (EU) 2019/44 (ECB/2020/4), Official Journal of the European Union, L 27I, 1.2.2020, pp. 6–8. European Central Bank. Eurosystem, Capital subscription, op. cit., pp. 3–5. European Central Bank. Eurosystem, ECB's subscribed capital to remain steady after Bank of England leaves the European System of Central Banks. Press release, 30 January 2020, https://www.ecb.europa.eu/, pp. 1–4 [accessed: 27 September 2020]. H.K. Scheller, Europejski Bank Centralny. Historia, rola i funkcje [The European Central Bank. The history, role and functions], Warszawa 2006, pp. 118–119.

98 Euro is irreversible, declares European Central Bank president Mario Draghi. ECB will do 'whatever it takes' to preserve the currency, https://www.theguardian.com/business/2012/jul/26/euro-irreversible-mario-draghi-ecb, p. 1 [accessed: 10 January 2023]. For the European Parliament's publication referring to that event ten years later, cf. European Parliament. 10 years after "whatever it takes": fragmentation risk in the current

of the easing of monetary policy, also referred to as quantitative easing (QE). The easing of monetary policy consisted in purchasing larger amounts of debt instruments from the secondary market in order to stimulate economic growth, primarily in the euro area Member States affected by the debt crisis. At Draghi's initiative, the European Central Bank prepared a special programme for purchasing securities in the euro area (Asset Purchase Programme – APP). In its final version, the APP was composed of four projects launched successively in 2014–2016. The first one was the third covered bond purchase programme (CBPP3) implemented from 20 October 2014. The second project, launched on 21 November 2014, was the asset-backed securities purchase programme (ABSPP), i.e. a programme for purchasing securities issued as a result of the securitisation of bank loans. The third component of the APP was the Public Sector Purchase Programme (PSPP), initiated on 15 March 2015. Finally, the fourth project, launched on 8 June 2016, was a programme for purchasing bonds and commercial papers issued by non-financial corporations located in the euro area Member States, referred to as the Corporate Sector Purchase Programme (CSPP)[99].

But the breakthrough event for the implementation of all the four components of the APP was the launch of the PSPP, established under Decision (EU) 2015/774 of the European Central Bank of 4 March 2015 on a secondary markets public sector asset purchase programme. Under the programme, the European Central Bank and the euro area national central banks, together forming the monetary authority of the euro area called the Eurosystem[100], purchased, in the secondary markets, securities issued by central governments of the euro area Member States and recognised agencies located in the euro area (Article 3(1) of the ECB Decision). Where the envisaged purchase amount could not be attained, those entities could also purchase securities issued by international organisations and 'multilateral development banks' located in the euro area (Article 3(1)

---

context. Compilation of papers. Monetary Dialogue Papers June 2022, Directorate-General for Internal Policies PE 703.367 – June 2022, pp. 1–115, https://www.europarl.europa.eu/RegData/etudes/STUD/2022/703367/IPOL_STU(2022)703367_EN. pdf [accessed: 10 January 2023].

99 European Central Bank. Eurosystem, Asset purchase programmes, https://www.ecb.europa.eu/, pp. 1–3 [accessed: 27 September 2022].

100 The primary objectives of the Eurosystem include the maintenance of price stability and the promotion of financial integration in the euro area, cf. European Central Bank. Eurosystem, Eurosystem mission, p. 1, https://www.ecb.europa.eu/ecb/ [accessed: 27 September 2022].

of the ECB Decision)[101]. Furthermore, the euro area national central banks only purchased securities of their own respective jurisdictions and in proportions reflecting their respective shares in the ECB's capital key. At the same time, pursuant to Article 123(1) TFEU, neither the ECB nor the euro area NCBs could purchase securities in the primary markets, i.e. directly from the governments of the euro area Member States. The purchase of securities by the ECB and the NCBs from commercial banks was supposed to push up securities prices and to increase the money supply in the banking system. Therefore, interest rates charged on various financial instruments, including loans, should go down. That should stimulate expenditure by individuals and corporations on investment and consumption, which in turn should boost economic growth and employment in the euro area Member States[102].

The NCBs' share of the book value of purchases was 90%, whereas only 10% would be purchased by the ECB. As regards issuers, the euro area governments and recognised agencies represented the highest proportion. Government and Agency bonds accounted for as much as 90% of the purchases, whereas the remaining 10% would be of bonds issued by international organisations and multilateral development banks[103]. In 2015–2018, the total amount assigned to

---

101 Decision (EU) 2015/774 of the European Central Bank of 4 March 2015 on a secondary markets public sector asset purchase programme (ECB/2015/10), Official Journal of the European Union, L 121, 14.5.2015, p. 20–24. The multilateral development banks recognised by the Eurosystem included the European Investment Bank, the European Bank for Reconstruction and Development, the International Bank for Reconstruction and Development, the Nordic Investment Bank and the Council of Europe Development Bank. At the same time, the international organisations recognised by the Eurosystem encompassed: the European Union, the International Monetary Fund, the Bank for International Settlements and, as discussed below, the European Financial Stability Facility and the European Stability Mechanism (Article 2 of the ECB Decision), cf. ibidem, p. 21. Regulation (EU) No 575/2013 of the European Parliament and of the Council of 26 June 2013 on prudential requirements for credit institutions and investment firms and amending Regulation (EU) No 648/2012, Official Journal of the European Union, L 176, 27.6.2013, p. 78.

102 Decision (EU) 2015/774 of the European Central Bank, op. cit. pp. 1, 24. For an interpretation of Decision (EU) 2015/774 of the European Central Bank, cf. European Central Bank. Eurosystem, How quantitative easing works, https://www.ecb.europa.eu/ecb/educational/explainers/show-me/html/app_infographic.en.html, pp. 1–3 [accessed: 27 September 2022].

103 Central Bank of Ireland. The Public Sector Purchase Programme (PSPP), p. 1, https://www.ecb.europa.eu/ecb/educational/explainers/show-me/html/app_infographic.en.html, [accessed: 27 September 2022].

securities purchases in the euro area under the APP was as much as EUR 2.6 trillion, with the highest share of the PSPP. On 1 November 2019, the asset purchase programme was restarted, albeit to a limited extent; it ended on 1 July 2022[104].

The public sector purchase programme raised significant controversy in the Northern Member States of the euro area, especially in Germany. Specifically, German opponents to the PSPP argued that quantitative easing by the European Central Bank transgressed the boundary between permitted monetary policy and the financing, prohibited under Article 123(1) TFEU, of debts of the euro area Member States affected by the debt crisis through the ECB's purchasing their bonds. Critics of the PSPP also pointed out that the highest contribution to the financing of that debt would be made by the Deutsche Bundesbank (Germany's central bank), due to its share of the subscribed capital of the ECB (27%). Therefore, groups critical of the PSPP filed four constitutional complaints with Germany's Federal Constitutional Court (*Bundesverfassungsgericht*, BVerfG). On 5 May 2020, the BVerfG ruled that Decision (EU) 2015/774 of the European Central Bank of 4 March 2015 on a secondary markets public sector asset purchase programme, amended by Decision (EU) 2017/100 of the ECB of 11 January 2017[105], as well as the judgment of the Court of Justice of the European Union (CJEU) of 11 December 2018 accepting quantitative easing by the ECB[106] were acts issued outside the scope of competence, i.e. amounting to *ultra vires* acts, regarding them as partly contrary to EU law. The BVerfG expressly submitted that the Governing Council of the ECB had infringed the EU principle

---

104 Bank of Italy. The Eurosystem's asset purchase programmes, p. 3, https://www.bancaditalia.it/ [accessed: 27 September 2022].

105 Decision (EU) 2015/774 of the European Central Bank, op. cit. pp. 20–24. Decision (EU) 2017/100 of the European Central Bank of 11 January 2017 amending Decision (EU) 2015/774 on a secondary markets public sector asset purchase programme (ECB/2017/1), Official Journal of the European Union, L 16, 20.1.2017, pp. 51–52.

106 The judgment of the Court of Justice of the EU was given on 11 December 2018, as a preliminary ruling requested by the BVerfG in 2017 with regard to quantitative easing. The Grand Chamber of the Court of Justice of the EU then ruled, *inter alia*, that the PSPP did not exceed the ECB's mandate as the programme concerned the area of the Union's exclusive competence for the euro area Member States and did not infringe the principle of proportionality, cf. Judgment of the Court (Grand Chamber) of 11 December 2018, Case C-493/17, ECLI:EU:C:2018:1000, https://curia.europa.eu/juris/document [accessed: 25 September 2022]. Court of Justice of the European Union. Press release No 192/18, Luxembourg, 11 December 2018, Judgment in Case C-493/17, Heinrich Weiss and Others, https://curia.europa.eu/jcms/, pp. 1–3 (here: p. 2) [accessed: 27 September 2022].

of proportionality and additionally held that the Governing Council of the ECB and the Court of Justice of the EU had breached the principle of conferral of powers.

According to the BVerfG, the ECB exceeded its mandate as it failed to conduct a sufficient 'proportionality analysis' for the PSPP. The BVerfG ruled that maintaining the competences of the European Union was essential to guaranteeing the principle of democracy, whereas the integration process must not lead to an actual cancellation of the principle of limited conferred powers as one of the fundamental principles of the European Union (paragraph 158). At the same time, the principle of proportionality in the delimitation of competences between the European Union and the Member States and the related overall assessment were relevant to the principles of democracy and national sovereignty. Neglecting them might shift the foundations of the competences of the European Union and undermine the principle of limited conferred powers (paragraph 158). The proportionality of the government bond purchase programme, in addition to its adequacy to the attainment of the intended purpose and necessity, required identifying, weighting and balancing the monetary policy objective against the resulting economic policy effects. But the unconditional pursuit of the monetary policy objective, ignoring the PSPP-related economic policy effects, was manifestly contrary to the principle of proportionality set out in Article 5(1) and (4) TEU (paragraph 165).

The BVerfG also found that the public sector asset purchase programme was partly contrary to the *Grundgesetz* (Basic Law) of the FRG, submitting that the German Federal Government and the Bundestag had infringed the German Constitution in their failure to scrutinise whether or not purchases of government bonds of the euro area Member States exceeded the powers of the ECB. Further, the BVerfG required that the state authorities of the FRG, including the Deutsche Bundesbank, no longer participate in the implementation of the PSPP if it should continue to infringe the principle of conferral of powers, unless the Governing Council of the ECB should demonstrate in a new decision, in a comprehensible manner, that the monetary policy objectives pursued by it under the PSPP were not disproportionate to the related economic and fiscal policies. In addition, the Federal Constitutional Court ruled that the Federal Government and the Bundestag, due to their responsibility for integration, were obliged to take measures aimed at the ECB's conducting an assessment of proportionality. It also required that the authorities concerned present to the European Central Bank their legal opinion or otherwise ensure restoring conditions compatible with the Treaty (paragraph 232). The BVerfG took the view that the constitutional authorities, public authorities and courts (of the FRG) must not participate in the creation, implementation, enforcement or operationalisation of any *ultra vires* acts, which concerned the Bundesbank as well (paragraph 234)[107]. As the PSPP was regarded as an *ultra vires* act to the extent to which the ECB had failed to assess its proportionality, the German Federal Government and the Bundestag, as the authorities responsible for integration, were required to take measures aimed at the ECB's carrying out such an assessment. As argued by the BVerfG, the requirement did not infringe the independence of the ECB or the Bundesbank (Article 130, Article 282 TFEU, Article 88 second sentence of the *Grundgesetz*). Therefore, the Federal Government and the Bundestag had a duty to clearly present to the ECB their legal position or to otherwise ensure restoring conditions compatible with the Treaty[108]. On the other hand, however, the BVerfG refused to agree with the criticism by the German opponents to the PSPP that quantitative easing infringed Article 123(1) TFEU on the prohibition of the financing of the Member States' budgets[109]. Nevertheless, the ruling of the German Federal Constitutional Court of 5 May 2020 established a very important precedent as for the first time in the history of the European Union the BVerfG so explicitly objected to a judgment of the Court of Justice of the EU and

107 BverfG. 2 BvR 859/15, 2 BvR 1651/15, 2 BvR 2006/15, 2 BvR 980/16. Leitsätze zum Urteil vom 5. Mai 2020, https://www.Bundesverfassungsgericht.de/, pp. 1–3 [accessed: 25 September 2022]. BVerfG. 2 BvR 859/15, 2 BvR 1651/15, 2 BvR 2006/15, 2 BvR 980/16. Urteil vom 5. Mai 2020, https://www.Bundesverfassungsgericht.de/, pp. 86–88 [accessed: 25 September 2022].

108 BVerfG ... Urteil, op. cit., p. 112.

109 Ibidem, pp. 71–72. For an interpretation of the BVerfG judgment of 5 May 2020, cf. M. Bainczyk, Glosa do wyroku FTK z 5 maja 2020 r. w sprawie obligacji EBC [An opinion on the the BVerfG judgment of 5 May 2020 on ECB bonds], 'Studia Prawnicze: Rozprawy i Materiały' 2020, no. 2, p. 258. Idem, Czy RFN może współtworzyć państwo europejskie? [Can the FRG co-create a European state?] 'Biuletyn Instytutu Zachodniego' 2022, no. 21, p. 5. C. Mik, Opinia prawna dotycząca orzeczenia Federalnego Trybunału Konstytucyjnego RFN w przedmiocie pierwszeństwa prawa UE [A legal opinion on the judgment by the Germany's Federal Constitutional Court with regard to the primacy of EU law], 'Zeszyty Prawnicze' 2020, no. 3, pp. 112–140. J. Górska-Szymczak, G. Górski, Orzeczenia ultra vires Trybunału Sprawiedliwości Unii Europejskiej i ich ocena w orzecznictwie niemieckiego Federalnego Trybunału Konstytucyjnego. Uwagi na marginesie orzeczenia z 5 maja 2020 r. [*Ultra vires* judgments of the Court of Justice of the European Union and their assessments in the case-law of the German Federal Constitutional Court. Remarks on the judgment of 5 May 2020], 'Przegląd Prawa Konstytucyjnego' 2021, no. 3, pp. 343–361.

even found that the judgment concerned did not bind the Federal Republic of Germany.

Therefore, the Deutsche Bundesbank requested explanations from the Governing Council of the ECB with regard to the proportionality assessment of the PSPP. At the meeting held on 3–4 June 2020, the Governing Council of the ECB adopted two decisions indicating and demonstrating that such a proportionality test, with a comprehensive assessment of interests considered and balancing the interests affected, including counter-arguments, had been conducted. On 26 June 2020, the Deutsche Bundesbank disclosed to the German Federal Ministry of Finance appropriate, including non-public, ECB documents in that regard, subsequently provided to the German Parliament. In the relevant letter to the Bundestag, the Ministry of Finance argued that the decision of the Governing Council of the ECB had been made after conducting a proportionality assessment of the PSPP and, as such, fully satisfied the requirements arising from the judgment of the Federal Constitutional Court of 5 May 2020.[110] On 2 July 2020, after reviewing all the documents received from the ECB, the Bundestag adopted, by a broad majority, a resolution declaring that the proportionality assessment conducted by the ECB's Governing Council satisfied the requirements set out in the judgment concerned[111].

Although the German Federal Government and the Bundestag, after considering all the documents provided by the ECB, including non-public information, found the proportionality assessment of the PSPP contained therein to be sufficient, on 9 June 2021 the European Commission launched an infringement procedure against Germany under Article 258 TFEU. The Commission also sent a 'letter of formal notice' to the German authorities, due to the BVerfG's having undermined the jurisdiction of the European Court of the EU and challenged the validity of the ECB Decision on bond purchases under the PSPP. However, after reviewing the German Federal Government's explanations provided in reply to the letter of formal notice and declaration containing commitments to observing the principles of autonomy, primacy, effectiveness and uniform application of

110 BVerfG. Pressemitteilung Nr. 38/2021. Erfolglose Vollstreckungsanträge zum Urteil des Zweiten Senats zu dem PSPP-Anleihekaufprogramm der EZB, Karlsruhe, 18. Mai 2021, https://www.bundesverfassungsgericht.de/, pp. 1–2.

111 The resolution was adopted against the votes of the *AfD* parliamentary group and with abstentions from the *Die Linke* parliamentary group. For information on the course of the debate, cf. Deutscher Bundestag, Verhandlungen des Deutschen Bundestages. Stenographische Berichte. 19. Wahlperiode. 170. Sitzung am 2. Juli 2020, pp. 21274–21283, https://www.bundestag.de/ [accessed: 22 July 2022].

Union law and the principle of sincere cooperation (duty of loyal cooperation) as well as regarding judgments of Court of Justice of the EU as final and binding, the European Commission decided to close the infringement procedure against Germany on 2 December 2021[112].

5. Taking stock of the implementation of the financial assistance and recovery programmes and of the Eurosystem projects

In 2010–2018, the fight against the euro area debt crisis cost a whopping EUR 415.66 billion; the countries affected received EUR 348.96 billion from the European Financial Stabilisation Mechanism, the European Financial Stability Facility and the European Stability Mechanism[113], EUR 61.90 billion from the International Monetary Fund and EUR 4.8 billion as bilateral loans from the non-euro area Member States (the United Kingdom, Sweden and Denmark). Greece was granted another EUR 73 billion as a temporary loan from the European Union Member States (EUR 52.9 billion) and the International Monetary Fund (EUR 20.1 billion) under the abovementioned first assistance programme. On the other hand, it must be emphasised that the actual scale of financial assistance for combating the crisis would be understated without the national funds assigned by Italy (EUR 20 billion) and Ireland (EUR 17.5 billion). Therefore, in 2010–2018, transfers of external and internal funds allocated to overcoming the crisis in the euro area totalled EUR 526.16 billion (cf. Table 2).

Table 2: Total transfers of external and internal funds allocated to overcoming the euro area crisis in 2010–2018 (EUR billion)

Country	Bilateral loans from the EU MSs	Loans from the IMF	EFSM loans	EFSF loans	ESM loans	National funds	Total
Greece	52.90	32.10	7.16	141.80	61.90		295.86
Cyprus		1.00			6.30		7.30

112 For more on the subject, cf. Th. Giegerich, Ende gut, alles gut? – Europäische Kommission stellt Vertragsverletzungsverfahren gegen Deutschland wegen des Karlsruher PSPP-Urteils ein, 3. Dezember 2021, https://jean-monnet-saar.eu/, p. 1 [accessed: 30 September 2022].

113 Including the short-term bridge loan of EUR 7.16 billion granted to Greece by the EFSM in 2015.

Country	Bilateral loans from the EU MSs	Loans from the IMF	EFSM loans	EFSF loans	ESM loans	National funds	Total
Ireland	4.80	22.50	22.50	17.70		17.50	85.00
Spain					41.30		41.30
Portugal		26.40	24.30	26.00			76.70
Italy						20.00	20.00
Total	57.70	82.00	53.96	185.50	109.50	37.50	526.16

Source: prepared by the author on the basis of: European Stability Mechanism. EFSF-ESM, op. cit., pp. 43–44, 46, 49. EFSF/ESM. Financial Assistance. Evaluation Report, op. cit., p. 38. C. Alcidi, D. Gros, J.N. Ferrer, D. Rinaldi, op. cit., p. 12. EFSF-ESM. Überblick, op. cit., pp. 4–9, 14–17.

As mentioned before, Germany was the largest net payer in financing the fight against the crisis among the European Union Member States. According to data of the German Federal Ministry of Finance, as at 31 December 2018, Germany's contribution to combating the crisis under temporary and permanent stabilisation mechanisms amounted to approx. EUR 90.44 billion[114]. With regard to the European Financial Stability Facility and the European Stability Mechanism, Germany contributed around EUR 79.65 billion[115], i.e. about 27% of the euro area Member States' total contributions according to the ECB's capital key[116], whereas in the case of the European Financial Stabilisation Mechanism – approx. EUR 10.79 billion[117], accounting for 20% of the overall contributions from the euro area Member States (in accordance with the share in the EU's general budget)[118]. Considering the loans of EUR 15.2 billion granted by the FRG under the first programme for Greece, Germany's total financial assistance to the indebted euro area economies in the form of loans amounted to EUR 105.64 billion (cf. Table 3)[119].

114 EFSF-ESM. Überblick, op. cit., pp. 2, 8.

115 Ibidem, pp. 4–7.

116 Cf. Narodowy Bank Polski [National Bank of Poland]. Departament Zagraniczny. Informacja na temat nowych zasad funkcjonowania Europejskiego Instrumentu Stabilności Finansowej oraz przyszłego kształtu Europejskiego Mechanizmu Stabilności [Information on the new principles and rules of the functioning of the European Financial Stability Facility and the future shape of the European Stability Mechanism], http://www.nbp.pl/, pp. 2–3 [accessed: 20 July 2022].

117 EFSF-ESM. Überblick, op. cit., pp. 2–17.

118 Ibidem, pp. 5–7.

119 For more on the influence of the German Federal Government on the dynamics of the debt crisis and the system reform of the Economic and Monetary Union, cf. J.J. Węc,

Table 3: Germany's financial contribution to the fight against the crisis (EUR billion)

Bilateral loans to Greece	Contributions to the EFSM and EFSF	Contributions to the ESM	Total
15.20	79.65	10.79	105.64

Source: prepared by the author on the basis of: EFSF-ESM. Überblick, op. cit., pp. 2–17.

Despite such significant funds, the introduction of most of the recovery reforms planned and the implementation of the Eurosystem programmes aimed at boosting growth, primarily in the indebted economies, the euro area debt crisis was hardly overcome in 2019. The majority of the Member States affected by the crisis had not been very successful in improving their public debt situations. After exiting their respective financial assistance programmes, all the countries under review continued to record significant public debt levels. Thus, having exited its financial assistance programmes in 2018, Greece remained the most indebted economy in the euro area. In spite of achieving in the same year the highest growth rate of GDP from the beginning of the crisis, at 1.7%, and a budget surplus of 1.0% of GDP, the Greek public debt was as much as 186.4% of GDP (cf. Table 1).

The Spanish, Portuguese and Italian economies performed slightly better. Having exited its financial assistance programmes in 2014, Spain entered a path of economic growth, recording a GDP growth rate of 2.3% in 2018. In 2017–2018, Spain also pushed down its budget deficit to a level satisfying the relevant convergence criterion under the Maastricht Treaty. But it still had not managed to meet the public debt requirement. In 2017 and 2018, the public debt levels in the Spanish economy were 101.8% and 100.4% of GDP respectively. Portugal, having also exited its financial assistance programmes in 2014, entered an economic growth path as well, noting a

Germany's Position, op. cit., pp. 180–216. Idem, Niemcy wobec reformy ustrojowej strefy euro [Germany and the system reform of the euro area], 'Roczniki Nauk Społecznych' 2016, no. 3, pp. 45–84. Idem, Die politische Debatte, op. cit., pp. 201–208. Idem, Debata w Niemczech na temat drugiej reformy ustrojowej Unii Europejskiej (2011–2012). Ewolucja programowa niemieckich partii politycznych w polityce europejskiej [The German debate on the second system reform of the European Union (2011–2012). The programme development of the German political parties in European politics], [in:] Dylematy strategiczne XXI wieku. Księga Jubileuszowa dedykowana Profesorowi Michałowi Chorośnickiemu z okazji czterdziestolecia pracy naukowej [The strategic dilemmas of the 21st century. The Professor Michał Chorośnicki Anniversary Volume honouring 40 years of his research work], B. Szlachta, J.J. Węc (eds.), Kraków 2013, pp. 431–452.

GDP growth rate of 2.8% in 2018. In 2016–2018, Portugal met the Maastricht convergence criterion with regard to budget deficit, but it still considerably exceeded the criterion of public debt. Between 2015 and 2018, the Portuguese economy noted debt-to-GDP ratios of 131.2%, 131.5%, 126.1% and 121.5% respectively. As mentioned before, Italy used no external financial assistance programme; in 2015–2018, the country also entered a path of economic growth and satisfied the Maastricht convergence criterion of budget deficit. Nevertheless, in the period in question, Italy was one of the two most indebted economies (in addition to Greece) in the euro area and the European Union as a whole. In 2015–2018, its public debt levels reached 135.3%, 134.8%, 134.2% and 134.4% of GDP respectively (cf. Table 1).

Simultaneously, an assessment of the economic performance of Cyprus must be ambivalent. Having exited its financial assistance programmes in 2016, the Cypriot economy entered a path of rapid economic growth, noting GDP growth rates of 5.7% and 5.6% in 2017 and 2018 respectively. In 2018, however, for the first time from 2014, Cyprus exceeded the Maastricht convergence criterion for budget deficit (-4.4% of GDP). But significant public debt remained the most challenging issue in the Cypriot economy, at 92.6% and 98.1% of GDP in 2017 and 2018 respectively. The only country to have recovered from the debt crisis was Ireland. Having exited its financial assistance programmes in 2013, the Irish economy entered a path of buoyant or even very strong economic growth. Between 2014 and 2018, its GDP grew at the respective rates of 8.6%, 24.4% (sic!), 2.0%, 9.0% and 8.5%. In 2015–2017, Ireland recorded an insignificant budget deficit that turned into a budget surplus of 0.1% of GDP in 2018. Simultaneously, its public debt only slightly exceeded the relevant Maastricht convergence criterion in 2015–2018 (cf. Table 1).

6. The economic consequences of the crisis

The euro area debt crisis was formally overcome in 2018 as all the Member States had exited their respective financial assistance programmes by then. But the affected economies continued to suffer its economic consequences for a long time. Those primarily took on three forms: (1) the still high public debt levels in the Southern euro area economies; (2) the dynamics of GDP *per capita* in the euro area and the European Union as a whole; and (3) the development of economic convergence in the EU.

In 2019–2021, the public debt levels in the Member States having experienced the debt crisis (with the exception of Ireland) remained very high, constituting a sort of 'pitfall' under the whole euro area. In 2019, the debt-to-GDP ratios in those countries were as follows: in Greece – 180.6%, in Italy – 134.1%, in Portugal – 116.6%, in Spain – 98.2% and in Cyprus – 90.4; in 2020, mostly due to the pandemic, those figures increased even further: to 206.3% in Greece, 154.9% in Italy, 134.9% in Portugal, 120.4% in Spain and 113.5% in Cyprus. It was not until 2021 that the public debt levels in the countries in question showed a slight decrease, but they still markedly exceeded the Maastricht criterion, at 194.5% of GDP in Greece, 150.3% of GDP in Italy, 125.5% of GDP in Portugal, 118.3% of GDP in Spain and 101.1% of GDP in Cyprus[120]. Between 2019 and 2021, only in Ireland the debt-to-GDP ratios satisfied the Maastricht criterion, at 57.0%, 58.4% and 55.4% respectively. On the other hand, all the countries under review remained on their economic growth paths in 2019, with the highest GDP growth rates noted by Cyprus (5.5%) and Ireland (5.4%) Furthermore, none of them, except for Spain (3.1% of GDP), noted a budget deficit exceeding the relevant Maastricht criterion. But the situation changed in 2020–2021, primarily due to the pandemic crisis. In the period in question, all the Member States under examination, including Ireland, noted significant budget deficits, particularly Spain (-10.1% and -6.9% of GDP), Greece (-9.9% and -7.5% of GDP) and Italy (-9.5% and -7.2% of GDP). Furthermore, in 2020, all the countries, except for Ireland, suffered substantial GDP contractions: Spain by 11.3%, Greece by 9.0%, Italy by 9.0%, Portugal by 8.3% and Cyprus by 4.4%. In the pandemic year, only Ireland noted economic growth at a rate of 6.2%. All the Member States concerned returned to economic growth paths in 2021, recording the following GDP growth rates: Ireland – 13.6%, Greece – 8.4%, Italy – 6.7%, Cyprus – 6.6%, Spain – 5.5%, Portugal – 5.5% (cf. Table 4).

The debt crisis as well as the pandemic crisis affected GDP *per capita* in the euro area and the European Union. Needless to say, some of those changes occurred during the debt crisis and persisted after overcoming it, being reflected in the following dimensions: GDP *per capita* in the euro area and in the European Union as a whole; differences in development between the South and the North of the European Union; and development disparities between the Central and Eastern European

120 Moreover, in 2019–2021, Belgium and France still recorded high public debt levels. In the period concerned, the respective GDP-to-debt ratios evolved from 97.6% through 112.0% to 109.2% in Belgium and from 97.4% through 115.0% to 112.8% in France. From the beginning of the debt crisis, the two Member States were characterised by high public debt levels. For Belgium, the GDP-to-debt ratios were as follows: 2010 – 100.3%; 2011 – 103.5%; 2012 – 104.8%; 2013 – 105.5%; 2014 – 107.0%; 2015 – 105.2%; 2016 – 105.0%; 2017 – 102.0%; and 2018 – 99.9%. In the same years, public debt in France was slightly lower, at 85.3%; 87.8%; 90.6%; 93.4%; 94.9%; 95.6%; 98.0%; 98.1%; and 97.8% of GDP respectively; cf. Eurostat. Government finance and EDP statistics. General government gross debt 2019–2021, Brussels 2022, https://ec.europa.eu/eurostat/en/, pp. 1–3 [accessed: 20 November 2022].

countries and the EU's South and North. Thus, in 2008–2009, 2012–2013 and 2020, both the euro area and the European Union suffered considerable contractions in GDP *per capita*, more abrupt in the euro area than in the EU. The growth rates of GDP *per capita* were also higher in the EU as a whole than in the euro area in 2010–2011, 2014–2019 and 2021 (cf. Chart 3)[121]. The years 2009–2021 saw widening differences in development between the South and the North of the EU. Whereas GDP *per capita* in the then weakest economies dropped by 22.1% in Greece, by 4.6% in Italy and by 1.7% in Spain in the period in question, Germany, Denmark and the Netherlands increased their GDP *per capita* by 9.8%, 9.4% and 5.4% respectively (cf. Chart 4). In 2009–2021, the development gap between the Central and Eastern European countries and the EU's South and North significantly narrowed (cf. Charts 5 and 6). The CEECs then enjoyed higher growth rates of GDP *per capita* than both the South and the North of the EU; for the fastest-growing economies of Poland, Lithuania, Estonia, Hungary, Latvia and Slovakia, the respective figures were 44.%, 40.%, 28.7%, 27.5%, 26.2% and 24.2%[122].

---

121 In comparing the dynamics of GDP *per capita* in the euro area and the European Union between 2004 and 2021, i.e. from the EU's first Eastern enlargement, it is worth pointing out that the overall growth rate of GDP *per capita* in the EU was 18.9%, whereas the GDP *per capita* of the euro area went up by 13.6%, cf. OECD.Stat. Growth in GDP per capita, productivity and ULC, https://stats.oecd.org/Index.aspx?DataSetCode=PDB_GR/, pp. 1–3. For information on the deterioration of the fiscal situations (budget deficit and public debt levels) in the new Member States (EU-10) in the aftermath of the euro area debt crisis, cf. E. Molendowski, P. Stanek, Globalny kryzys finansowo-gospodarczy i strefy euro a sytuacja fiskalna nowych państw członkowskich (UE-10) [The global and euro area financial and economic crisis and the fiscal situations of the new Member States (EU-10)], 'Acta Universitatis Lodziensis'. Folia Oeconomica, 2012, no. 273, pp. 267–284.

122 OECD.Stat. Growth in GDP per capita, productivity and ULC, pp. 1–3.

Table 4: Economic growth rates, deficit-to-GDP and debt-to-GDP ratios in selected euro area Member States in 2019–2021

Country	Year	GDP growth/ contraction (in %)	Budget deficit/surplus (in % of GDP)	Public debt (% of GDP)
Cyprus	2021	6.6	-1.7	101.1
	2020	-4.4	-5.8	113.5
	2019	5.5	1.3	90.4
Greece	2021	8.4	-7.5	194.5
	2020	-9.0	-9.9	206.3
	2019	1.9	1.1	180.6
Spain	2021	5.5	-6.9	118.3
	2020	-11.3	-10.1	120.4
	2019	2.0	-3.1	98.2
Ireland	2021	13.6	-1.7	55.4
	2020	6.2	-5.0	58.4
	2019	5.4	0.5	57.0
Portugal	2021	5.5	-2.9	125.5
	2020	-8.3	-5.8	134.9
	2019	2.7	0.1	116.6
Italy	2021	6.7	-7.2	150.3
	2020	-9.0	-9.5	154.9
	2019	0.5	-1.5	134.1
Belgium	2021	6.1	-5.6	109.2
	2020	-5.4	-9.0	112.0
	2019	2.2	-1.9	97.6
France	2021	6.8	-6.5	112.8
	2020	-7.8	-9.0	115.0
	2019	1.8	-3.1	97.4

Source: Eurostat. Real GDP growth rate – volume 2019–2021 (% change on previous period), Brussels 2022, https://ec.europa.eu/eurostat/en/, pp. 1–2 [accessed: 20 November 2022]. Eurostat. General government deficit/surplus 2019–2021 (% of GDP and million EUR), Brussels 2022, https://ec.europa.eu/eurostat/en/, pp. 1–2. [accessed: 20 November 2022]. Eurostat. Government finance and EDP statistics. General government gross debt 2019–2021, Brussels 2021, https://ec.europa.eu/eurostat/en, pp. 1–2 [accessed: 20 November 2022].

Chart 3: Growth rates of GDP *per capita* in the euro area and the EU in 2004–2021* (in %)

* Until 31 January 2020: the EU-28; from 1 February 2020: the EU-27

Source: prepared by the author on the basis of: OECD.Stat. Growth in GDP per capita, productivity and

ULC, https://stats.oecd.org/Index.aspx?DataSetCode=PDB_GR/ pp. 1–3.

Chart 4: Growth rates of GDP *per capita* in selected EU Member States in 2009–2021 (in %)

Source: prepared by the author on the basis of: OECD.Stat. Growth in GDP *per capita*, op. cit., pp. 1–3.

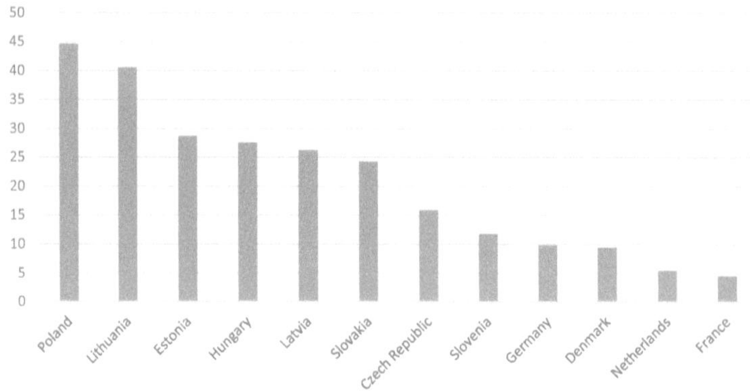

Chart 5: Growth rates of GDP *per capita* in the Northern European and Central and Eastern European Member States in 2009–2021 (in %)

Source: prepared by the author on the basis of: OECD.Stat. Growth in GDP *per capita*, op. cit., pp. 1–3.

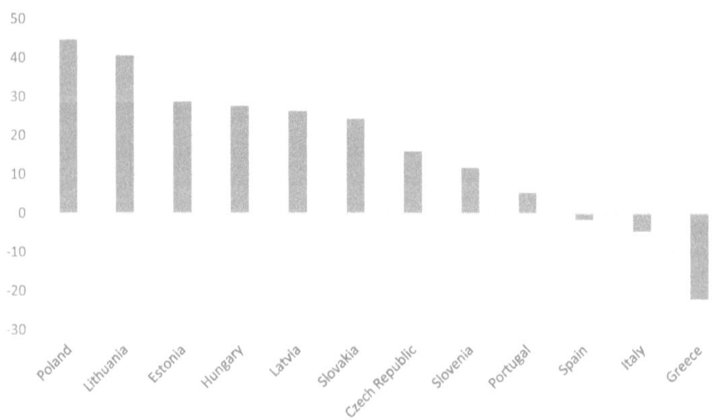

Chart 6: Rates of GDP *per capita* growth and contraction in the Southern European and Central and Eastern European Member States of the EU between 2009 and 2021 (in %)

Source: prepared by the author on the basis of: OECD.Stat. Growth in GDP *per capita*, op. cit., pp. 1–3.

In January 2022, mainly based on the World Bank data, the Polish Economic Institute performed an exegesis of the convergence process in the European Union between 1995 and 2022, taking into account the consequences of the euro area debt crisis. As concluded by the authors of the report, throughout the period in question, the EU basically met the challenges of economic and institutional convergence, although to a varying degree in particular Member States[123]. In contrast, there was hardly any structural convergence in the European Union as individual Member States followed different economic development paths: Western Europe largely developed technologically advanced sectors, Central and Eastern Europe was dominated by unsophisticated industries while starting to build modern business services, the Southern countries heavily relied on tourism[124].

In terms of economic convergence, the years 1995–2020 witnessed the fastest reduction in development differences between the CEECs and the rest of the EU[125]. As demonstrated by the authors of the report, in the period in question, the gap in GDP *per capita* in the EU-28 decreased by as much as 18%, mostly due to advancements in the fast-growing economies of Central and Eastern Europe[126]. In 1995–2020, GDP *per capita* in the countries in question grew at an annual average of 3.1%, whereas GDP *per capita* in the EU-15 only rose by 1% per year. As a result, the CEECs were catching up quickly with Western Europe in terms of living standards. On the other hand, low GDP *per capita* growth rates in

123 M. Klucznik, K. Marczewski, An EU of convergence…, op. cit., pp. 10–28. For an interpretation of the report, cf. T. Żółciak, 30 lat traktatu o UE. Różnice rozwojowe między krajami znów zaczęły się pogłębiać [30 years of the Treaty on EU. Development disparities between countries have started to widen again], 7 February 2022, https://www.gazetaprawna.pl/, pp. 1–3 [accessed: 20 July 2022].

124 M. Klucznik, K. Marczewski, An EU of convergence…, op. cit., pp. 15–19.

125 If the EU's largest economy, i.e. the German economy, should be adopted as a benchmark, the Central and Eastern European countries to catch up with Germany at the fastest pace were the Baltic States, Poland and Romania. For example, between 1995 and 2020, Lithuanian GDP *per capita* rose from 27% to 72% of the GDP *per capita* of Germany, whereas Polish and Romanian GDP *per capita* increased from 33% to 63% and from 31% to 56% of German GDP *per capita* respectively, cf. ibidem, p. 11. Institutional convergence in the European Union also advanced at the fastest pace in the Central and Eastern European countries (e.g. in terms of economic freedom, the Member States concerned reduced their distance from Western Europe to a mere fourth of the previous gap), whereas the South performed much worse in that regard, cf. ibidem, p. 15.

126 Ibidem, p. 11.

the EU-15 showed that those Member States were basically no longer converging economically[127], which was 'the opposite of the desired outcome'[128].

But as a consequence of the euro area debt crisis as well as of the pandemic crisis, economic convergence in the EU-28 slowed down considerably. In 2020–2021, the narrowing of economic development differences in the EU-28 was 2.5 times slower than in 1995–2010[129]. On the other hand, there was a significant widening of development disproportions between the South and the North of the EU-15. The average difference in GDP *per capita* in the EU-15 was 20% higher in 2020–2021 than in 1995, which implied that economic development disparities between those Member States increased as well[130]. In the period 2008–2013 alone, the difference in GDP *per capita* between the Southern and Northern countries of the EU-15 went up by an average of 33%, whereas the recession caused by the COVID-19 pandemic widened the disparities even further[131]. Consequently, there was a dramatic increase in developmental differences between the South and the North of the EU-15. According to the authors of the report, the euro area debt crisis and the pandemic crisis led to the emergence of a 'two-speed' Europe within the EU-15[132].

The analysis conducted substantiates formulating an opinion that the euro area debt crisis of 2010–2018 was only partly resolved. Having exited their respective financial assistance programmes, recovery programmes and Eurosystem projects, all the Member States affected by the crisis indeed entered economic growth paths, reduced their budget deficits and unemployment rates. But their public debt levels (with the exception of Ireland) remained very high even after

127 Ibidem, p. 13.

128 Ibidem.

129 Ibidem, p. 10.

130 The authors of the report deliberately excluded from the analysis two Member States of the EU-28 – Luxembourg and Ireland – in order to avoid understating the results or blurring trends in other countries. In their opinion, Luxembourg has an economy partly 'disconnected' from the rest of the EU-28. In 2020, the GDP *per capita* of Luxembourg was more than 2.6 times the EU average and nearly 4.3 times the figure for the EU's poorest Member State. At the same time, it only accounted for 0.14% of the EU population. As regards Ireland, following the debt crisis its economy relied on 'attracting foreign corporations with very low tax rates' and to a certain degree also 'separating' itself from the rest of the EU-28, cf. ibidem, p. 12.

131 Ibidem.

132 For instance, whereas Italy was as wealthy as Germany in 1995, it became nearly 25% poorer in 2020, cf. ibidem, pp. 13–14.

2018. Transfers of external and internal funds allocated to overcoming the crisis totalled a whopping EUR 526.16 billion, whereby the largest net payer was Germany. Simultaneously, the German and French governments had the most significant influence on the form of combating the crisis, not only affecting its dynamics but also indirectly or directly contributing to its exacerbation. The lack of success in fully overcoming the euro area debt crisis was determined by failed efforts by some of the Member States to implement their respective economic adjustment programmes, the outbreak of the coronavirus pandemic in the European Union in early 2020 and the ensuing economic and financial consequences as well as by the sluggish progress in reforming the Economic and Monetary Union after 2015.

Chapter II: The first stage of the system reform of the Economic and Monetary Union in 2010–2015

1. Strengthening economic and budgetary governance in the Economic and Monetary Union (2010–2012/13)

Soon after the onset of the euro area debt crisis, the European Union institutions and the governments of the euro area Member States launched various initiatives aimed at strengthening economic and budgetary governance in the Economic and Monetary Union. The following years witnessed the introduction, establishment or adoption of the 'European Semester', the Euro Plus Pact, the 'six-pack' and the 'two-pack', the Fiscal Compact, three new crisis management tools reinforcing the financial stability of the euro area Member States experiencing a crisis or economic difficulties and centralised supervision of financial markets of the European Union at macro- and micro-prudential levels.

1.1. The European Semester

As early as the first half of 2010, the European Commission issued two information documents: the Communication on reinforcing economic policy coordination (12 May 2010) and the Communication on enhancing economic policy coordination for stability, growth and jobs (30 June 2010)[133]. The latter also set out a roadmap for the European Semester, to enter into force on 1 January 2011[134]. The legal bases for the procedure included Articles 121 and 148 TFEU

---

133 Communication from the Commission to the European Parliament, the European Council, the Council, the European Central Bank, the European Economic and Social Committee and the Committee of the Regions of 12 May 2010: Reinforcing economic policy coordination, Brussels, 12.5.2010, COM(2010) 250 final. Communication from the Commission to the European Parliament, the Council, the European Central Bank, the European Economic and Social Committee and the Committee of the Regions: Enhancing economic policy coordination for stability, growth and jobs – Tools for stronger EU economic governance, Brussels, 30.6.2010, COM (2010) 367 final.

134 For more information on the circumstances of establishing the European Semester during the Belgian Presidency, cf. J.J. Węc, Nowe zasady sprawowania prezydencji w Radzie Unii Europejskiej. Bilans prezydencji belgijskiej [New rules for presiding the

and the 'six-pack' described below, i.e. a package of six legislative acts reforming the Stability and Growth Pact. As adopting the 'six-pack' took more time than expected, the procedure of the first European Semester was based on the above-mentioned roadmap of the European Commission.

Under the European Semester procedure, the European Union Member States coordinate *ex ante* their economic, fiscal, employment and social policies, in accordance with the rules laid down at the EU level. The coordination primarily concerns implementing structural reforms (especially promoting growth and employment), ensuring the sustainability of public finance under the Stability and Growth Pact and preventing excessive macroeconomic imbalances[135]. In that sense, the procedure also serves to deliver on the Europe 2020 strategy and the Euro Plus Pact. As the most important part of the procedure falls on the first six months of each calendar year, it is called a semester. In structural terms, the European Semester procedure comprises three parallel and interrelated paths: (1) macroeconomic surveillance; (2) thematic surveillance; and (3) fiscal surveillance. The macroeconomic surveillance and thematic surveillance paths concern National Reform Programmes prepared by all the EMU Member States, whereas the fiscal surveillance path applies to Stability Programmes submitted by euro area Member States and Convergence Programmes required from non-euro area Member States[136].

Council of the European Union. Taking stock of the Belgian Presidency], 'Przegląd Zachodni' 2011, no. 3, p. 13.

135 Following the proclamation of the European Pillar of Social Rights on 17 November 2017, social and employment policies have also been subject to coordination under the European Semester procedure.

136 Semestr Europejski [European Semester], Ministerstwo Gospodarki [Polish Ministry of Economy], http://www.mg.gov.pl, p. 1 [accessed: 20 July 2022]. Semestr europejski. Przewodnik po kluczowych dokumentach (stan na 4 czerwca 2012 r.) [European Semester. A guide to key documents (as at 4 June 2012)], Ośrodek Informacji i Dokumentacji Europejskiej Sejmu RP, http://libr.sejm.gov.pl, pp. 1–5 [accessed: 20 July 2022]. Ministerstwo Gospodarki RP. Semestr europejski. Okres oceny i koordynacji polityki gospodarczej w UE [European Semester. The economic policy assessment and coordination period in the EU], Warszawa 2014, pp. 8–9. Semestr europejski. Przebieg cyklu koordynacji na poziomie Unii i Polski (2011–2016) (stan prawny na 30 listopada 2015) [European Semester. The coordination cycle at the Union and Poland's level (legal status as at 30 November 2015)], Ośrodek Informacji i Dokumentacji Europejskiej. Biblioteka Sejmowa, https://oide.sejm.gov.pl, pp. 1–5 [accessed: 20 July 2022]. In the past, European Union institutions conducted assessments of Member States' economic policies in the spring and of their fiscal frameworks in the autumn.

The European Semester procedure is described in detail below. In November of the year preceding the calendar year concerned, the European Commission does the analysis of budgetary and structural policies and macroeconomic imbalances, if any. Next, in December, the Commission presents an Annual Growth Survey (AGS, also called an Annual Sustainable Growth Survey – ASGS) and an Alert Mechanism Report (AMR) on any discovered macroeconomic imbalances. Such an Annual Growth Survey comprises three economic policy components: macroeconomic and budgetary policies, structural reforms and growth-enhancing measures. It is also a tool for the European Commission to propose the EU's general economic priorities for the coming year. In its Alert Mechanism Report, the Commission presents the macroeconomic situations of particular Member States, identifying those at risk of macroeconomic imbalances and in need of analysis in an in-depth review (IDR). Based on its Annual Growth Survey, the Commission formulates a draft recommendation for the euro area. In February of the calendar year concerned, the European Parliament provides an opinion on employment guidelines, whereas the Council of the European Union studies the Commission's Annual Growth Survey and euro area recommendation, followed by the adoption of political conclusions in the form of a report on the EU's economic policy priorities for the coming year. In March, on that basis, the European Council endorses the priorities report and provides policy orientations. In mid-April, but no later than the end of April, the EMU Member States submit, for the European Commission's assessment, their updated National Reform Programmes, Stability or Convergence Programmes taking into account the priorities approved and policy orientations provided by the European Council. Such National Reform Programmes contain all the EMU Member States' plans concerning structural reforms as well as growth- and employment-enhancing measures[137]. Stability Programmes of euro area Member States or Convergence Programmes of non-euro area Member States include their national commitments to ensuring sound, resilient and sustainable public finances. In May of the calendar year concerned, based on those documents and having assessed

---

The fulfilment of obligations imposed on the Member States at the EU level was only reviewed ex post. It implied that decisions regarding economic policy objectives were made without necessarily knowing the amount of actually available funds.

137 National Reform Programmes represent the main tool for the implementation of the Europe 2020 strategy by the EMU Member States. According to the European Semester procedure, National Reform Programmes must be updated on an annual basis and submitted to the European Commission in April, together with updated Stability and Convergence Programmes.

them, the European Commission drafts country-specific recommendations for the EMU Member States and subsequently, at the turn of May and June, presents them to the Council of the European Union, indicating the progress made and any failures to implement the measures agreed. In June, the Council of the European Union agrees on the final versions of country-specific recommendations. Later that month, the European Council endorses them. In July, the Council of the European Union adopts the recommendations with an opinion on the National Reform Programmes, Stability or Convergence Programmes. From that time, the Member States must take into account the above-mentioned recommendations in their draft budgets for the forthcoming year. The last component of the European Semester procedure is the European Parliament's debate concluding with the adoption of a resolution on the Member States' implementation of the priorities for the fiscal year concerned[138].

The European Semester cycle is coordinated with the interparliamentary dialogue of the European Union Member States. From 2013, in January or February of the calendar year concerned, after the European Commission's presentation of its Annual Growth Survey, Interparliamentary Committee Meetings (ICMs) are held in Brussels, for the relevant committees of the European Parliament and of national parliaments. The ICMs are organised as part of the European Parliamentary Week and address economic governance in the Economic and Monetary Union. Furthermore, from 2013, the Interparliamentary Conference on Stability, Economic Coordination and Governance in the European Union takes place alternately in Brussels (within the European Parliamentary Week) and in the capital cities of other EMU Member States[139]. The establishment of the IPC SECG implemented the provisions of Article 13 of the Fiscal Compact, providing for the organisation of a conference of representatives of a joint committee of the European Parliament and of national Parliaments, aimed at discussing budgetary policies and other issues covered by the intergovernmental

---

138 Regulation (EU) No 1175/2011 of the European Parliament and of the Council of 16 November 2011 amending Council Regulation (EC) No 1466/97 on the strengthening of the surveillance of budgetary positions and the surveillance and coordination of economic policies, Official Journal of the European Union, L 306, 23.11.2011, pp. 12–24. European Council. Council of the European Union. Who does what in the European Semester, https://www.consilium.europa.eu/en/infographics/european-semester/, p. 1.

139 Europejski Tydzień Parlamentarny [European Parliamentary Week], Ośrodek Informacji i Dokumentacji Europejskiej, https://oide.sejm.gov.pl/oide, pp. 1–2 [accessed: 28 October 2022].

agreement (Treaty). The Conference is attended by representatives of particular national parliaments and of the European Parliament[140].

1.2. The Euro Plus Pact

On 24–25 March 2011, the European Council endorsed a plan for reforming the Economic and Monetary Union, referred to as the Euro Plus Pact[141]. It was based on proposals submitted by the euro area Heads of State or Government two weeks before[142]. The Euro Plus Pact also referred to 'Europe 2020: A strategy for smart, sustainable and inclusive growth' announced by the European Commission on 3 March 2010, including a plan for the Economic and Monetary Union to recover from the debt crisis and for boosting economic growth in the following decade[143]. Formally, the Pact was concluded outside the European Union, but it

---

140 Cf. Konferencja Międzyparlamentarna ds. Stabilności, Koordynacji i Zarządzania Gospodarczego w Unii Europejskiej [Interparliamentary Conference on Stability, Economic Coordination and Governance in the European Union], Ośrodek Informacji i Dokumentacji Europejskiej, https://oide.sejm.gov.pl/oide, pp. 1–2 [accessed: 28 October 2022]. Spotkania Konferencji Międzyparlamentarnej ds. Stabilności, Koordynacji i Zarządzania Gospodarczego w Unii Europejskiej [Meetings of the Interparliamentary Conference on Stability, Economic Coordination and Governance in the European Union], Ośrodek Informacji i Dokumentacji Europejskiej, https://oide.sejm.gov.pl/oide, pp. 1–2 [accessed: 28 October 2022]. The Conference emerged from previous meetings of the finance or economic committee chairpersons, held every six months by the Presidency Parliament. Cf. T. Woźnicki, Współpraca międzyparlamentarna w świetle art. 13. Traktatu o stabilności, koordynacji i zarządzaniu w Unii Gospodarczej i Walutowej [Interparliamentary cooperation in the light of Article 13 of the Treaty on Stability, Coordination and Governance in the Economic and Monetary Union], 'Przegląd Europejski' 2015, no. 3, pp. 137–138.

141 European Council, 24/25 March 2011, Conclusions, Brussels, 20 April 2011, EUCO 10/1/11/ REV 1. Annex I: The Euro Plus Pact. Stronger economic policy coordination for competitiveness and convergence, pp. 13–20.

142 European Council. Conclusions of the Heads of State or Government of the Euro area of 11 March 2011, Brussels, 11 March 2011, http://www.consilium.europa.eu, pp. 1–15 [accessed: 20 July 2022].

143 The Europe 2020 strategy was announced by the European Commission on 3 March 2010 and approved by the European Council on 17 June 2010, as a follow-up to the Lisbon Strategy of 2000. Cf. European Commission. Communication from the Commission: Europe 2020. A strategy for smart, sustainable and inclusive growth, Brussels, 3 March 2010, COM(2010) 2020 final. European Council, 17 June 2010, Conclusions, pp. 2–3. Pakt Euro Plus z Polską [The Euro Plus Pact with Poland], EURACTIV, 28 March 2011, p. 1, http://www.for.org.pl [accessed: 20 July 2022].

still constituted a political commitment made 'at the highest political level'[144], i.e. that of the Heads of State or Government of the signatory Member States. Despite being an intergovernmental agreement, it had no legal effect. It was signed by all the euro area Member States and six non-euro area Member States – Bulgaria, Denmark, Lithuania, Latvia, Poland and Romania (hence the name: the Euro Plus Pact). It remained open for the other four Member States of the European Union to join.

Under the Euro Plus Pact, the signatory Member States committed to the implementation of national reforms and stronger economic policy coordination for improving the competitiveness of their economies, increasing employment and enhancing public finance and budgetary sustainability. Another area of cooperation should also be tax policy coordination[145]. The renewed effort should be based on four guiding rules: (1) the Pact was supposed to 'be in line with and strengthen the existing economic governance in the EU'; it should be consistent with existing instruments such as the Europe 2020 strategy, the European Semester, the Stability and Growth Pact and the new macroeconomic surveillance framework; (2) the Pact covered 'priority policy areas', 'essential for fostering competitiveness and convergence'; (3) each year, concrete national commitments would be undertaken by each Head of State or Government, whereas the implementation of commitments would be monitored politically by the Heads of State or Government of the euro area and participating countries on a yearly basis, on the basis of a report by the Commission; (4) participating Member States should be fully committed to the completion of the Single Market, being 'key to enhancing the competitiveness in the EU and the euro area'[146].

1.3. New crisis management tools reinforcing the financial stability of the euro area

In the process of strengthening economic and budgetary governance in the euro area, three new crisis management tools were established. Those were as follows: the European Financial Stabilisation Mechanism (2010) and the European Financial Stability Facility (2010) as temporary crisis instruments and the European Stability Mechanism (2012) as a permanent international organisation for the euro area as a whole. All the three economic and budgetary governance

---

144 J. Barcz, Główne kierunki, op. cit., p. 142.
145 European Council, 24/25 March 2011, Conclusions... Annex I, op. cit., pp. 13–20.
146 Ibidem, pp. 13–15.

tools aimed at reinforcing the financial stability of the euro area Member States. However, as mentioned before, the EFSM and the EFSF only provided assistance to three euro area Member States, i.e. Greece, Portugal and Ireland, the hardest hit countries at that time, experiencing the most serious economic difficulties, whereas the ESM was supposed to financially support all the euro area Member States.

The legal bases of the functioning of the EFSM and the EFSF were the above-mentioned acts: Council Regulation (EU) No 407/2010 of 11 May 2010 establishing a European financial stabilisation mechanism under Article 122(2) TFEU and the EFSF Treaty of 7 June 2010, signed by the Finance Ministers of the 16 euro area Member States at Luxembourg[147]. The whole temporary stabilisation function of the European Union could provide credit guarantees of up to EUR 500 billion: EUR 60 billion from the EFSM and EUR 440 billion from the EFSF. An additional support of EUR 250 billion was guaranteed by the International Monetary Fund. Whereas EFSM loans came from the general budget of the European Union, EFSF loans were financed from the national budgets of the euro area Member States, in accordance with the ECB's capital key. Assistance from the EFSM was approved by the Council of the European Union, whereas that under the EFSF – by the Eurogroup. In both cases, funds were disbursed in tranches, depending on the progress made in the implementation of recovery programmes agreed with the Troika, i.e. representatives of the European Commission, the European Central Bank and the International Monetary Fund[148].

The EFSF was a limited liability company owned by the 16 euro area Member States as the signatories to the Treaty, established in Luxembourg under the laws of the Grand-Duchy of Luxembourg. The euro area Member States contributed by providing guarantees of up to the total amount of EUR 440 billion. On 4 August 2010, after the Treaty had been ratified by 90% of the signatories, the EFSF started operations. Initially, its effective lending capacity was EUR 250 billion. Decisions on granting loans were made by the Board of Directors of the EFSF, composed of high-level representatives (deputy ministers, secretaries of state or director generals of national treasuries) of the euro area Member States. Representatives of the European Central Bank and the European Commission could attend meetings of the EFSF Board as observers. On the basis of the

147 Council Regulation (EU) No 407/2010, op. cit., pp. 1–4. Decision of the 16 euro area Member States, op. cit., p. 1. For an analysis of the provisions of the two documents, cf. J.J. Węc, Pierwsza polska prezydencja, op. cit., pp. 134–136.

148 J.J. Węc, Pierwsza polska prezydencja, op. cit., p. 135.

above-mentioned guarantees from the euro area Member States, the EFSF issued bonds and bills to raise funds for the euro area countries experiencing serious financial difficulties[149].

In the face of the deteriorating euro area debt crisis, the effectiveness of the existing stabilisation instruments proved to be limited. Therefore, in 2011 the EU decided to make the EFSF more effective. The most important decisions in that regard were taken during three meetings of the Heads of State or Government of the 17 euro area Member States:[150] on 11 March, 21 July and 26 October 2011. The effective lending capacity of the EFSF was increased from EUR 250 billion to EUR 440 billion, the maximum amount of guarantees by the euro area Member States was raised from EUR 440 billion to EUR 780 billion, the EFSF was empowered to intervene (in exceptional cases) in the primary and secondary debt markets, the rate of interest charged on EFSF loans was reduced to 3.5%, whereas their maturities were extended from 7.5 years to 15 years[151].

At the same time, the EU institutions started work on establishing a permanent crisis mechanism for the whole euro area as soon as possible. A political decision on its establishment was made by the European Council on 28–29 October 2010. However, it required amending Article 136(3) TFEU. Therefore, on

149 J.J. Węc, Nowe zasady sprawowania prezydencji w Radzie Unii Europejskiej..., pp. 12–13.

150 On 1 January 2011, Estonia joined the euro area as the 17th Member State of the EU.

151 Narodowy Bank Polski. Departament Zagraniczny. Informacja na temat nowych zasad funkcjonowania Europejskiego Instrumentu Stabilności Finansowej, op. cit., pp. 1–3. European Council. Conclusions of the Heads of State or Government of the Euro area of 11 March 2011, op. cit., pp. 1–15; European Council Statement by the Heads of State or Government of the Euro area and EU institutions, Brussels, 21 July 2011, http://www.consilium.europa.eu, pp. 1–4 [accessed: 20 July 2022]. European Council. Press release. Remarks by President Van Rompuy at the press conference following the Eurozone Summit, Brussels, 21 July 2011, EUCO 54/11, p. 1; European Council – 2011. Statement of EU Heads of State or Government, Brussels, 26 October 2011, Publications Office of the European Union, Luxembourg 2012, pp. 62–66. The lowering of the interest rates of EFSF loans to 3.5% was proposed by the Polish Presidency, cf. Sejm Rzeczypospolitej Polskiej [Sejm of the Republic of Poland]. VII kadencja. Interpelacje, zapytania, pytania i oświadczenia. Odpowiedź podsekretarza stanu w Ministerstwie Finansów na zapytanie nr 205 w sprawie realizacji priorytetów polskiej prezydencji z obszarów działania Ministerstwa Finansów [Reply of the Under-Secretary of State at the Ministry of Finance to question no. 205 on the implementation of the priorities of the Polish Presidency in the areas of competence of the Ministry of Finance], http://orka2.sejm.gov.pl, p. 2 [accessed: 20 July 2022].

16 December 2010, the Belgian government, performing the function of Presidency at the time, submitted to the European Council a proposal for revising the provisions in question, in accordance with a simplified revision procedure laid down in Article 48(6) TEU. Later that day, the European Council requested opinions from the European Parliament, the European Commission and the European Central Bank on the proposal put forward by the Belgian Presidency. Having obtained positive opinions from the three institutions, on 25 March 2011, the European Council unanimously decided to revise Article 136(3) TFEU in accordance with the simplified revision procedure (Article 48(6) TEU), which enabled the establishment of the European Stability Mechanism. The amendment consisted in adding to Article 136 TFEU the following paragraph 3: *The Member States whose currency is the euro may establish a stability mechanism to be activated if indispensable to safeguard the stability of the euro area as a whole. The granting of any required financial assistance under the mechanism will be made subject to strict conditionality*[152].

It is emphasised in the literature that the provisions of Article 136(3) TFEU did not explicitly establish a European Stability Mechanism; rather, they only stipulated that the euro area Member States had the competence to establish such a mechanism, thus confirming the compatibility of establishing such a mechanism with Union law[153]. Under the provisions in question, on 11 July 2011, the Finance Ministers of the 17 euro area Member States signed the Treaty establishing the European Stability Mechanism as an international organisation separate from the European Union. But on account of the dynamics of crisis developments, first on 21 July and next on 9 December 2011, the euro area Heads of State or Government needed to agree on revising the Treaty with a view to increasing the effectiveness of the ESM. Subsequently, on 2 February 2012, the representatives of the euro area Member States concluded a new Treaty establishing the European Stability Mechanism[154]. Finally, the Treaty entered into force on 27

---

152 European Council Decision of 25 March 2011 amending Article 136 of the Treaty on the Functioning of the European Union with regard to a stability mechanism for Member States whose currency is the euro, Official Journal of the European Union, L 91, 6.4.2011, p. 1–2. Cf. also: European Council, 24/25 March 2011, Conclusions, Brussels, 20 April 2011, EUCO 10/1/11/ REV 1. Annex II: Term Sheet on the ESM, pp. 21–34.

153 Cf. J. Barcz, Główne kierunki, op. cit., p. 137.

154 Treaty establishing the European Stability Mechanism between the Kingdom of Belgium, the Federal Republic of Germany, the Republic of Estonia, Ireland, the Hellenic Republic, the Kingdom of Spain, the French Republic, the Italian Republic, the

September 2012, after it had been ratified by the euro area Member States representing at least 90% of the ESM capital[155]. The European Stability Mechanism

---

Republic of Cyprus, the Grand Duchy of Luxembourg, Malta, the Kingdom of the Netherlands, the Republic of Austria, the Portuguese Republic, the Republic of Slovenia, the Slovak Republic, the Republic of Finland, http://www.european-council.europa.eu, pp. 1–62 [accessed: 20 July 2022].

155 The longest ratification process was that in the Federal Republic of Germany. Although the Bundestag and the Bundesrat consented to the conclusion of the ESM Treaty and the Fiscal Compact on 29 June 2012, as many as six actions were brought against those acts before the BVerfG. Objections were raised by applicants such as *Die Linke*, Peter Gauweiler (CSU) and *Mehr Demokratie*. In such circumstances, President Joachim Gauck postponed ratification until the relevant ruling given by the BVerfG. On 12 September 2012, the Federal Constitutional Court found both Treaties and the European Council Decision of 25 March 2011 amending Article 136 TFEU (by adding paragraph 3) compatible with the German Basic Law. However, the BVerfG also ruled that the FRG could only join the ESM Treaty on certain conditions, e.g. the provision of guarantees under international law that if Germany's financial commitments to the ESM should exceed EUR 190 billion, it would always require the German Parliament's consent. It implied that increasing funds for the purposes of the ESM would be impossible without a prior consent given by the Bundestag in every case. On 13 September 2012, President Gauck signed the relevant ratification acts, but with the reservation that the process of ratifying the ESM Treaty would be completed upon the meeting by the Federal Government of the requirements set out by the BVerfG. On the following day, the Finance Ministers of the euro area Member States agreed on a declaration interpreting the provisions of the Treaty addressed by the BVerfG. On 27 September 2012, it was adopted by the governments of all the euro area Member States. Later that day, President Gauck signed the ratification act and deposited the relevant instruments with the Depositary. Cf. M. Ferber, Verfassungsklagen verzögern den Euro-Rettungsfonds, 'Augsburger Allgemeine', 1. Juli 2012, https://www.augsburger-allgemeine.de/, p. 1 [accessed: 20 July 2022]. ESM und Fiskalpakt: Bundesverfassungsgericht entscheidet über Eilklagen, 'Augsburger Allgemeine', 3. Juli 2012, https://www.augsburger-allgemeine.de/, p. 1, [accessed: 20 July 2022]. M. Sievers, Verfassungsgericht vor seiner schwersten Entscheidung, 'Frankfurter Rundschau', 10. Juli 2012, p. 1, https://www.fr.de/ [accessed: 20 July 2022]. Der Europäische Stabilitätsmechanismus und der Fiskalpakt. Übersicht über den Stand der Ratifikation, Stiftung Wissenschaft und Politik. Deutsches Institut für Internationale Politik und Sicherheit, http://www.swp-berlin.org/de, p. 1 [accessed: 20 July 2022]. Der Bundespräsident. Ausfertigung der Gesetze zum 'Euro-Rettungsschirm', Berlin, 13. September 2012, p. 1. https://www.bundespraesident.de/ SharedDocs /Pressemitteilungen/DE/2012/09/120913-Rettungsschirm.html [accessed: 20 July 2022]. A.-L. Kirch, D. Schwarzer, *Die Ratifizierung des Fiskalpakts und des ESM in den Ländern der Eurozone – rechtliche*

started operations later that year, on 8 October. The initial assumption was that the ESM would replace both the EFSF and the EFSM as early as 2013; in March 2012, however, it was decided that the EFSF would continue to function, limiting its activities to the management of the financial assistance programmes in the course of implementation, with no new lending operations[156].

The establishment of the European Stability Mechanism as an international organisation separate from the European Union but still to a certain extent involving EU institutions raised controversy with regard to compatibility with EU law. Those doubts were called into question by the CJEU in its judgment of 27 November 2012 in Case C-370/12 Thomas Pringle v Government of Ireland and Others, confirming that the European Council had followed the procedure laid down in Article 48(6) TEU in its adoption of Decision 2011/199/EU and declaring the ESM Treaty compatible with EU law. According to Jan Barcz, the establishment of the European Stability Mechanism outside the institutional and legal framework of the EU as a separate international organisation whose members could only be the euro area Member States, in spite of the judgment of the Court of Justice of the European Union, indicated 'walking a tightrope' – with regard to such intergovernmental measures – between the fragmentation of the European Union and the autonomisation of the euro area. Therefore, only a subsequent incorporation of the ESM Treaty into European Union law could prevent such a risk and enhance the EU system coherence at the same time[157].

The European Stability Mechanism is an international (intergovernmental) organisation established under public international law and based in Luxembourg. Its tasks include lending to the ESM Members, providing financial assistance and precautionary financial assistance where needed, purchasing bonds of beneficiary ESM Members in the primary and secondary markets and granting loans for the re-capitalisation of financial institutions. The authorised capital stock of the ESM is EUR 704.8 billion, divided into paid-in capital with the aggregate nominal value of EUR 80.5 billion and unpaid (callable) capital of EUR 624.3 billion, declared and guaranteed by the euro area Member States[158]. The

---

und politische Rahmenbedingungen, Arbeitspapier der Forschungsgruppe 1, 2012, Nr. 2, p. 4.

156 M. Cichocki, Europejski Mechanizm Stabilności – główne zasady działania i próba oceny [The European Stability Mechanism – the main principles of functioning and an attempt at assessment], 'International Journal of Management and Economics' 2013, no. 37, pp. 88–90.

157 J. Barcz, Główne kierunki, op. cit., p. 138.

158 EFSF-ESM. Überblick, op. cit., p. 10.

contribution key of the European Stability Mechanism is based on the key for the subscription of the ECB capital, whereby the euro area Member States with GDP *per capita* below 75% of the EU average GDP *per capita* are entitled to benefit from a temporary correction for a period of 12 years after their joining the euro area[159]. The effective lending capacity of the ESM is set at a maximum amount of EUR 500 billion, reviewed regularly and at least every five years[160].

The European Stability Mechanism bodies are as follows: the Board of Governors, the Board of Directors and the Managing Director (Article 4(1) of the ESM Treaty)[161]. The Board of Governors is composed of Governors being members of governments with responsibility for finance and of alternate Governors. The latter have full power to act on behalf of the former when the Governors

---

159 The contribution key of the European Stability Mechanism based on the key for the subscription of the ECB capital for the 17 euro area Member States, in %, was initially adopted as follows: Austria – 2.783; Belgium – 3.477; Cyprus – 0.196; Estonia – 0.186; Finland – 1.797; France – 20.386; Germany – 27.146; Greece – 2.817; Ireland – 1.592; Italy – 17.914; Luxembourg – 0.250; Malta – 0.073; the Netherlands – 5.717; Portugal – 2.509; Slovakia – 0.824; Slovenia – 0.428; Spain – 11.904. The temporary correction would be three quarters of the difference between GNI and ECB capital shares (or effectively: 75% of the GNI share and 25% of the ECB capital share), according to the following formula: ESM share = ECB key share - 0.75 (ECB key share - GNI share). The downward compensation on those countries would be redistributed among all the other countries according to their ECB key shares. Cf. European Council, 24/25 March 2011, Conclusions..., Annex II..., p. 34. But the final arrangement for the contribution key adopted in the ESM Treaty of 2012 was modified as follows: Austria – 2.7644; Belgium – 3.4534; Cyprus – 0.1949; Estonia – 0.1847; Finland – 1.7852; France – 20.2471; Germany – 26.9616; Greece – 2.7975; Ireland – 1.5814; Italy – 17.7917; Latvia – 0.2746, Lithuania – 0.4063, Luxembourg – 0.2487; Malta – 0.0726; the Netherlands – 5.6781; Portugal – 2.4921; Slovakia – 0.8184; Slovenia – 0.4247; Spain – 11.8227. Cf. Annex I to the Treaty establishing the European Stability Mechanism, op. cit., p. 61. Pursuant to Article 42(2)(a) and (b), the formula for the temporary correction of the contribution key was also simplified to the sum of 25% of the ECB capital share and 75% of the GNI share. Cf. Treaty establishing the European Stability Mechanism, op. cit., pp. 55–56.

160 Treaty establishing the European Stability Mechanism, op. cit., pp. 21–26. Any losses arising from the ESM operations would be charged, firstly, against the reserve fund in which the proceeds of the financial sanctions received from the euro area Member States under the multilateral surveillance procedure, the excessive deficit procedure and the macroeconomic imbalances procedure should be put aside. For more on the subject cf. J.J. Węc, Pierwsza polska prezydencja, op. cit., pp. 135–136, 148–150.

161 Treaty establishing the European Stability Mechanism, op. cit., p. 11.

are not present. The Board of Governors elects a Chairperson and a Vice-Chairperson from among its members for a term of two years, with a possible re-election, or decides to be chaired by the President of the Eurogroup (referred to as the 'Euro Group' in the ESM Treaty). The meetings of the Board of Governors may be attended, as observers, by following: the member of the European Commission in charge of economic and monetary affairs, the President of the ECB and the President of the Eurogroup (if he or she is not the Chairperson of the Board of Governors) as well as representatives of non-euro area Member States participating in stability support operations for euro area Member States when this stability support and its monitoring will be discussed (Article 5(1) to (4) of the ESM Treaty). The Board of Governors takes decisions in matters such as: (1) providing stability support; (2) establishing the choice of instruments and the financial terms and conditions of such support; (3) adapting the maximum lending volume of the ESM; and (4) changing the list of financial assistance instruments (Article 5(6) and (7) of the ESM Treaty). Its decisions are taken in accordance with four different procedures: by mutual agreement, i.e. unanimously (whereby abstentions do not prevent the adoption of a decision by mutual agreement); by qualified majority (80% of the votes cast); by qualified majority in an emergency procedure (85% of the votes cast); or by simple majority. All decisions require a quorum of ⅔ of the members with voting rights representing at least ⅔ of the voting rights. Each ESM Member has voting rights equal to the number of shares allocated to it in the authorised capital stock of the ESM. If any ESM Member fails to pay any part of the amount due in respect of its obligations in relation to paid-in shares or calls of capital of the ESM, or in relation to the reimbursement of the financial assistance, such an ESM Member may be unable to exercise its voting rights (Article 4(2) to (8) of the ESM Treaty). An emergency voting procedure is used in exceptional cases, i.e. where the lack of a decision by the Board of Governors would threaten the economic or financial sustainability of the euro area[162].

The Board of Directors is composed of representatives of particular Member States (each represented by one Director and one alternate Director). The meetings of the Board of Directors may also be attended, as observers, by representatives of the European Commission and of the European Central Bank. Representatives of non-euro area Member States participating in a financial assistance operation for a euro area Member State should also be invited to participate, as observers, in the meetings of the Board of Directors when this financial

162 Ibidem, pp. 11–13. European Council, 24/25 March 2011..., Annex II..., pp. 21–34.

assistance and its monitoring will be discussed (Article 6(1) to (6) of the ESM Treaty). The Board of Directors performs all tasks on the basis of powers delegated to it by the Board of Governors. It takes all decisions by mutual agreement (whereby abstentions do not prevent the adoption of a decision by mutual agreement), by qualified majority (80% of the votes cast) or by simple majority. As in the case of the Board of Governors, all decisions require a quorum of ⅔ of the members with voting rights representing at least ⅔ of the voting rights (Article 4(2) and (3), (5) to (7) of the ESM Treaty)[163].

The Managing Director is appointed by the Board of Governors from among representatives of the ESM Members, for a term of office of five years, and he or she may be re-appointed once. The successful candidate must have relevant international experience and a high level of competence in economic and financial matters. He or she chairs the meetings of the Board of Directors, participates in the meetings of the Board of Governors and conducts, under the direction of the Board of Directors, the current business of the ESM (Article 7(1) to (5) of the ESM Treaty) (cf. Figure 2)[164].

A procedure for granting stability support under the European Stability Mechanism takes a total of three to four weeks, being initiated on receipt by the Chairperson of the Board of Governors of a request from an ESM Member indicating the financial assistance instrument(s) to be considered. The Chairperson of the Board of Governors entrusts the European Commission, in liaison with the ECB, with the tasks to assess: (1) the existence of a risk to the financial stability of the euro area as a whole or of its Member States, unless the ECB has already submitted an analysis concerning support in the form of purchasing government bonds in the secondary market; (2) whether public debt is sustainable – wherever appropriate and possible, such an assessment should be conducted together with the IMF; and (3) the actual or potential financing needs of the ESM Member concerned. Next, the Board of Governors takes a decision on granting stability support, entrusting the European Commission – in liaison with the ECB and, wherever possible, together with the IMF – with the task of negotiating, with the ESM Member concerned, a memorandum of understanding detailing the conditionality (e.g. the necessary reforms) attached to the financial assistance facility. Further, the Managing Director prepares a proposal for such a financial assistance facility agreement, whereas the European Commission signs the Memorandum of Understanding on behalf of the ESM, subject to prior approval

163 Treaty establishing the European Stability Mechanism, op. cit., pp. 11–13.
164 Ibidem, pp. 20–21.

by the Board of Governors. The Commission is also responsible for monitoring compliance by the ESM Member concerned with the conditionality attached to the financial assistance facility (in liaison with the ECB and, wherever possible, together with the IMF). The stability support is provided to the beneficiary ESM Member in one or more tranches and each tranche may include one or more disbursements (Article 13(1) to (7) of the ESM Treaty)[165].

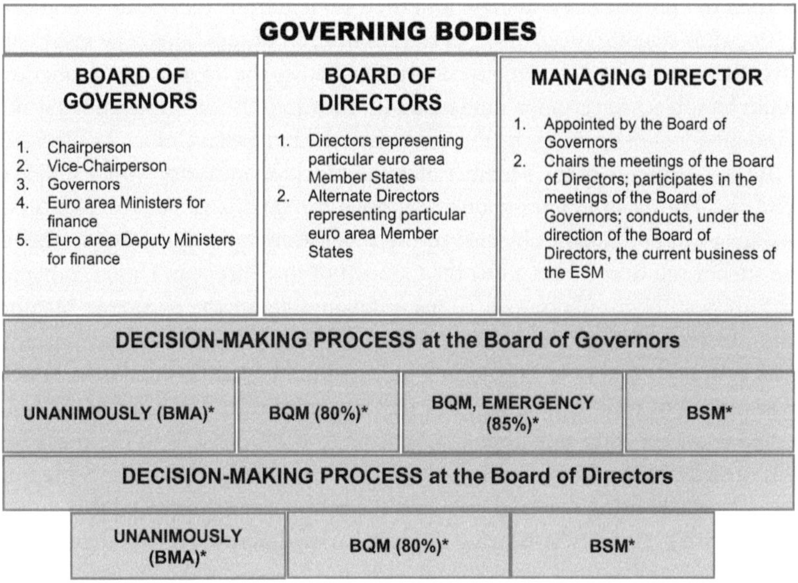

Figure 2: The organisational structure and the decision-making process in the European Stability Mechanism

* All decisions require a quorum of ⅔ of the members with voting rights representing at least ⅔ of the voting rights. Each ESM Member has voting rights equal to the number of shares allocated to it in the authorised capital stock of the ESM.

Source: prepared by the author on the basis of: Treaty establishing the European Stability Mechanism, op. cit., pp. 11–13, 20–34.

165 Ibidem, pp. 28–30. Cf. also: A. Trzcińska, Europejski Mechanizm Stabilności jako stabilizator w planowanej unii finansowej [The European Stability Mechanism as a stabiliser in the planned financial union], 25 March 2013, https://www.nbp.pl/, pp. 21–22 [accessed: 20 July 2022].

1.4. From the 'six-pack' to the 'two-pack'

Negotiations on the 'six-pack', or six legislative acts reforming the Stability and Growth Pact, were lengthy and, as a result, took more than twelve months. The main reason for the delay was the fact that the European Parliament proposed over 2,000 amendments to all the draft legislative acts of the European Commission. Adopting the 'six-pack' was also hindered by a dispute having arisen between the European Parliament and the Council of the European Union over the decision-making mechanism in the application of sanctions. The most controversial issue was addressing the question whether the imposition of sanctions should be subject to certain automatism, i.e. the extent to which sanctions would be independent of decisions by the Council of the European Union. As suggested by the governments of the Member States, a blocking minority would suffice to reject the European Commission's proposals for sanctions. Representatives of the European Parliament objected to the suggestion and argued that in the future such a solution would allow the Council of the European Union to bypass the European Commission's decisions unfavourable for the euro area Member States. Instead, they proposed that Finance Ministers should have the power to reject proposals from the European Commission by qualified majority. Finally, it was not until mid-September 2011 that a compromise was reached whereby decisions on applying sanctions (amounting to 0.2% of GDP in the preceding year, initially in the form of a deposit and subsequently a non-refundable fine) would be made using reversed qualified majority voting. It implied that a decision requiring an interest-bearing deposit, a non-interest-bearing deposit or a fine from a Member State would be taken by the Council of the European Union if – within ten days of the European Commission's adopting a relevant recommendation – the Council should not reject it by qualified majority[166]. Such a solution added certain automatism to sanctions, which reduced the influence of political factors on decision making in that regard.

166 Regulation (EU) No 1173/2011 of the European Parliament and of the Council of 16 November 2011 on the effective enforcement of budgetary surveillance in the euro area, Official Journal of the European Union, L 306, 23.11.2011, pp. 4–5. On 21 July 2011, the euro area Heads of State or Government declared that euro area Member States would 'fully support the Polish Presidency in order to reach agreement with the European Parliament on voting rules in the preventive arm of the Pact', cf. European Council. Statement by the Heads of State or Government of the Euro area and EU institutions, Brussels, 21 July 2011, op. cit., p. 4.

Only arriving at the compromise on the decision-making mechanism for the application of sanctions enabled the adoption of the package of six legislative acts on 8 and 16 November 2011. Those were as follows: (1) Council Regulation (EU) No 1177/2011 of 8 November 2011 amending Council Regulation (EC) No 1467/97 on speeding up and clarifying the implementation of the excessive deficit procedure[167]; (2) Regulation (EU) No 1175/2011 of the European Parliament and of the Council of 16 November 2011 amending Council Regulation (EC) No 1466/97 on the strengthening of the surveillance of budgetary positions and the surveillance and coordination of economic policies[168]; (3) Regulation (EU) No 1173/2011 of the European Parliament and of the Council of 16 November 2011 on the effective enforcement of budgetary surveillance in the euro area[169]; (4) Regulation (EU) No 1176/2011 of the European Parliament and of the Council of 16 November 2011 on the prevention and correction of macroeconomic imbalances[170]; (5) Regulation (EU) No 1174/2011 of the European Parliament and of the Council of 16 November 2011 on enforcement measures to correct excessive macroeconomic imbalances in the euro area[171]; (6) Council Directive 2011/85/EU of 8 November 2011 on requirements for budgetary frameworks of the Member States[172].

The package of six new legislative acts, entering into force on 13 December 2011, provided for tightening fiscal rules, primarily in the euro area Member States, but also for strengthening the coordination of economic policies of all the

167 Council Regulation (EU) No 1177/2011 of 8 November 2011 amending Regulation (EC) No 1467/97 on speeding up and clarifying the implementation of the excessive deficit procedure, Official Journal of the European Union, L 306, 23.11.2011, pp. 33–40.

168 Regulation (EU) No 1175/2011 of the European Parliament and of the Council, op. cit., pp. 12–24.

169 Regulation (EU) No 1173/2011 of the European Parliament and of the Council …, pp. 1–7.

170 Regulation (EU) No 1176/2011 of the European Parliament and of the Council of 16 November 2011 on the prevention and correction of macroeconomic imbalances, Official Journal of the European Union, 2011, L 306, 23.11.2011, pp. 25–32.

171 Regulation (EU) No 1174/2011 of the European Parliament and of the Council of 16 November 2011 on enforcement measures to correct excessive macroeconomic imbalances in the euro area, Official Journal of the European Union, 2011, L 306, 23.11.2011, pp. 8–11.

172 Council Directive 2011/85/EU of 8 November 2011 on requirements for budgetary frameworks of the Member States, Official Journal of the European Union, L 306, 23.11.2011, pp. 41–47.

EMU Member States. Three acts concerning public finance reformed and reinforced both basic arms of the Stability and Growth Pact in the 1997 version, i.e. the preventive and corrective arms[173]. The multilateral surveillance procedure was also revised by the fourth and fifth legislative acts, i.e. Regulation (EU) No 1176/2011 of the European Parliament and of the Council on the prevention and correction of macroeconomic imbalances and Regulation (EU) No 1174/ 2011 of the European Parliament and of the Council on enforcement measures to correct excessive macroeconomic imbalances in the euro area. Regulation No 1176/2011 introduced two new procedures: the macroeconomic imbalance procedure (MIP) and the excessive macroeconomic imbalance procedure (EMIP). At the same time, Regulation No 1174/2011 laid down a system of sanctions only applicable to the euro area Member States. The two procedures were introduced because the development of the financial and economic crisis showed that imbalances in one Member State, such as a high current account deficit or a real estate bubble, could have negative spill-over effects on other Member States of the EU. The MIP should identify and prevent internal imbalances (e.g. those arising from public or private indebtedness), likely to adversely affect the economic stability in the EU Member State concerned, the euro area or the EU as a whole. It is used under the European Semester. Conversely, the EMIP should be applied in more serious cases, i.e. with excessive macroeconomic imbalances already identified in a Member State, with a view to addressing and eliminating them. Both procedures involve the European Commission, the Council of the European Union, the European Parliament and the Eurogroup. If, under the EMIP, the Commission considers that a Member State is experiencing excessive macroeconomic imbalances, it informs the European Parliament, the Council and the Eurogroup accordingly. Acting on a recommendation from the Commission, the Council of the European Union may adopt a recommendation establishing the existence of an excessive imbalance. The Council also requires the Member State concerned to take corrective action. Its government then prepares and submits to the Council and the Commission a corrective action plan

173 Lastly, the sixth legislative act, or the new Directive on requirements for budgetary frameworks, was aimed to ensure that national solutions should be conducive to strengthening fiscal discipline in the European Union, cf. Council Directive 2011/85/ EU, op. cit., pp. 44–47; Najważniejsze rezultaty prac prezydencji Polski w Radzie Unii Europejskiej. Komunikat prasowy, 22 grudnia 2011 r. [The most important results of the work of the Polish Presidency at the European Council. Press release, 22 December 2011], http://www.pl2011.eu, p. 1 [accessed: 20 July 2022].

based on the Council's recommendation. If, upon a Commission recommendation, the Council considers the corrective action plan sufficient, it endorses the plan by way of a recommendation. Otherwise, the Council recommends that the Member State concerned submit a new corrective action plan. The Commission monitors the implementation of the Council's recommendation by that Member State. If the Council, on a recommendation from the Commission, considers that the Member State concerned is no longer affected by excessive imbalances, the procedure should be closed[174]. In the case of excessive macroeconomic imbalances in the euro area Member States, the Council of the European Union may impose sanctions for the lack of discipline, in the form of an interest-bearing deposit or an annual fine equal to 0.1% of the GDP in the preceding year of the Member State concerned[175].

The reform of the Stability and Growth Pact basically consisted in making the multilateral surveillance procedure and the excessive deficit procedure more restrictive. Sanctions against the euro area Member States for failure to comply with budgetary policy rules and principles were extended and could be imposed at an earlier stage than before. They would be applied within both the preventive arm (interest-bearing deposits of 0.2% of GDP) and the corrective arm (non-interest-bearing deposits or even fines of 0.2% of GDP) of the Stability and Growth Pact. Fines would also be imposed on Member States manipulating public debt and budget deficit statistics. There would be less discretion in the decision-making procedure concerning sanctions, with a significantly reinforced role to be played by the European Commission. Furthermore, much greater emphasis – strengthening the corrective arm of the Stability and Growth Pact – was placed on the mechanism for controlling the debt criterion, previously less relevant than budget deficit control. Pursuant to the new provisions, public debt exceeding the threshold of 60% of GDP should be treated with the same degree of severity as situations of budget deficit in excess of 3% of GDP (recommendations, notices to take remedial measures or even fines)[176]. The amendments

174 Regulation (EU) No 1176/2011 of the European Parliament and of the Council ..., pp. 28–32.

175 Regulation (EU) No 1174/2011 of the European Parliament and of the Council ..., pp. 10–11. For an assessment of the macroeconomic imbalance procedure in the context of the EU Member States' external debt service capacities, cf. A. Afonso, F. Huart, J. Tovar Jalles, P. Stanek, Assessing the sustainability of external imbalances in the European Union, 'The World Economy', 2019, pp. 320–348.

176 A Member State with public debt exceeding 60% of GDP could only be 'freed' from the excessive deficit procedure if it should manage to reduce its budget deficit below

introduced also concerned enhancing the economic dialogue between the European Union institutions (specifically, between the European Parliament, the Council of the European Union and the European Commission) and establishing two new procedures: a procedure for preventing macroeconomic imbalances and a procedure for excessive macroeconomic imbalances.

Although the adoption of the 'six-pack' closed the period of building the economic and budgetary governance system in the Economic and Monetary Union, designed by the European Commission in 2010–2011, the new system proved to be insufficient as well. The euro area debt crisis persisted and posed a real threat of spreading from one euro area Member State to another. Therefore, on 23 November 2011, the European Commission submitted proposals for two new legislative acts to supplement the 'six-pack' and to strengthen the surveillance mechanisms in the euro area[177]. The legislative work on the proposals took more than eighteen months. Both regulations, also called a 'two-pack', were adopted by the European Parliament and by the Council of the European Union on 21 May 2013 and entered into force on 30 May of the same year[178].

3% of GDP or to decrease its debt-to-GDP ratio at a satisfactory pace, i.e. if the differential with respect to the reference value (of 60%) should have decreased over the previous three years at an average rate of one-twentieth per year as a benchmark, cf. R. Poliński, Strefa euro, op. cit., p. 11. Cf. also: Regulation (EU) No 1175/2011 of the European Parliament and of the Council …, pp. 15–24; Regulation (EU) No 1173/2011 of the European Parliament and of the Council …, pp. 3–7; Council Regulation (EU) No 1177/2011 …, pp. 35–40. No fines could be imposed on non-euro area countries; Member States outside the euro area could only be given recommendations or notices for the correction of situations of excessive deficit or debt.

177 European Commission. Proposal for a Regulation of the European Parliament and of the Council on common provisions for monitoring and assessing draft budgetary plans and ensuring the correction of excessive deficit of the Member States in the euro area, Brussels, 23.11.2011, COM(2011) 821 final, pp. 1–11; European Commission. Proposal for a Regulation of the European Parliament and of the Council on the strengthening of economic and budgetary surveillance of Member States experiencing or threatened with serious difficulties with respect to their financial stability in the euro area, Brussels, 23.11.2011, COM(2011) 819 final, pp. 1–9.

178 Whereas the 'six-pack' concerned both the euro area Member States (Regulation (EU) No 1173/2011 of the European Parliament and of the Council, Regulation (EU) No 1174/2011 of the European Parliament and of the Council) and the Member States outside the euro area (Regulation (EU) No 1175/2011 of the European Parliament and of the Council, Council Regulation (EU) No 1177/2011, Regulation (EU) No 1176/2011 of the European Parliament and of the Council, Council Directive 2011/85/EU), the 'two-pack' only applied to the euro area Member States.

The first act, Regulation (EU) No 472/2013 of the European Parliament and of the Council, laid down provisions for strengthening the European Union's economic and budgetary surveillance of Member States in the euro area in the following two cases: (1) where those Member States experienced (or were threatened with) serious difficulties with respect to their 'financial stability or to the sustainability of their public finances', leading to 'potential adverse spill-over effects on other Member States in the euro area'; (2) where those Member States requested or received 'financial assistance' from one or several other Member States or third countries, the EFSM, the EFSF, the ESM and the IMF. The Regulation in question introduced greater differentiation among the euro area Member States in terms of supervisory obligations they were subject to, leading to the formation of three different types of surveillance[179].

The second act, Regulation (EU) No 473/2013 of the European Parliament and of the Council, introduced provisions for closer monitoring and coordination of budgetary policies in the euro area, already laid down in the Stability and Growth Pact and the European Semester procedure. It set up a common budgetary timeline for the euro area Member States, ensuring better synchronisation of the key steps in the preparation of their national budgets. Preferably by 15 April of each year, the euro area Member States should present to the European Commission, together with their stability programmes, their medium-term fiscal plans, or national fiscal plans for the following three years, prepared on the basis of independent macroeconomic forecasts. By 15 October of each year, those Member States should submit to the European Commission and to the Eurogroup their draft budgetary plans for the forthcoming year. Closer monitoring would apply to the euro area Member States subject to an excessive deficit procedure, to facilitate the European Commission's identifying risks in compliance with the relevant deadlines for correcting such excessive deficits. The euro area Member States experiencing serious difficulties with respect to their financial stability or receiving financial assistance on a precautionary basis would require even closer surveillance than those subject to an excessive deficit

179 Regulation (EU) No 472/2013 of the European Parliament and of the Council of 21 May 2013 on the strengthening of economic and budgetary surveillance of Member States in the euro area experiencing or threatened with serious difficulties with respect to their financial stability, Official Journal of the European Union, L 140, 27.5.2013, pp. 1–10 (here: pp. 3–6). Cf. also: M. Koczor, op. cit., pp. 247–248.

procedure. Both Regulations were supposed to enhance the effectiveness of the European Semester procedure[180].

It must be concluded that the 'six-pack' and the 'two-pack' introduced seven innovative solutions to economic and budgetary governance in the Economic and Monetary Union. Firstly, they reinforced both arms of the Stability and Growth Pact, but particularly strengthening its preventive arm. Secondly, they increased automatism in making decisions imposing sanctions against euro area Member States for failure to comply with budgetary policy rules and principles, thus limiting discretion and the influence of political factors on the process. Thirdly, the scope of applying sanctions was extended: they could be imposed in both the preventive and corrective arms of the Stability and Growth Pact. Fourthly, fines would also be required from Member States manipulating public debt and budget deficit statistics. Fifthly, the mechanism for controlling the debt criterion significantly gained in importance, previously much less relevant than budget deficit control. The modification strengthened the corrective arm of the Stability and Growth Pact. Sixthly, the acts in question conferred new powers: on the Commission – to assess the euro area Member States' medium-term fiscal plans (for the following three years), on the Commission and on the Eurogroup – to assess draft budgetary plans of those countries for the forthcoming year. Furthermore, the Commission became responsible for closer monitoring with regard to the euro area Member States subject to an excessive deficit procedure. Seventhly and lastly, the provisions laid down two new procedures: a procedure for preventing macroeconomic imbalances and a procedure for excessive macroeconomic imbalances. In the procedure, new powers were conferred on the European Commission and on the Council of the European Union. The Council of the European Union, on a recommendation from the Commission, could adopt a recommendation establishing the existence of an excessive imbalance and recommending that the Member State concerned take corrective action, subsequently endorsing or rejecting the corrective action plan on the basis

180 Regulation (EU) No 473/2013 of the European Parliament and of the Council of 21 May 2013 on common provisions for monitoring and assessing draft budgetary plans and ensuring the correction of excessive deficit of the Member States in the euro area, Official Journal of the European Union, L 140, 27.5.2013, pp. 11–23 (here: 17–20). Cf. also: M. Kawalec, Wpływ kryzysu finansowego na możliwość wprowadzenia federalizmu fiskalnego w strefie euro [The effects of the financial crisis on the possibility to introduce fiscal federalism in the euro area], 'Zeszyty Naukowe Uniwersytetu Ekonomicznego w Krakowie' 2017, no. 9, p. 43.

of a Commission report. Further, the Commission would monitor the implementation of the Council's recommendations by that Member State.

1.5. New tools for the supervision of financial markets in the European Union

With a view to mitigating the risk of another financial crisis, a centralised system was established for the supervision of financial markets in the European Union at the macro- and micro-prudential levels. The system is composed of the European Systemic Risk Board, in charge of monitoring systemic risks, and three new supervisory authorities for the banking, capital and insurance sectors: the European Banking Authority, the European Securities and Markets Authority and the European Insurance and Occupational Pensions Authority.

1 January 2011 marked the launch of the European System of Financial Supervision, coordinating operations of national regulatory authorities, ensuring the consistent application of Union law applicable to the financial sector to preserve financial stability and protecting the customers of financial services. As mentioned before, the European System of Financial Supervision comprises the following: the European Systemic Risk Board (ESRB) seated in Frankfurt am Main and three sectoral supervisory authorities: the European Banking Authority (EBA) seated in London, the European Securities and Markets Authority (ESMA) seated in Paris and the European Insurance and Occupational Pensions Authority (EIOPA) seated in Frankfurt am Main. The European System of Financial Supervision also includes the Joint Committee of the European Supervisory Authorities and national supervisory authorities. Whereas the European Systemic Risk Board is responsible for the macro-prudential oversight of the financial system within the European Union, the sectoral authorities perform tasks related to the micro-prudential supervision of the banking, capital and insurance sectors (Figure 3)[181].

181 Regulation (EU) No 1092/2010 of the European Parliament and of the Council of 24 November 2010 on European Union macro-prudential oversight of the financial system and establishing a European Systemic Risk Board, Official Journal of the European Union, L 331, 15.12.2010, pp. 1–11. Regulation (EU) No 1093/2010 of the European Parliament and of the Council of 24 November 2010 establishing a European Supervisory Authority (European Banking Authority), amending Decision No 716/2009/EC and repealing Commission Decision 2009/78/EC, Official Journal of the European Union, L 331, 15.12.2010, pp 12–47. Regulation (EU) No 1094/2010 of the European Parliament and of the Council of 24 November 2010 establishing a European Supervisory Authority (European Insurance and Occupational Pensions

AUTHORITIES			
EUROPEAN SYSTEMIC RISK BOARD (ESRB)	**EUROPEAN BANKING AUTHORITY (EBA)**	**EUROPEAN SECURITIES AND MARKETS AUTHORITY (ESMA)**	**EUROPEAN INSURANCE AND OCCUPATIONAL PENSIONS AUTHORITY (EIOPA)**
Macro-prudential oversight	**Micro-prudential supervision**	**Micro-prudential supervision**	**Micro-prudential supervision**
1. General Board 2. Steering Committee 3. Secretariat 4. Advisory Technical Committee 5. Advisory Scientific Committee	1. EBA Board of Supervisors 2. EBA Management Board 3. EBA Chairperson 4. EBA Executive Director 5. EBA Board of Appeal	1. ESMA Board of Supervisors 2. ESMA Management Board 3. ESMA Chairperson 4. ESMA Executive Director 5. ESMA Board of Appeal	1. EIOPA Board of Supervisors 2. EIOPA Management Board 3. EIOPA Chairperson 4. EIOPA Executive Director 5. EIOPA Board of Appeal
	Joint Committee of the European Supervisory Authorities (EBA, ESMA, EIOPA) **Micro-prudential supervision**		

Figure 3: The organisational structure of the European System of Financial Supervision

Source: prepared by the author on the basis of: Regulation (EU) No 1092/2010 of the European Parliament and of the Council ..., pp. 6–10. Regulation (EU) No 1093/2010 of the European Parliament and of the Council ..., pp. 22–23. Regulation (EU) No 1094/2010 of the European Parliament and of the Council ..., pp. 59–60. Regulation (EU) No 1095/2010 of the European Parliament and of the Council ..., pp. 95–96.

The European Systemic Risk Board is an independent body of the European Union. Its tasks include the prevention or mitigation of systemic risks to financial

Authority), amending Decision No 716/2009/EC and repealing Commission Decision 2009/79/EC, Official Journal of the European Union, L 331, 15.12.2010, pp. 48–83. Regulation (EU) No 1095/2010 of the European Parliament and of the Council of 24 November 2010 establishing a European Supervisory Authority (European Securities and Markets Authority), amending Decision No 716/2009/EC and repealing Commission Decision 2009/77/EC, Official Journal of the European Union, L 331, 15.12.2010, pp. 84–119. Council Regulation (EU) No 1096/2010 of 17 November 2010 conferring specific tasks upon the European Central Bank concerning the functioning of the European Systemic Risk Board, Official Journal of the European Union, L 331, 15.12.2010, pp. 162–164. European Commission. Press release. EU Economic governance: a major step forward, Brussels, 31 May 2011, MEMO/11/364, p. 10; cf. Narodowy Bank Polski. System finansowy [The financial system], http://www.nbp.pl/home.aspx?f=/systemfinansowy/esrb.html, p. 1. [accessed: 20 July 2022]. J.J. Węc, Nowe zasady sprawowania prezydencji w Radzie Unii Europejskiej..., pp. 12–13.

stability in the European Union, arising from the interconnectedness of financial institutions and markets or from macroeconomic and structural conditions. The ESRB issues warnings regarding identified systemic risks and recommendations for remedial action to be taken by the Member States' competent authorities. It cooperates closely with the European Central Bank, providing analytical, statistical, administrative and logistical support to the ESRB. The decision-making body of the ESRB is the General Board. The other bodies of the ESRB are as follows: the Steering Committee, the Secretariat, the Advisory Technical Committee and the Advisory Scientific Committee. Members of the General Board with voting rights comprise the President and the Vice-President of the ECB, the Governors of the national central banks of all the European Union Member States, the Chairpersons of the EBA, the ESMA and the EIOPA as well as the Chairs of the Advisory Technical Committee and of the Advisory Scientific Committee. Each of the European Supervisory Authorities comprises the following bodies: the Board of Supervisors, the Management Board, the Chairperson, the Executive Director and the Board of Appeal. The decision-making body of each ESA is the Board of Supervisors, composed of representatives of all the competent national supervisory authorities[182]. The Joint Committee of the European Supervisory Authorities ensures the cross-sectoral coordination of the activities of the three supervisory authorities: the EBA, the ESMA and the EIOPA[183].

1.6. The Fiscal Compact

On 23 October 2011, the European Council endorsed the proposal from the Heads of State or Government of the euro area for the strengthening of economic convergence within the euro area and for improving fiscal discipline and deepening economic union. It was also an indication of developing a fiscal agreement in the future. On the other hand, the European Council pointed to the 'need for coherence of the activities of the euro area and the European Union, with due

182 Komisja Nadzoru Finansowego [Polish Financial Supervision Authority]. Europejski System Nadzoru Finansowego [European System of Financial Supervision], http://www.knf.gov.pl/, p. 1 [accessed: 20 July 2022]. European Systemic Risk Board (ESRB), http://www.esrb.europa.eu, p. 1 [accessed: 20 July 2022].

183 Regulation (EU) No 1092/2010 of the European Parliament and of the Council ..., pp. 6–10. Regulation (EU) No 1093/2010 of the European Parliament and of the Council ..., pp. 22–23. Regulation (EU) No 1094/2010 of the European Parliament and of the Council ..., pp. 59–60. Regulation (EU) No 1095/2010 of the European Parliament and of the Council ..., pp. 95–96.

respect for the integrity of the European Union as a whole'[184]. Subsequently, at the Brussels European Council meeting held on 8–9 December 2011, the Heads of State or Government of the 25 European Union Member States agreed on a new 'fiscal compact'. In addition to the euro area countries, Bulgaria, Denmark, Lithuania, Latvia, Poland and Romania also indicated the possibility to take part in the process. Before the European Council meeting ended, similar declarations were made by Hungary, the Czech Republic and Sweden. The participants also decided that the signatories to such a new fiscal compact would provide, in the form of loans from their national central banks, EUR 200 billion to the International Monetary Fund to ensure that the IMF should have adequate resources to assist euro area Member States threatened by the crisis[185].

The main advocates of tightening fiscal discipline and the related sanctions for non-compliance were German Chancellor Angela Merkel and French President Nicolas Sarkozy. They argued that the changes to be introduced under the 'six-pack', entering into force in several days, were insufficient in the face of the deteriorating euro area debt crisis and permanent non-compliance by the majority of the EMU Member States with the convergence criteria, particularly with the fiscal criterion. In 2011, as many as 19 Member States of the EMU recorded budget deficits above 3% of GDP, whereas 14 countries had public debts exceeding 60% of GDP[186]. Chancellor Merkel insisted that the new fiscal provisions should be incorporated into EU primary law. However, as the United Kingdom, initially supported by Hungary, the Czech Republic and Sweden, refused to accept such

184 European Council, 23 October 2011, Conclusions, Brussels, 30 November 2011, EUCO 52/1/11, REV 1, p. 5.

185 K. Zachariasz, Czechy, Szwecja, Wielka Brytania, Węgry – kto się waha i dlaczego? [The Czech Republic, Sweden, the United Kingdom, Hungary – who is hesitating and why?], 'Gazeta Wyborcza', 9 December 2011, p. 1, https://wyborcza.pl [accessed: 20 July 2022]. I. Sudak, Jest porozumienie na szczycie UE. Wielka Brytania stawia się poza Unią [The EU summit has reached an agreement. The United Kingdom placing itself outside the EU], 'Gazeta Wyborcza', 9 December 2011, p. 1, https://wyborcza.pl [accessed: 20 July 2022]. For a critical analysis of the decisions made by the European Council, cf. T.G. Grosse, Reformy antykryzysowe czy zmiana kierunku integracji europejskiej? Ocena skutków szczytu UE 8–9 grudnia 2011 r. [Anti-crisis reforms or a reorientation of European integration? An assessment of the results of the EU summit of 8–9 December 2011], Brief programowy Instytutu Kościuszki, pp. 1–5, https://ik.org.pl, [accessed: 20 July 2022].

186 Monitor konwergencji nominalnej [Nominal Convergence Monitor]. Ministerstwo Finansów [Polish Ministry of Finance]. Departament Polityki Finansowej, Analiz i Statystyki, 2012, no. 4, p. 3.

a solution, new provisions were supposed to be adopted in the form of an intergovernmental agreement[187].

The European Council's decisions were endorsed and particularised by the euro area Heads of State or Government on 9 December 2011. They agreed that a new fiscal compact, strengthened economic policy coordination and further development of existing stabilisation tools were indispensable steps towards a stronger economic union[188]. They also decided that the signatories to the fiscal compact would consider, and confirm within ten days, the provision of additional resources for the International Monetary Fund of up EUR 200 billion, in the form of bilateral loans, to reinforce its measures aimed at dealing with the euro area debt crisis[189].

Subsequently, at the Brussels European Council meeting held on 2 March 2012, the Heads of State or Government of the 25 European Union Member States – with the exception of the United Kingdom and the Czech Republic – signed an intergovernmental agreement referred to as the Fiscal Compact[190]. Pursuant to Article 14(2) of the Fiscal Compact, it entered into force on 1 January 2013. Within five years of the date of its entry into force, the substance of the Fiscal Compact should be incorporated into European Union law (Article 16 of the Treaty)[191]. The Fiscal Compact imposed on the euro area Member States new requirements concerning their national budgetary policies, whereas compliance was voluntary for the other contracting parties. In general, the Treaty introduced provisions aimed to guarantee that (1) the general government budgetary positions of the euro area Member States should be balanced or in surplus;

187 J.J. Węc, Pierwsza polska prezydencja…, op. cit., pp. 144–145.

188 European Council. Statement by the Euro area Heads of State or Government, Brussels, 9 December 2011, http://www.consilium.europa.eu, pp. 2–4 [accessed: 20 July 2022].

189 Ibidem, pp. 2–4, 7.

190 European Council, 1/2 March 2012, Conclusions, Brussels, 26 April 2012, EUCO 4/2/12, REV 2, p. 1.

191 Treaty on Stability, Coordination and Governance in the Economic and Monetary Union between the Kingdom of Belgium, the Republic of Bulgaria, the Kingdom of Denmark, the Federal Republic of Germany, the Republic of Estonia, Ireland, the Hellenic Republic, the Kingdom of Spain, the French Republic, the Italian Republic, the Republic of Cyprus, the Republic of Latvia, the Republic of Lithuania, the Grand Duchy of Luxembourg, Hungary, Malta, the Kingdom of the Netherlands, Republic of Austria, the Republic of Poland, the Portuguese Republic, Romania, the Republic of Slovenia, the Slovak Republic, the Republic of Finland and the Kingdom of Sweden, http://european-council.europa.eu, pp. 18, 21–22, 24.

(2) the European Commission should play an increased role in the excessive deficit procedure with respect to the euro area Member States; (3) economic policy coordination should be strengthened within the euro area. The provisions of the Fiscal Compact primarily reflected the diplomatic success of two governments: those of Germany and France; from the beginning, their representatives strongly advocated strengthening budgetary discipline in the euro area Member States by transposing the 'golden rule' (the balanced budget rule), described in detail below, into their national legal systems and by making financial assistance under the ESM conditional on the ratification of the new international agreement. In contrast to Germany, France was satisfied with the intergovernmental status of the Treaty.

With a view to ensuring balanced budgets, the Fiscal Compact introduced the 'golden rule' according to which the annual structural balance (deficit) of the general government of a euro area Member State must not exceed 0.5% of GDP (Article 3(1)(b) of the Fiscal Compact)[192]. The guardian of balanced budgets would be a correction mechanism triggered automatically (Article 3(1)(e) and Article 3(2) of the Fiscal Compact). Temporary deviations from the balanced budget rule would be possible in exceptional circumstances only (Article 3(1)(c) of the Fiscal Compact). For example, such a circumstance could be a period of severe economic downturn. On the other hand, if public debt should be significantly below 60% of GDP, the lower limit of the medium-term objective for the structural deficit could be increased to 1% of GDP (Article 3(1)(d) of the Fiscal Compact). Such an automatic correction mechanism should take effect in the national legal systems 'at the latest one year after the entry into force' of the Fiscal Compact, 'through provisions of binding force and permanent character, preferably constitutional', 'on the basis of common principles to be proposed by the European Commission'[193]. In the event of failure to comply with those requirements, the matter could be brought to the CJEU. Where the European Commission or a euro area Member State should consider that another Member State had failed to transpose into its national law the provisions regarding the correction mechanism, the Member State concerned or a group of euro area Member States, but not the European Commission, would be entitled to bring the matter to the

192 The structural deficit of the general government refers to the annual cyclically-adjusted balance net of one-off and temporary government measures (such as higher expenditure on unemployment benefits during an economic slump).

193 Treaty on Stability, Coordination and Governance in the Economic and Monetary Union, op. cit., pp. 11–12.

Court of Justice. In both cases, the judgment of the CJEU should be binding on the parties to the proceedings. However, if the Court of Justice should find failure by the Member State concerned to comply with its judgment, it might impose on it a lump sum or a penalty payment appropriate in the circumstances, up to 0.1% of its GDP. The penalty amounts imposed on the euro area Member State concerned would be payable to the European Stability Mechanism or to the general budget of the EU (Article 8(1) and (2) of the Fiscal Compact)[194].

In order to strengthen the excessive deficit procedure, the euro area Member States committed to supporting all the proposals or recommendations submitted by the European Commission to the Council of the European Union during the relevant vote unless the Council should reject the decision proposed or recommended by the Commission by qualified majority. The position of the Member State concerned, i.e. that subject to the procedure, would not be taken into account (Article 7 of the Fiscal Compact). With a view to enhancing economic policy synergy in the euro area, the contracting parties agreed to discuss and coordinate *ex ante* all major economic policy reforms to be undertaken by them (Article 11 of the Fiscal Compact). Furthermore, the Member States' governments should report in advance on their public debt issuance plans (i.e. borrowing the necessary funds from bondholders) to the European Commission and to the Council of the European Union (Article 6 of the Fiscal Compact). With the aim of strengthening economic governance, the contracting parties agreed that the euro area Heads of State or Government and the President of the European Commission should meet informally at least twice a year. The President of the ECB should be invited to take part in such Euro Summit meetings. Under the provisions of the Fiscal Compact, the 'President of the Euro Summit' should be appointed by the euro area Heads of State or Government for a term of two and a half years. In close cooperation with the President of the European Commission, he or she should ensure the preparation and continuity of the above-mentioned Euro Summit meetings. The appointment should be made at the same time as the European Council elects its President and for the same term of office. The Eurogroup (referred to as the 'Euro Group' in the Fiscal Compact) was also indicated as the body responsible for the preparation of and follow up to the Euro Summit meetings, whereas its President should be invited to attend such meetings. The non-euro area Heads of State or Government should participate 'in discussions of Euro Summit meetings' addressing competitiveness, future modifications of the global architecture of the euro area, 'as well as, when appropriate

194 Ibidem, p. 16.

and at least once a year, in discussions on specific issues of implementation' of the Fiscal Compact (Article 12(1) to (4) of the Fiscal Compact). Therefore, the Euro Summit became a new non-contractual body of the European Union. With a view to strengthening interparliamentary dialogue, the Fiscal Compact also provided for the organisation and promotion of a conference (the Interparliamentary Conference on Stability, Economic Coordination and Governance in the European Union) of representatives of particular national parliaments and of the European Parliament. As mentioned before, the Conference should analyse and discuss budgetary policies and other issues covered by the Treaty (Article 13 of the Fiscal Compact).

To recapitulate, it must be emphasised that the Fiscal Compact imposed on the participating Member States five new requirements concerning stability, coordination as well as economic and budgetary governance in the euro area, whereas the other EMU Member States could comply with those on a voluntary basis. Firstly, as compared to the Stability and Growth Pact revised in 2011, the Fiscal Compact introduced the 'golden rule' that the annual structural balance (deficit) of the general government of a euro area Member State could not exceed 0.5% of its GDP. Thus, it lowered the previously applicable general threshold for the structural deficit from 1% to 0.5% of GDP. Secondly, the Fiscal Compact required the transposition of an automatic correction mechanism into national legal systems. Thirdly, the Treaty extended the euro area Member States' obligation to comply with the European Commission's recommendations concerning the excessive deficit procedure as the contracting parties explicitly committed to supporting all the proposals or recommendations submitted by the European Commission to the Council of the European Union during the relevant vote unless the Council should reject the decision proposed or recommended by the Commission by qualified majority. Fourthly, the Fiscal Compact basically strengthened budgetary discipline and economic policy coordination in the euro area. Fifthly, the Treaty introduced a possibility of bringing an action to the CJEU if the European Commission or a euro area Member State should conclude that another Member State had failed to transpose into its national legislation the provisions regarding the automatic correction mechanism. However, such an action could be brought by one or more euro area Member States only, not by the European Commission.

Opinions on the role of the Fiscal Compact vary in the literature. Some lawyers take the view that at least two articles of the Fiscal Compact, namely Article 8(1) to (3) and Article 7, are incompatible with Article 126(1) to (14) TFEU, constituting the legal basis for the excessive deficit procedure. One argument is that Article 8(3) of the Fiscal Compact empowers the CJEU to take action under the procedure pursuant to Article 273 TFEU. In accordance with Article 273 TFEU, the Court of Justice has jurisdiction in any dispute between Member States relating to the subject-matter of the Treaties if the dispute is submitted to the CJEU under a special agreement between the parties. However, in the opinion of the above-mentioned experts, it must not be applied in the procedure in question as its legal basis, Article 126(10) TFEU, expressly excludes a possibility of bringing an action to the CJEU against a Member State having failed to fulfil its obligations under the procedure. It also concerns a situation where such an action should be brought by one or more euro area governments (pursuant to Article 8(1) and (2) of the Fiscal Compact) rather than by the European Commission[195]. Further, it is argued that Article 7 of the Fiscal Compact contains an explicit commitment by the euro area Member States to supporting the European Commission's proposals or recommendations concerning the excessive deficit procedure (except if the Council of the European Union should reject such proposals or recommendations by qualified majority), which is in turn contrary to Article 126(13) TFEU, imposing no such obligation on the euro area governments[196]. Other experts consider that the Fiscal Compact introduced no modifications to the excessive deficit procedure, being purely declarative in nature and containing 'non-binding commitments' arising from the intergovernmental agreement in question[197]. Moreover, in accordance with the case-law of the CJEU, European Union law takes precedence over international agreements, including intergovernmental treaties. The establishment of an automatically triggered correction mechanism (Article 3(1)(e) and Article 3(2) of the Fiscal Compact) and the adoption of provisions facilitating the imposition of sanctions under the excessive deficit procedure (Article 8(1) to (3) of the Fiscal Compact) were solutions strengthening budgetary discipline; on the other hand, as an intergovernmental agreement, the Fiscal Compact did not fully guarantee

---

195 Pakt fiskalny. Analiza z dnia 26 marca 2012 r. Forum Obywatelskiego Rozwoju, Centrum für Europäische Politik [The Fiscal Compact. Analysis of 26 March 2012. Civil Development Forum, Centrum für Europäische Politik], http://www.for.org.pl/, pp. 3–4 [accessed: 20 July 2022]. D. Kabat-Rudnicka, Traktat o stabilności, koordynacji i zarządzaniu w Unii Gospodarczej i Walutowej – Analiza krytyczna [The Treaty on Stability, Coordination and Governance in the Economic and Monetary Union – A critical analysis], 'Krakowskie Studia Międzynarodowe' 2012, no. 3, pp. 89–93.

196 Pakt fiskalny. Analiza..., op. cit., p. 4.

197 D. Adamski, Pakt fiskalny a prawo europejskie i polska konstytucja [The Fiscal Compact, European law and the Polish Constitution], 'Europejski Przegląd Sądowy', December 2013, pp. 10–12, 17–20.

the transposition of such a correction mechanism into national legal systems or proper compliance, whereas the euro area Member States' commitment to supporting the European Commission's recommendations could be treated as a political declaration only as it would otherwise infringe European Union law[198]. With regard to Article 7 of the Fiscal Compact, only a 'soft' interpretation would be possible as well, or interpreting it as a political commitment, not subject to the jurisdiction of the Court of Justice. According to experts taking the view concerned, the provisions of the Fiscal Compact were intended as a tool for creating a culture of stability in the EU Member States; therefore, rather than being incompatible with EU law, they supplemented the legal instruments envisaged in the EU's legal framework[199].

In agreement here with the latter group of experts, it must be concluded that the signatories to the Fiscal Compact did not actually establish measures for taking effective action if the governments of particular euro area Member States should refuse to comply with the correction mechanism rules. The situation would remain unchanged until the incorporation of the provisions of the Fiscal Compact into the European Union's primary law, which would most probably involve revising the Treaties. On the other hand, it would be important to incorporate those rules into EU law, as in the case of the above-mentioned Treaty establishing the ESM, also with a view to preventing the fragmentation of the EU, thus reinforcing the coherence of the EU system.

2. Herman Van Rompuy's report approved on 14 December 2012. The system reforms proposed

The policy framework for reforming the Economic and Monetary Union in 2012–2015 was laid down in political and legal acts adopted by the European Union institutions, specifically by the European Council, the European Commission and the European Central Bank. On 14 December 2012, the European Council approved the report presented by its President Herman Van Rompuy and entitled '*Towards a genuine Economic and Monetary Union*', as the basis for further work aimed at completing the process of establishing the Economic and Monetary Union. In its December 2012 Conclusions, the European Council set out the most important objectives and scope of the proposed modifications to

198 Pakt fiskalny. Analiza..., op. cit., p. 4.
199 Ibidem.

the EMU system, with a view to overcoming the debt crisis[200]. A few months before, on 6 September 2012, the Governing Council of the ECB had decided on the introduction of a programme of unlimited purchases (with no limits as to time or scale of operations) in secondary markets for sovereign bonds, with maturities of one to three years, issued by the euro area Member States benefiting from financial assistance under EFSF or ESM programmes. Becoming a creditor of the countries concerned, the ECB still did not infringe Article 123(1) TFEU prohibiting the financing of Member States' national budgets as it would be done through the secondary market[201]. On 28 November 2012, the European Commission published its own 'Blueprint' for fighting the debt crisis, largely consistent with the assumptions of the report by Van Rompuy[202].

---

200 European Council, 13/14 December 2012, Conclusions, Brussels, 14 December 2012, EUCO 205/12, pp. 1–5. In June, October and December 2012, Rompuy submitted three different versions of his report, prepared in collaboration with José Manuel Barroso, President of the European Commission, Jean-Claude Juncker, President of the Eurogroup and Mario Draghi, President of the European Central Bank. Therefore, the documents are sometimes referred to as the Four Presidents' reports. The third version, announced on 5 December 2012 as the final report, was approved by the European Council. Cf. European Council. The President. Towards a genuine Economic and Monetary Union. [Final report], Brussels, 5 December 2012, http://www.consilium.europa.eu/, pp. 1–18 [accessed: 22 July 2022]. Cf. also: European Council. Report by President of the European Council Herman Van Rompuy. Towards a genuine Economic and Monetary Union. Press release, Brussels, 26 June 2012, EUCO 120/12, p. 3. European Council. The President. Towards a genuine Economic and Monetary Union. Interim Report, Brussels, 12 October 2012, http://www.consilium.europa.eu, pp. 1–8 [accessed: 22 July 2022].

201 The ECB's operations aimed at overcoming the crisis had started before the collapse of Lehman Brothers and consisted in the quantitative easing of monetary policy described below (2007–2012) and cutting interest rates (2008–2012). At the same time, the period 2010–2012 saw the implementation of a temporary securities markets programme for purchases of euro area government bonds in the secondary market and of private debt securities in the primary and secondary markets. Established under a decision of the Governing Council of the ECB of 10 May 2010, the programme ended on 12 September 2012. Cf. P. Panfil, Polityka Europejskiego Banku Centralnego w dobie kryzysu [The policy of the European Central Bank in the days of the crisis], 2012, https://www.law.muni.cz/sborniky/, pp. 5–9 [accessed: 21 October 2022]. J. Kozłowska, Polityka Europejskiego Banku Centralnego w dobie kryzysu finansowego [The policy of the European Central Bank in the days of the financial crisis], 'Zeszyty Naukowe Firma i Rynek' 2015, no. 1, pp. 19–22.

202 European Commission. A Blueprint for a deep and genuine Economic and Monetary Union: Launching a European debate. Press release, Brussels, 28 November 2012, IP/

The report by Van Rompuy approved on 14 December 2012 and the European Commission's Blueprint of 28 November 2012 assumed the establishment of three new structures in the Economic and Monetary Union: (1) an integrated financial framework; (2) an integrated budgetary framework; and (3) an integrated economic policy framework for the euro area Member States. The underlying concept of the integrated financial framework was that of a Financial Union, the integrated budgetary framework implied a Fiscal Union, whereas the integrated economic policy framework should be understood as a genuine Economic Union. The establishment of the new structures would involve serious limitations on the sovereignty of the euro area Member States. Therefore, in his report, Van Rompuy proposed a rather vague mechanism of legitimacy and accountability. The intention behind the enigmatic concept was that of extending the powers of the European Union's institutions, primarily those of the European Parliament as well as of national Parliaments in the euro area, in accordance with Article 13 of the Fiscal Compact and the Protocol (No 1) on the role of national Parliaments in the European Union, annexed to the TEU, the TFEU and the Euratom Treaty.

The adoption of the report by Van Rompuy and of the European Commission's Blueprint as the policy bases for the reform also involved moving away from the design considered in certain Member States in 2011–2012, i.e. transforming the European Union into a Political Union with a view to overcoming the debt crisis. Such a proposal was first put forward by representatives of the German Federal Government as early as October 2011, leading to a public debate on the subject in both Germany and the European Union[203]. It was also reflected in the

---

12/1272, pp. 1–3. For a broader analysis of the report by Van Rompuy, the European Commission's Blueprint and the European Central Bank's programme, cf. J.J. Węc, The European Union Debate, op. cit., pp. 22, 25–29.

203 In 2011–2012, there was a public debate in Germany, as the first European Union Member State, on the necessity to implement deep changes to the EU system with the aim of combating the euro area debt crisis. Representatives of the Federal Government (e.g. Angela Merkel and Wolfgang Schäuble) and certain political parties (CDU, FDP, SPD) even advocated the transformation of the European Union into a Political Union. Germany's proposal for establishing a Political Union as a remedy for the debt crisis was backed by Polish Foreign Minister Radosław Sikorski on 28 November 2011 and by Belgian Foreign Minister Didier Reynders on 9 August 2012. In contrast, French President François Hollande objected to it, declaring on 22 June 2012 that France would not agree to a Political Union. However, the debate in Germany and in the European Union diminished in importance as most governments of the Member States but also the EU's institutions were increasingly critical of the

Final Report of the Future of Europe Group of 17 September 2012, prepared by the Foreign Ministers of the following 11 European Union Member States: the Federal Republic of Germany, France, Belgium, the Netherlands, Luxembourg, Poland, Austria, Denmark, Italy, Spain and Portugal. The Report of the Future of Europe Group not only contained proposals for system changes to the Economic and Monetary Union, but it also envisaged a comprehensive reform of the European Union as a whole, resulting in its transformation into a Political Union[204].

As envisaged in the report by Van Rompuy and in the European Commission's Blueprint, the system reform of the Economic and Monetary Union would be implemented in three stages. Stage 1 would end in 2012–2013; Stage 2 would cover the period 2013–2014, whereas Stage 3 would start after 2014 and complete the process of change. The first step towards a Financial Union should be the establishment of a Banking Union. It should be based on three pillars: a Single Supervisory Mechanism; a Single Resolution Mechanism; and the harmonisation of national deposit guarantee frameworks[205].

A Fiscal Union would be established in several stages. First, it would be necessary to finalise the implementation of the 'six-pack', the 'two-pack' and the Fiscal Compact; as mentioned before, their objectives included *ex ante* coordination of annual budgets of the euro area Member States. It should be followed by an agreement on the annual budget balance and public debt limits for the

---

German proposals. A 'breakthrough' role for the debate was played, especially, by Van Rompuy's report adopted on 14 December 2012 and the European Commission's Blueprint of 28 November 2012. The documents only recommended introducing system changes to the euro area rather than to the European Union as a whole, as a priority task in fighting the crisis. Therefore, the system reform of the Economic and Monetary Union implemented in 2012–2015 was based on that scenario and not on Germany's proposals. Its roadmap was set out in the European Council decisions of December 2012 and of March and June 2013. For more on the subject, cf. J.J. Węc, Die politische Debatte, op. cit., pp. 201–208. Idem, Debata w Unii Europejskiej na temat drugiej reformy ustrojowej (2011–2012) [The debate in the European Union on the second system reform (2011–2012)], 'Przegląd Zachodni' 2013, no. 1, pp. 9–12, 14.

204 For more on the subject, cf. J.J. Węc, The European Union Debate..., op. cit., pp. 18–21. J.J. Węc, Niemcy wobec reformy ustrojowej strefy euro, op. cit., pp. 45–48.

205 The harmonisation of national deposit guarantee schemes was supposed to ensure that 'sufficiently robust national deposit insurance systems are set up in each Member State, thereby limiting the spill-over effects associated with deposit flight between institutions and across countries, and ensuring an appropriate degree of depositor protection in the European Union', cf. European Council. The President. Towards a genuine Economic and Monetary Union. [Final report], op. cit., p. 8.

euro area Member States, which would allow for the common issuance of public debt without resorting to the mutualisation of sovereign debt. Any public debt issued in excess of the mutually agreed limit would need justification and prior approval by the European Union's institutions. In the long term, it would be necessary to agree on a separate budget for the euro area, called by Van Rompuy, somewhat enigmatically, 'fiscal capacity', and to establish a Treasury function 'with clearly defined responsibilities'[206].

The Economic Union should complement the Financial Union and the Fiscal Union. In the short term, it would be vital to complete the building of the Single Market. Based on the European Semester and the Euro Plus Pact, the coordination of major economic policy reforms should be enhanced. It would involve the establishment of a framework for *ex ante* coordination of such reforms pursuant to Article 11 of the Fiscal Compact and the setting up of a mechanism for stronger coordination, convergence and enforcement of structural policies for promoting growth and jobs in accordance with the Europe 2020 strategy[207]. Under the latter mechanism, the euro area Member States concerned would enter into contractual arrangements with the EU institutions on the reforms they would commit to implementing with a view to strengthening their economic competitiveness, boosting economic growth and reducing unemployment. In return, they would be provided financial support from the European Union budget (cf. Figure 4)[208].

3. The implementation of the assumptions of Van Rompuy's report in 2012/13–2015

Early measures aimed at implementing the provisions of Van Rompuy's report included actions for establishing a Banking Union as a component of a future Financial Union. The course and outcome of legislative negotiations on the establishment of a Banking Union were largely determined by the German and French governments. Initially, the Banking Union was supposed to be a supranational institution, but the German and French governments together with those of several other Member States rejected the European Commission's proposal, which

206 Such a separate euro area budget (fiscal capacity) would also perform the asymmetric shock absorption function, cf. ibidem, pp. 8–12.

207 European Council. The President. Towards a genuine Economic and Monetary Union. [Final report], op. cit., p. 13.

208 Ibidem, pp. 14–16.

led to the weakening of the competences of the new structure in the euro area[209]. The final decision was that the Banking Union would be a structure based on three pillars and two legal orders: EU law and public international law. Detailed regulations concerning the rules of the functioning of the Banking Union were also agreed under significant influence of the German and French governments. Having pushed through various safeguards for the restructuring of euro area banks, the two countries strengthened their positions in the decision-making process while simultaneously complicating the functioning of the Banking Union. Their efforts resulted in a voting method at the Single Resolution Board (SRB), i.e. the body of the second pillar of the Banking Union, that allowed for Germany and France to form blocking coalitions for the resolution of banks in need of financial assistance exceeding EUR 5 billion or including institutions established in at least one euro area Member State and in at least one non-euro area country (referred to as a 'group resolution'). Furthermore, as the largest contributors to the Single Resolution Fund (SRF), Germany and France secured the casting vote in all essential bank resolution processes, thus a major influence on the reform orientations in Member States affected by the financial crisis[210].

At its meetings in March and June 2013, the European Council agreed that the key priority in further work would be completing the Banking Union, of fundamental importance to ensuring financial stability in the euro area Member States[211]. Therefore, between 2013 and 2015, an agreement was reached on a

---

209 For more on the subject, cf. J.J. Węc, Proces konstytuowania Unii Bankowej, op. cit., pp. 43–44.

210 A resolution plan for euro area banks could be blocked by Member States representing at least one-third of capital. Germany, likely to account for 18.8% to 25.7% of capital (depending on the number of the EU Member States to join the Banking Union and on the amount of capital contributed), together with France, would be able to block solutions considered unfavourable. Cf. K. Popławski, Kształt unii bankowej potwierdza uprzywilejowaną pozycję Berlina w strefie euro [The shape of the banking union confirms Berlin's privileged position in the euro area], Komentarze OSW, 10 January 2014, pp. 1–6.

211 European Council, 14/15 March 2013, Conclusions, Brussels, 14 March 2013, EUCO 23/13, p. 9. European Council, 27/28 June 2013, Conclusions, Brussels, 28 June 2013, EUCO 104/2/13, REV 2, pp. 9–10. In March 2014, the European Council urged the European Parliament and the Council of the European Union to adopt the Regulation establishing a Single Resolution Mechanism as soon as possible and invited the euro area Member States to complete negotiations on the intergovernmental agreement on the establishment of a Single Resolution Fund, cf. European Council, 20/21 March 2014, Conclusions, Brussels, 21 March 2014, EUCO 7/1/14, REV 1, p. 2.

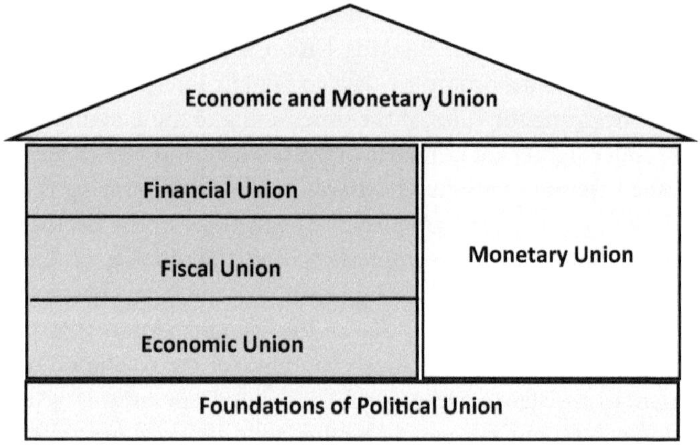

Figure 4: The organisational structure of the Economic and Monetary Union in 2025 according to the report by Herman Van Rompuy

Source: prepared by the author on the basis of: European Council. The President. Towards a genuine Economic and Monetary Union. [Final report], op. cit., pp. 1–5. J.J. Węc, The European Union Debate, op. cit., pp. 22, 25–29.

single rulebook for all the European Union Member States with regard to the functioning of banks and the financial market as a whole and the legal bases for the Banking Union were codified. By mid-2014, the single rulebook was introduced as a set of the following four legislative acts: (1) Capital Requirements Directive 2013/36/EU of the European Parliament and of the Council of 26 June 2013 (CRD IV)[212]; (2) Capital Requirements Regulation (EU) No 575/2013 of the European Parliament and of the Council of 26 June 2013 (CRR)[213]; (3) Bank Recovery and Resolution Directive 2014/59/EU of the European Parliament and of the Council of 15 May 2014, also referred to as the BRRD[214]; and (4) Deposit

212 Directive 2013/36/EU of the European Parliament and of the Council of 26 June 2013 on access to the activity of credit institutions and the prudential supervision of credit institutions and investment firms, amending Directive 2002/87/EC and repealing Directives 2006/48/EC and 2006/49/EC, Official Journal of the European Union, L 176, 27.6.2013, pp. 338–436.

213 Regulation (EU) No 575/2013 of the European Parliament and of the Council ..., pp. 1–337.

214 The abbreviation comes from the title of the Directive: the Bank Recovery and Resolution Directive – BRRD. Cf. Directive 2014/59/EU of the European Parliament and of the Council of 15 May 2014 establishing a framework for the recovery and resolution

Guarantee Schemes Directive 2014/49/EU of the European Parliament and of the Council of 16 April 2014 (DGSD)[215]. The provisions in question were intended to guarantee better functioning of the European Union's financial market as a whole and to increase the effectiveness of the Banking Union.

The CRD IV/CRR legislative package concerned prudential requirements for banks and investment firms. CRD IV defined conditions for the establishment of banks, capital buffers, the principles of supervision, standards of management and corporate governance. The CRR set out uniform rules for own funds, capital requirements, liquidity, etc.[216] The BRRD on crisis management laid down a harmonised legal framework for the resolution of credit institutions, including banks, in all the EU Member States. It contains provisions requiring all the EU Member States to establish national resolution funds. All financial institutions should contribute to such funds. Institutions' contributions should be calculated in proportion to their size and risk profile. The bank resolution provisions guarantee that shareholders and creditors of banks bear an appropriate part of the costs through the bail-in mechanism. If it should be insufficient, national resolution funds provide the necessary funding of the relevant bank under resolution. As aptly pointed out by Marcin Borsuk and Kamil Klupa, the EU Member States were left a certain margin of discretion in the management of their national financial systems, primarily due to the fact that no Common Financial Backstop was established at the EU level for crisis situations in local financial markets, whereas the budgetary consequences of financial crises would ultimately be suffered by the Member States only[217].

---

of credit institutions and investment firms and amending Council Directive 82/891/EEC, and Directives 2001/24/EC, 2002/47/EC, 2004/25/EC, 2005/56/EC, 2007/36/EC, 2011/35/EU, 2012/30/EU and 2013/36/EU, and Regulations (EU) No 1093/2010 and (EU) No 648/2012, of the European Parliament and of the Council, Official Journal of the European Union, L 173, 12.6.2014, pp. 190–348.

215 The abbreviation comes from the title of the Directive: the Deposit Guarantee Schemes Directive – DGSD, cf. Directive 2014/49/EU of the European Parliament and of the Council of 16 April 2014 on deposit guarantee schemes, Official Journal of the European Union, L 173, 12.6.2014, pp. 149–178.

216 A. Jurkowska-Zeidler, Europejski System Gwarantowania Depozytów: trzeci brakujący filar do dokończenia Unii Bankowej [The European Deposit Insurance Scheme: the third missing pillar for completing the Banking Union], 'Annales Universitatis Marie Curie-Sklodowska Lublin – Polonia'. Sectio H, 2016, Vol. L 4, p. 175.

217 M. Borsuk, K. Klupa, Europejski system gwarantowania depozytów (EDIS) jako trzeci filar unii bankowej i jego wpływ na państwa spoza strefy euro – perspektywa Polski [The European Deposit Insurance Scheme (EDIS) as the third pillar of the banking

The DGSD introduced five significant changes to the functioning of national deposit guarantee schemes. Firstly, it created a consistent set of rules for providing to depositors throughout the European Union a uniform level of protection against the consequences of the insolvency of credit institutions, including banks[218]. It should be the main function of the third pillar of the Banking Union. Secondly, the Directive requires the Member States to ensure that coverage level for the aggregate deposits of each depositor is EUR 100,000 in the event of deposits being unavailable[219]. Thirdly, the amounts repayable to depositors under DGSs should be available sooner, namely within seven business days rather than 20 business days as before. Fourthly, national deposit guarantee schemes should have at their disposal more funds than before as the new provisions introduced a higher level of *ex-ante* financing by banks. After 10 years, the available financial means of DGSs should reach 0.8% of the amount of covered deposits. If *ex-ante* financing should appear to be insufficient, *ex-post* contributions to the relevant national deposit guarantee schemes should be made immediately. Fifthly, the DGSD provides for the establishment of a mechanism for national DGSs to lend money to each other on a voluntary basis[220].

The legal bases for the Banking Union are the provisions of the European Union's primary and secondary law and intergovernmental agreement entered into by 26 EMU Member States (including those with a derogation). In primary law, those include Article 114(1) to (10) and Article 127(6) TFEU[221]. Pursuant to Article 114(1) TFEU, the European Parliament and the Council may, acting in accordance with the ordinary legislative procedure, adopt the measures for the harmonisation ('approximation') of the provisions laid down by law, regulation or administrative action in Member States which have as their object the establishment and functioning of the internal market. Article 127(6) TFEU stipulates

---

union and its influence on the non-euro area Member States – the perspective of Poland], 'Czasopismo Zarządzanie i Finanse – Journal of Management and Finance' 2017, no. 1, p. 19.

218 Directive 2014/49/EU of the European Parliament and of the Council, op. cit., p. 150.

219 Ibidem, p. 160.

220 An important role in ensuring consistent application of the DGSD is played by the above-mentioned EBA, empowered to issue recommendations and guidelines on the functioning of deposit guarantee scheme for common, uniform and consistent application of the DGSD throughout the European Union, cf. ibidem, pp. 174–175.

221 Treaty of Lisbon, op. cit., pp. 90, 124, 134–135. For a broader discussion of the issue, including acts of secondary law establishing the existing structures of the Banking Union, cf. J.J. Węc, Proces konstytuowania Unii Bankowej, op. cit., pp. 35–37.

that the Council of the European Union, acting in accordance with a special legislative procedure, may adopt a regulation conferring specific tasks on the European Central Bank concerning policies relating to the prudential supervision of credit institutions and other financial institutions with the exception of insurance undertakings. The Council must then act unanimously and after consulting the European Parliament and the European Central Bank.

With regard to secondary law, the relevant legislative acts are as follows: (1) Council Regulation (EU) No 1024/2013 of 15 October 2013 conferring specific tasks on the European Central Bank concerning policies relating to the prudential supervision of credit institutions[222]; (2) Regulation (EU) No 806/2014 of the European Parliament and of the Council of 15 July 2014 establishing uniform rules and a uniform procedure for the resolution of credit institutions and certain investment firms in the framework of a Single Resolution Mechanism and a Single Resolution Fund and amending Regulation (EU) No 1093/2010[223]; (3) Directive 2014/49/EU of the European Parliament and of the Council of 16 April 2014 on deposit guarantee schemes, also referred to as the DGSD[224]. The intergovernmental agreement signed on 21 May 2014 was aimed to govern the transfer and mutualisation of contributions to the Single Resolution Fund. Its conclusion was obligatory for the euro area governments and voluntary for the non-euro area Member States intending to join the first and second pillars of the Banking Union (excluding the United Kingdom and Sweden)[225].

222 Council Regulation (EU) No 1024/2013 of 15 October 2013 conferring specific tasks on the European Central Bank concerning policies relating to the prudential supervision of credit institutions, Official Journal of the European Union, L 287, 29.10.2013, pp. 63–89.

223 Regulation (EU) No 806/2014 of the European Parliament and of the Council of 15 July 2014 establishing uniform rules and a uniform procedure for the resolution of credit institutions and certain investment firms in the framework of a Single Resolution Mechanism and a Single Resolution Fund and amending Regulation (EU) No 1093/2010, Official Journal of the European Union, L 225, 30.7.2014, pp. 1–90.

224 Directive 2014/49/EU of the European Parliament and of the Council, op. cit., pp. 149–178.

225 Agreement on the transfer and mutualisation of contributions to the Single Resolution Fund between the Kingdom of Belgium, the Republic of Bulgaria, the Czech Republic, the Kingdom of Denmark, the Federal Republic of Germany, the Republic of Estonia, Ireland, the Hellenic Republic, the Kingdom of Spain, the French Republic, the Republic of Croatia, the Italian Republic, the Republic of Cyprus, the Republic of Latvia, the Republic of Lithuania, the Grand Duchy of Luxembourg, Hungary, the Republic of Malta, the Kingdom of the Netherlands, the Republic of Austria, the Republic of

In spite of undoubted legislative achievements, between 2013 and 2015 the process of establishing the Banking Union was significantly delayed. Only two out of the three pillars designed were created. The first pillar, or the Single Supervisory Mechanism (SSM), was established as late as 4 November 2014 rather than – as had been planned – earlier that year, on 1 January (according to the report by Van Rompuy). The creation of the second pillar, composed of the Single Resolution Mechanism (SRM) and the above-mentioned Single Resolution Fund (SRF), was also considerably delayed: the SRM was established on 1 January 2015, whereas the SRF did not become operational until 1 January 2016. In the meantime, the third pillar was still *in statu nascendi* as its legal basis, the DGSD, had not been transposed into the legal systems of the Member States participating in the Banking within the time limit set, i.e. by 3 July 2015. The fundamental difference between the third pillar and the other two pillars of the Banking Union was that it would not be mutualised. Its component, the deposit guarantee scheme, was supposed to be based on the harmonisation of national laws, which only implied enhanced coordination of operations of national DGSs (Article 4(1) DGSD)[226]. Some of the Member States, led by Germany, advocated the harmonisation of existing national legislations and simultaneously objected their unification. That group of countries pushed through their position during negotiations on the establishment of the third pillar[227].

The Banking Union supervises euro area credit institutions, including banks; on the other hand, it also guarantees that the institutions concerned could be wound up in a controlled manner, without detriment to national financial systems or costs previously borne by taxpayers. The structures existing within the Banking Union were created for the euro area Member States, but the Regulation establishing the Single Supervisory Mechanism provided for an opt-in (the possibility to voluntarily join the first pillar, which involved joining the second pillar

Poland, the Portuguese Republic, Romania, the Republic of Slovenia, the Slovak Republic and the Republic of Finland, Brussels, 21 May 2014, EU/SRF, pp. 1–45.

226 Pursuant to Article 4(1) DGSD, each 'Member State shall ensure that within its territory one or more DGSs are introduced and officially recognised. This shall not preclude the merger of DGSs of different Member States or the establishment of cross-border DGSs. Approval of such cross-border or merged DGSs shall be obtained from the Member States where the DGSs concerned are established', cf. Directive 2014/49/EU of the European Parliament and of the Council, op. cit., p. 158. Cf. also: J. Koleśnik, op. cit., pp. 101–103. A. Jurkowska-Zeidler, Fundamentalne zmiany ..., pp. 189–192.

227 Cf. Directive 2014/49/EU of the European Parliament and of the Council, op. cit., pp. 149–178.

as well) by the other European Union Member States by establishing 'close cooperation' with the European Central Bank. Nevertheless, the EU Member States with a derogation within the meaning of Article 139(1) TFEU were supposed to become full members of the first and second pillars upon joining the euro area (cf. Figure 5)[228].

The Single Supervisory Mechanism is composed of the European Central Bank and competent national supervisory authorities (NCAs) of participating Member States and of non-participating Member States having joined it in the model of 'close cooperation' with the European Central Bank[229]. The Single Supervisory Mechanism directly supervises the 120 largest banks in the euro area, accounting for approx. 82% of the euro area bank assets[230].

The bodies entrusted with supervisory tasks are joint teams composed of staff members from the ECB and from the NCAs (Joint Supervisory Teams – JSTs). The remaining 3,500 banks are supervised by the NCAs, although – ultimately – the ECB is also responsible for the supervision. However, its powers in that regard only consist in authorising credit institutions and withdrawing authorisations of credit institutions as well as in assessing notifications of the acquisition and disposal of qualifying holdings in such banks (cf. Figure 6). The main objectives of the Single Supervisory Mechanism include enhancing the supervision of the largest euro area banks, ensuring their safety and soundness as well as safeguarding financial stability in the euro area and in the single market. Specifically, the Single Supervisory Mechanism aims to verify compliance with

---

228 Odpowiedź sekretarza stanu w Ministerstwie Finansów [Izabeli Leszczyny] – z upoważnienia prezesa Rady Ministrów – na interpelację nr 30121 w sprawie stanowiska rządu PO-PSL w sprawie unii bankowej [Reply of the Secretary of State at the Ministry of Finance [Izabela Leszczyna] – as authorised by the Prime Minister – to question no. 30121 on the position of the PO-PSL government on the banking union], 3 February 2015, https://www.sejm.gov.pl/sejm7.nsf/InterpelacjaTresc.xsp?key=2117A115.

229 On 1 October 2020, Bulgaria and Croatia – as the first two non-euro area Member States – established 'close cooperation' with the ECB, thus joining the first and second pillars of the Banking Union.

230 The initial assumption concerned 128 banks representing 85% of bank assets. Cf. Europejski Bank Centralny – rozpoczęcie nadzorowania banków strefy euro przez Europejski Bank Centralny [The European Central Bank – The commencement of the supervision of euro area banks by the European Central Bank], 'Przegląd Spraw Europejskich' 2014, no. 11, p. 15. J.J. Węc, Proces konstytuowania Unii Bankowej, op. cit., p. 38.

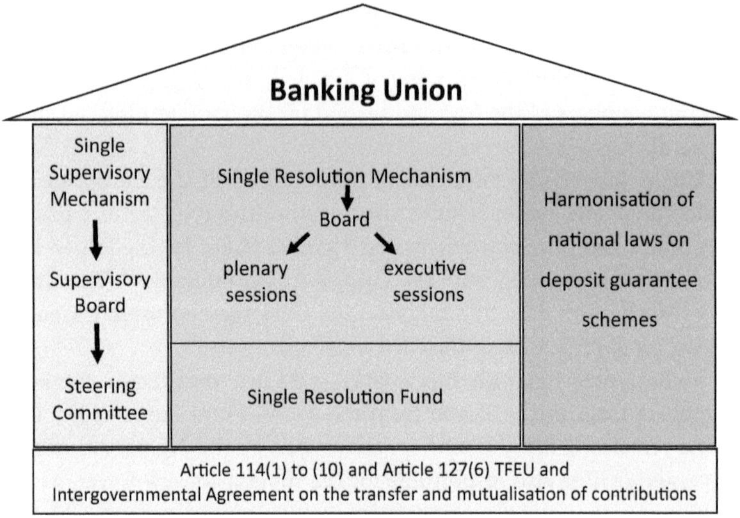

Figure 5: The organisational structure of the Banking Union

Source: prepared by the author on the basis of: Treaty of Lisbon, op. cit., pp. 90, 124, 134–135. Agreement on the transfer and mutualisation of contributions, op. cit., pp. 1–45. Council Regulation (EU) No 1024/2013, op. cit., pp. 1–45. Regulation (EU) No 806/2014 of the European Parliament and of the Council ..., op. cit., pp. 1–90. Directive 2014/49/EU of the European Parliament and of the Council, op. cit., pp. 150–163.

prudential requirements for credit institutions, detect their weaknesses at an early stage and prevent threats to overall financial stability. The effective and consistent functioning of the Single Supervisory Mechanism is the responsibility of the European Central Bank, acting in cooperation with the national competent authorities. The Single Supervisory Mechanism is supported by the second pillar of the Banking Union, i.e. the Single Resolution Mechanism[231].

The Single Resolution Mechanism, also called the insolvency and recovery mechanism, is composed of the Single Resolution Board (SRB) and the national resolution authorities. Its functioning involves the Council of the European Union, the European Commission and the European Central Bank. The Single Resolution

231 Europejski Bank Centralny – rozpoczęcie nadzorowania banków strefy euro przez Europejski Bank Centralny [The European Central Bank – The commencement of the supervision of euro area banks by the European Central Bank], 'Przegląd Spraw Europejskich' 2014, no. 11, p. 15.

GOVERNING BODIES	
SUPERVISORY BOARD 1. **Chair** 2. **Vice-Chair** 3. **Representatives of the ECB (4)** 4. **Representatives of the national supervisory authorities (1 for each participating Member State)**	**STEERING COMMITTEE** **Established by the Supervisory Board to give opinions and to execute coordination tasks**
DECISION-MAKING PROCESS AT THE **SUPERVISORY BOARD** **BSM*, the Chair has a casting vote** 1. **Draft decisions for the Governing Council of the ECB** 2. **Implementing decisions of the Supervisory Board**	

Figure 6: Single supervisory mechanism

* BSM – by simple majority

Source: prepared by the author on the basis of: Council Regulation (EU) No 1024/2013, op. cit. pp. 1–45.

Mechanism may only be used in Member States participating in the Single Supervisory Mechanism. It aims to guarantee that any future bankruptcies of credit institutions, including banks, in the euro area would only entail minimised costs of the resolution of such failed entities borne by the taxpayers. In the Member States not participating in the Banking Union, insolvency and recovery measures are taken by the relevant national resolution authorities[232].

The Single Resolution Fund, also called the insolvency and recovery fund, provides emergency assistance, i.e. it is only intended for crisis situations (cf. Figure 7). It may only be used for the purpose of ensuring the efficient application of the resolution tools for failing banks after other options, such as the bail-in tool, have been exhausted. It should be gradually built during eight years, from 1 January 2016. In the transitional period of eight years from the entry into force of the Regulation, i.e. until 31 December 2023, it should function as a dual system, composed of national sub-funds and the mutualised part of the SRF. Under the Intergovernmental Agreement

232 Regulation (EU) No 806/2014 of the European Parliament and of the Council of 15 July 2014, op. cit., pp. 1–90. The Single Resolution Mechanism is a centralised resolution mechanism for all banks operating in the Member States participating in the Single Supervisory Mechanism, cf. A. Jurkowska-Zeidler, Europejski System Gwarantowania Depozytów, op. cit., p. 172.

of 21 May 2014, constituting the legal basis for the SRF, contributions to the Single Resolution Fund are collected from banks located in particular Member States by the relevant national resolution authorities and subsequently transferred to the SRF. Initially, the funds raised should be pooled in envelopes (referred to as 'compartments') corresponding to each participating Member State and solely earmarked for the bail-out of banks established in the Member State concerned. However, after a period of eight years, or from 1 January 2024, they will be fully mutualised and available for the resolution of any euro area bank. In the first and second years of operation, 40% and another 20%, respectively, of the funds raised were subject to mutualisation, whereas the rest should be gradually mutualised during the subsequent six years. Individual contributions from particular banks to the Single Resolution Fund are calculated pro-rata to their liabilities and in proportion to the risk profile of the institutions concerned[233]. By the end of the transitional period, i.e. from 1 January 2024, the available financial means of the SRF should reach at least 1% of the amount of the covered deposits of all credit institutions authorised in all of the Member States participating in the Banking Union. In July 2021, it was approx. EUR 52 billion, but the target level should be around EUR 55 billion[234]. According to Anna Trzcińska, it means that the SRF will only be able to cover the costs involved in the resolution of individual banks (e.g. two to five medium-sized banks in large financial systems and four to six small banks in smaller systems), but it will be unable to bear the costs of a systemic crisis[235]. Therefore, as early as this stage of the reform, it has become clear that the SRF should be filled from other sources as well. The resolution procedure was codified in Article 18(1) to (10) of Regulation (EU) No 806/2014 of the European Parliament and of the Council of 15 July 2014. It is only initiated where the relevant supervisory action taken within the first pillar of the Banking Union has proven to be insufficient. In such an event, the Single Resolution Board may adopt a resolution decision for such a failing bank. The relevant

---

233 Agreement on the transfer and mutualisation of contributions, op. cit., pp. 22–23, 27. The individual contribution of each bank is calculated pro-rata to the amount of its liabilities (excluding own funds and covered deposits), with respect to the aggregate liabilities (excluding own funds and covered deposits) of all of the credit institutions and investment firms authorised in the territories of all of the 21 Member States participating in the Banking Union. Cf. Single Resolution Board. Single Resolution Fund, https://www.srb.europa.eu/en/content/single-resolution-fund, pp. 1–3 [accessed: 28 July 2022].

234 Regulation (EU) No 806/2014 of the European Parliament and of the Council, op. cit., p. 77.

235 A. Trzcińska, op. cit., p. 53.

procedure includes the steps described below. The European Central Bank, as the supervisory authority, assesses whether a bank 'is failing or is likely to fail'. Where the assessment confirms that the above condition is met, the ECB immediately notifies the European Commission and the Single Resolution Board. Such an assessment can also be made by the executive session of the Single Resolution Board on its own initiative, but only if, after having been informed by the SRB of its intention, the ECB does not make such an assessment within three calendar days of the receipt of that information. Furthermore, during its executive session, the Board decides 'whether a private solution is possible and whether the resolution is necessary in the public interest'. If the conditions for resolution are not met, the bank concerned is wound up in accordance with national law. Otherwise, the Board adopts a resolution scheme, setting out the resolution tools and the use of the Single Resolution Fund, and subsequently transmits the resolution scheme to the European Commission. The scheme 'enters into force within 24 hours of its approval by the Board'. During that period, the European Commission either endorses the scheme or objects to it with regard to its discretionary aspects. It may also propose to the Council of the European Union to object 'on the grounds that the resolution is not necessary in the public interest'. In such a situation, the Council of the European Union acts by simple majority. The European Commission may also propose to the Council of the European Union 'to approve or object to a material modification of the amount of the Fund'. A material change is considered to be that of '5% or more to the amount of the Fund compared with the original proposal of the Board'. If the European Commission intends to propose to the Council of the European Union to object, the Commission must 'do so within 12 hours of the Board's approval of the resolution scheme, enabling the Council to take a decision within the next 12 hours'. If the Council of the European Union 'objects to the placing of an institution under resolution, that institution is wound up in accordance to the applicable national law'[236].

With regard to the third pillar of the Banking Union, under the provisions of the DGSD, responsibility for deposit guarantee schemes in the euro area will continue to lie with the national authorities, although the supervision of and taking a resolution decision for a bank will be the powers of the European Central Bank. On the one hand, banks likely to fail will be forced to protect their depositors; on the other hand, they will also be able to use some of the funds covered by the

236 Regulation (EU) No 806/2014 of the European Parliament and of the Council, op. cit., pp. 41–43. Single Resolution Mechanism, https://www.consilium.europa.eu/en/, pp. 1–3 [accessed: 28 July 2022].

GOVERNING BODY	FUND
Single Resolution Board 1. Chair 2. Members (4) 3. Representatives of the national resolution authorities (1 for each participating Member State)	**Single Resolution Fund** 1. Contributions raised from banks by the relevant national resolution authorities. Initially, pooled in national envelopes ('compartments'), subject to mutualisation after 8 years (EUR 55 billion from 2024) 2. Establishment process in 2016–2023 ('transitional period') 3. Resolution costs should be borne by particular entities in the following order: shareholders, creditors, holders of deposits in excess of EUR 100,000, the Single Resolution Fund and the Common Backstop
Decision-making process at the **Single Resolution Board** 1. Plenary session: • As a rule, BSM*; in the event of a tie, the Chair has a casting vote • BSM* of the Board members representing at least 30% of contributions of the Member States participating in the SRF, with regard to decisions concerning financial assistance above the threshold of EUR 5 billion or group resolution (involving one euro area Member State + one non-euro area Member State) 2. Executive session: • As a rule, joint agreement by consensus, decisions concerning financial assistance not exceeding EUR 5 billion • BSM* (no joint agreement by consensus); in the event of a tie, the Chair has a casting vote	

Figure 7: Single resolution mechanism

* BSM – by simple majority

Source: prepared by the author on the basis of: Regulation (EU) No 806/2014 of the European Parliament and of the Council ..., pp. 1–90. Agreement on the transfer and mutualisation of contributions, op. cit., pp. 1–45.

above-mentioned guarantees to finance measures aimed to avoid their failure[237].

---

237 Directive 2014/49/EU of the European Parliament and of the Council, op. cit., pp. 150, 160–163. Klaudia Zielińska aptly points out that those provisions of the Directive strongly incentivise banks to take greater investment risk, cf. K. Zielińska, Drogi do unii bankowej – reformy systemu regulacji systemu bankowego [The ways towards the banking union – reforming the regulatory system for the banking system], 'Ekonomia Międzynarodowa' 2013, Issue 4, p. 35. Cf. also: T. Beck, Banking union for Europe – risks and challenges, [in:] Banking union for Europe – risks and challenges, T. Beck (ed.), London 2012, pp. 9–18. Ch. Wyplosz, Banking union as a crisis-management tool, [in:] Banking union for Europe – risks and challenges, T. Beck (ed.), London 2012, pp. 19–23. C. M. Buch, B. Weigert, Legacy problems in transition to a banking union, [in:] Banking union for Europe – risks and challenges, T. Beck (ed.), London

Therefore, with regard to failures of banks, the functioning of the Single Resolution Mechanism and the Single Resolution Fund should be closely connected with the DGSD. Pursuant to Article 15(1) to (4) of Regulation (EU) No 806/2014 of the European Parliament and of the Council of 15 July 2014 establishing... a Single Resolution Mechanism and a Single Resolution Fund, losses caused by banks' failures are borne first by shareholders and creditors, followed by clients or, specifically, by holders of deposits exceeding EUR 100,000, whereas the Single Resolution Fund is used as a last resort (in the event of insufficient funds)[238].

4. The legitimacy of system changes to the Economic and Monetary Union in 2010–2015

The legitimacy of system changes implemented in the Economic and Monetary Union at the first stage of the reform in 2010–2015 was reflected in the conferral of new powers on the European Union's institutions, bodies and authorities as well as on the national parliaments. Under the Banking Union, new powers were mostly conferred on the European Central Bank and the Council of the European Union as well as – to a lesser degree – on the European Commission, the European Parliament, the Court of Auditors and the national parliaments. Thus, in the first pillar, the European Central Bank became competent to carry out micro-prudential supervision tasks relating to the largest euro area banks participating in the Banking Union, including the following powers in particular: (1) to carry out supervisory reviews, on-site inspections and investigations; (2) to authorise banks and to withdraw authorisations of banks (in cooperation with national competent authorities), to impose fines on banks for failure to comply with the applicable provisions; (3) to assess the acquisition and disposal of significant holdings in banks; (4) to ensure compliance with the EU's prudential requirements; (5) to apply higher capital requirements (buffers) in order to handle financial threats; (6) to monitor the supervision of smaller banks by the national supervisors, or even to take over direct supervision of any bank in a Member State participating in the Banking Union. In the second pillar of the Banking Union, the powers conferred on the ECB included informing the Single

2012, pp. 25–35. T. Beck, Why the rush? Short-term crisis resolution and long-term bank stability, [in:] Banking union for Europe – risks and challenges, T. Beck (ed.), London 2012, pp. 37–43.

238 Regulation (EU) No 806/2014 of the European Parliament and of the Council, op. cit., pp. 39–40.

Resolution Board that a bank is failing or is likely to fail. As regards the Council of the European Union, the powers conferred on it under the first and second pillars comprised the following: (1) controlling supervisory action by the ECB and the Supervisory Board; approving the resolution scheme adopted by the Single Resolution Board; (2) appointing the Chair and the Vice-Chair of the Supervisory Board at the request of the ECB and members of the Single Resolution Board; and (3) deciding on how the banking sector should transfer *ex-ante* contributions to the Single Resolution Fund (by way of an implementing act). Under the second pillar, the European Commission became competent to either endorse or object to the resolution scheme adopted by the Single Resolution Board. Furthermore, the Commission may propose to the Council to object if the resolution scheme concerned is not necessary in the public interest or to approve or object to a material modification of the amount of the Fund provided for in the resolution scheme of the Board. Under the first and second pillars of the Banking Union, the powers conferred on the European Parliament comprised control of supervisory action by the ECB and the Supervisory Board and of activities of the Single Resolution Board. The European Parliament also became competent to approve the appointment by the Council of the European Union of the Chair and the Vice-Chair of the Supervisory Board. The power of audit with regard to supervisory action by the ECB was conferred on the Court of Auditors. New powers were also conferred on the national parliaments: the European Central Bank and the Single Resolution Board became obliged to submit to those parliaments annual reports on the performance of their respective supervisory tasks in the euro area[239].

In the ongoing process of establishing the Fiscal Union and completing a genuine Economic Union, new powers were conferred on the EU's institutions, bodies and authorities as well as on the national parliaments: mainly on the European Commission and the Council of the European Union, and to a lesser extent on the European Council, the European Parliament, the Court of Justice of the EU and the Eurogroup. Thus, the European Commission became competent to perform the following tasks: (1) to prepare and present an Annual Growth Survey for the EMU Member States and to formulate a draft recommendation

239 Council Regulation (EU) No 1024/2013, op. cit., pp. 1–45. Regulation (EU) No 806/2014 of the European Parliament and of the Council ..., pp. 1–90. Directive 2014/49/EU of the European Parliament and of the Council, op. cit., pp. 150–163. Agreement on the transfer and mutualisation of contributions, op. cit., pp. 1–45. Single Resolution Mechanism, op. cit., pp. 1–3.

for the euro area under the European Semester procedure (Fiscal Union); (2) to prepare an Alert Mechanism Report on any discovered macroeconomic imbalances in the EMU Member States under the European Semester procedure (Fiscal Union); (3) to assess, on an annual basis, National Reform Programmes, Stability or Convergence Programmes and, based on such assessments, to draft country-specific recommendations for the EMU Member States under the European Semester procedure (Fiscal Union); (4) to exercise strengthened budgetary surveillance of the EMU Member States under the 'six-pack' (Fiscal Union); (5) to inform the European Parliament, the Council of the European Union and the Eurogroup of the occurrence of macroeconomic imbalances or excessive macroeconomic imbalances in an EMU Member State under two new procedures: the MIP and the EMIP (Fiscal Union and Economic Union); (6) to prepare annual reports containing qualitative economic and financial assessments of the EU Member States and of the euro area under the macroeconomic imbalance procedure (Fiscal Union and Economic Union); (7) to adopt a report to serve as the basis for the Council of the European Union to either endorse or reject the relevant corrective action plan under the excessive macroeconomic imbalance procedure (Fiscal Union and Economic Union); (8) to monitor the implementation of the relevant recommendation from the Council of the European Union by the Member State subject to the excessive macroeconomic imbalance procedure (Fiscal Union and Economic Union); (9) to prepare recommendations concerning the imposition by the Council of the European Union of sanctions on a euro area Member State for the lack of discipline under the relevant excessive macroeconomic imbalance procedure (Fiscal Union and Economic Union); (10) to evaluate the euro area Member States' medium-term fiscal plans for the following three years, to monitor, assess and issue recommendations for draft budgetary plans for the forthcoming year before their adoption by the euro area Member States concerned, under the European Semester procedure and the 'two-pack' (Fiscal Union); (11) to exercise closer monitoring of the euro area Member States subject to an excessive deficit procedure under the 'two-pack' (Fiscal Union); (12) to formulate recommendations for the euro area Member States within the framework of an excessive deficit procedure under the Fiscal Compact (Fiscal Union); (13) to prepare annual reports on the implementation of the provisions of the Euro Plus Pact and to present them for assessment to the Heads of State or Government of the signatory Member States (Economic Union); (14) to exercise strengthened surveillance of the euro area Member States' public debt issuance plans under the Fiscal Compact (Fiscal Union); (15) to coordinate the activities of and cooperate with the National Competitiveness Boards under the European Semester procedure, e.g. with regard to the Annual

Growth Survey and the relevant excessive imbalance procedure under the Fiscal Compact (Fiscal Union); (16) to prepare common principles for the functioning of the automatic correction mechanism, concerning in particular the nature, size and time-frame of the corrective action to be undertaken, under the Fiscal Compact (Fiscal Union); (17) to monitor the putting in place at the national level of the correction mechanism under the Fiscal Compact (Fiscal Union); (18) to monitor the implementation by a Member State subject to an excessive deficit procedure of the relevant budgetary and economic partnership programme and the yearly budgetary plans consistent with it under the Fiscal Compact (Fiscal Union); (19) to receive *ex ante* reports by the signatory Member States on their debt issuance plans under the Fiscal Compact (Fiscal Union). Furthermore, the European Commission's role in the excessive deficit procedure was strengthened: the euro area Member States committed to supporting its proposals or recommendations submitted to the Council of the European Union unless a qualified majority of the Council members should object to the Commission's position (Fiscal Union)[240].

The Council of the European Union became competent to perform the following tasks: (1) to study the Commission's Annual Growth Survey and euro area recommendations and to adopt, based on the documents in question, political conclusions in the form of a priorities report under the European Semester procedure (Fiscal Union); (2) to adopt country-specific recommendations for the EMU Member States based on assessments of their respective National Reform Programmes, Stability or Convergence Programmes under the European

240 European Council. Council of the European Union. Who does what in the European Semester, op. cit., p. 1. Europejski Tydzień Parlamentarny, op. cit., pp. 1–2. Konferencja Międzyparlamentarna ds. Stabilności, Koordynacji i Zarządzania Gospodarczego, op. cit., pp. 1–2. Spotkania Konferencji Międzyparlamentarnej ds. Stabilności, Koordynacji i Zarządzania Gospodarczego, op. cit., pp. 1–2. European Council, 24/25 March 2011, Conclusions..., Annex I, op. cit., pp. 13–20. Regulation (EU) No 1176/2011 of the European Parliament and of the Council …, op. cit., pp. 28–32. Regulation (EU) No 1174/2011 of the European Parliament and of the Council…, op. cit., pp. 10–11. Council Regulation (EU) No 1177/2011, op. cit., pp. 33–40. Regulation (EU) No 1175/ 2011 of the European Parliament and of the Council…, op. cit., pp. 12–24. Regulation (EU) No 1173/2011 of the European Parliament and of the Council …, op. cit., pp. 1–7. Regulation (EU) No 472/2013 of the European Parliament and of the Council…, op. cit., pp. 17–23. Regulation (EU) No 473/2013 of the European Parliament and of the Council…, op. cit., pp. 1–10. Treaty on Stability, Coordination and Governance in the Economic and Monetary Union, op. cit., pp. 1–24.

Semester procedure, whereby the governments of the Member States concerned must take into account the above-mentioned recommendations in their draft budgets for the forthcoming year (Fiscal Union); (3) acting on a recommendation from the European Commission, to adopt a recommendation establishing the existence of an excessive (macroeconomic) imbalance in an EU or euro area Member State and to require the Member State concerned to take corrective action under the excessive imbalance procedure (Fiscal Union and Economic Union); (4) to endorse or reject, on the basis of a Commission report, the relevant corrective action plan submitted by the EU or euro area Member State concerned under the excessive imbalance procedure (Fiscal Union and Economic Union); (5) to decide on the imposition of sanctions against a euro area Member State for the lack of discipline under the excessive imbalance procedure, in the form of an interest-bearing deposit or an annual fine equal to 0.1% of the GDP in the preceding fiscal year of the Member State concerned (Fiscal Union and Economic Union); (6) to endorse the relevant budgetary and economic partnership programme submitted by a Member State subject to an excessive deficit procedure and including a detailed description of the structural reforms which should lead to an 'effective and durable correction' of its excessive deficit, under the Fiscal Compact (Fiscal Union); (7) to monitor the implementation by a Member State subject to an excessive deficit procedure of the relevant budgetary and economic partnership programme and the yearly budgetary plans consistent with it (Fiscal Union); (8) to receive *ex ante* reports by the signatory Member States on their debt issuance plans under the Fiscal Compact (Fiscal Union).

The new powers conferred on the European Parliament included the provision of opinions on employment guidelines in the euro area Member States (Economic Union) as well as the organisation of debates and the adoption of resolutions on the implementation by the EMU Member States of priorities for the fiscal year concerned with regard to their economic growth and macroeconomic situations, under the European Semester procedure (Fiscal Union). Under the Fiscal Compact, the President of the Euro Summit must present a report to the European Parliament after each Euro Summit meeting (Fiscal Union). Furthermore, dialogue between the European Parliament and the national parliaments should be strengthened by the establishment of the Interparliamentary Committee Meetings addressing economic governance in the EU as well as by the organisation of the Interparliamentary Conference on Stability, Economic Coordination and Governance in the European Union (Fiscal Union). The 'six-pack' also enhanced the economic dialogue between the EU institutions, particularly between the European Commission, the European Parliament and the Council of the European Union (Fiscal Union and Economic Union).

The European Council became competent to adopt conclusions endorsing the relevant report by the Council of the European Union on euro area priorities for the following fiscal year under the European Semester procedure (Fiscal Union) and to adopt conclusions endorsing country-specific recommendations by the Council of the European Union for the EMU Member States with regard to their respective National Reform Programmes, Stability or Convergence Programmes under the European Semester procedure (Fiscal Union). The new powers conferred on the Court of Justice of the European Union included jurisdiction in matters brought by one or more euro area Member States against other Member States having failed to transpose into their respective legal systems the provisions regarding the correction mechanism under the Fiscal Compact. If the Court of Justice should find failure by the Member State concerned to comply with its judgment, it might impose on it a lump sum or a penalty payment appropriate in the circumstances, up to 0.1% of its GDP (Fiscal Union). The Eurogroup became competent to assess draft budgetary plans for the forthcoming year submitted by the euro area Member States under the 'two-pack' (Fiscal Union). The Fiscal Compact established the Euro Summit as a new non-contractual body of the euro area and the EMU. Lastly, new powers were also conferred on the national parliaments, within the framework of the Interparliamentary Committee Meetings and the Interparliamentary Conference on Stability, Economic Coordination and Governance in the EU (Fiscal Union) (cf. Table 5).

Table 5: New powers conferred on the European Union's institutions, bodies and authorities as well as on the national parliaments at the first stage of the system reform of the Economic and Monetary Union in 2010–2015

Institution	Powers
European Council	1. Adoption of conclusions endorsing the relevant report by the Council of the European Union on euro area priorities for the following fiscal year under the European Semester procedure (Fiscal Union) 2. Adoption of conclusions endorsing country-specific recommendations by the Council of the European Union for the EMU Member States with regard to their respective National Reform Programmes, Stability or Convergence Programmes under the European Semester procedure (Fiscal Union)

Institution	Powers
Council of the European Union	1. Control of supervisory action by the ECB and the Supervisory Board (Banking Union) 2. Approval of the resolution scheme adopted by the Single Resolution Board (Banking Union) 3. Appointment of the Chair and the Vice-Chair of the Supervisory Board at the request of the ECB and members of the Single Resolution Board (Banking Union) 4. Deciding on how the banking sector should transfer *ex-ante* contributions to the Single Resolution Fund (by way of an implementing act) (Banking Union) 5. Study of the Commission's Annual Growth Survey and of euro area recommendations as well as the adoption, based on the documents in question, of political conclusions in the form of a priorities report under the European Semester procedure (Fiscal Union) 6. Adoption of country-specific recommendations for the EU or euro area Member States based on assessments of their respective National Reform Programmes, Stability or Convergence Programmes under the European Semester procedure. The governments of the Member States concerned must take into account the above-mentioned recommendations in their draft budgets for the forthcoming year (Fiscal Union) 7. Adoption, acting on a recommendation from the European Commission, of a recommendation establishing the existence of an excessive (macroeconomic) imbalance in an EU or euro area Member State and requiring the Member State concerned to take corrective action under the excessive imbalance procedure (Fiscal Union and Economic Union) 8. Endorsement or rejection, on the basis of a Commission report, of the relevant corrective action plan submitted by the EU or euro area Member State concerned under the excessive imbalance procedure (Fiscal Union and Economic Union) 9. Adoption of a decision imposing sanctions against a euro area Member State for the lack of discipline under the excessive imbalance procedure, in the form of an interest-bearing deposit or an annual fine equal to 0.1% of the GDP in the preceding fiscal year of the Member State concerned (Fiscal Union and Economic Union)

Institution	Powers
	10. Endorsement of the relevant budgetary and economic partnership programme submitted by a Member State subject to an excessive deficit procedure and including a detailed description of the structural reforms which should lead to an 'effective and durable correction' of its excessive deficit, under the Fiscal Compact (Fiscal Union) 11. Monitoring of the implementation by a Member State subject to an excessive deficit procedure of the relevant budgetary and economic partnership programme and the yearly budgetary plans consistent with it (Fiscal Union) 12. Receipt of *ex ante* reports by the signatory Member States on their debt issuance plans under the Fiscal Compact (Fiscal Union) 13. Enhanced economic dialogue between the EU institutions, particularly between the European Parliament, the Council of the European Union and the European Commission, under the 'six-pack' (Fiscal Union and Economic Union)
European Commission	1. Endorsement of or objection to the resolution scheme adopted by the Single Resolution Board. The Commission may also propose to the Council to object if the resolution scheme concerned is not necessary in the public interest or to approve or object to a material modification of the amount of the Fund provided for in the resolution scheme of the Board (Banking Union) 2. Preparation and presentation of an Annual Growth Survey for the EU or euro area Member States and of a draft recommendation for the euro area under the European Semester procedure (Fiscal Union) 3. Adoption of annual reports containing qualitative economic and financial assessments of the EU Member States and of the euro area under the macroeconomic imbalance procedure (Fiscal Union and Economic Union) 4. Assessment, on an annual basis, of National Reform Programmes, Stability or Convergence Programmes and, based thereon, the drafting of country-specific recommendations for the EMU States under the European Semester procedure (Fiscal Union and Economic Union) 5. Monitoring, assessment of and issuing recommendations for draft budgetary plans for the forthcoming year before their adoption by the euro area Member States concerned, under the Euro Plus Pact, the European Semester procedure and the 'two-pack' (Fiscal Union) 6. Exercise of strengthened budgetary surveillance of the EMU Member States under the 'six-pack' (Fiscal Union)

Institution	Powers
	7. Informing the European Parliament, the Council of the European Union and the Eurogroup of the occurrence of macroeconomic imbalances or excessive macroeconomic imbalances in an EU or euro area Member State under the two new procedures: MIP and EMIP (Fiscal Union and Economic Union) 8. Preparation of a recommendation establishing the existence of an excessive imbalance in an EU or euro area Member State and the adoption of a report to serve as the basis for the Council to either endorse or reject the relevant corrective action plan under the excessive imbalance procedure (Fiscal Union and Economic Union) 9. Monitoring of the implementation of the Council's recommendation by the Member State subject to an excessive imbalance procedure (Fiscal Union and Economic Union) 10. Preparation of recommendations concerning the imposition by the Council of sanctions on a euro area Member State for the lack of discipline under the excessive imbalance procedure (Fiscal Union and Economic Union) 11. Evaluation of the euro area Member States' medium-term fiscal plans for the following three years and the assessment of draft budgetary plans for the forthcoming year under the 'two-pack' (Fiscal Union) 12. Exercise of closer monitoring of the euro area Member States subject to an excessive deficit procedure under the 'two-pack' (Fiscal Union) 13. Issuing of recommendations for the euro area Member States in the framework of an excessive deficit procedure under the Fiscal Compact (Fiscal Union) 14. Preparation of annual reports on the implementation of the provisions of the Euro Plus Pact and their presentation for assessment to the Heads of State or Government of the signatory Member States (Economic Union) 15. Exercise of strengthened surveillance of the euro area Member States' public debt issuance plans under the Fiscal Compact (Fiscal Union) 16. Coordination of the activities of and cooperation with the National Competitiveness Boards under the European Semester procedure, e.g. with regard to the Annual Growth Survey and the macroeconomic imbalance procedure (Fiscal Union)

Institution	Powers
	17. Preparation of common principles for the functioning of the automatic correction mechanism (the nature, size and time-frame of the corrective action to be undertaken) under the Fiscal Compact (Fiscal Union) 18. Monitoring of the implementation by a Member State subject to an excessive deficit procedure of the relevant budgetary and economic partnership programme and the yearly budgetary plans consistent with it under the Fiscal Compact (Fiscal Union) 19. Receipt of *ex ante* reports by the signatory Member States on their debt issuance plans under the Fiscal Compact (Fiscal Union) 20. Monitoring of the putting in place at the national level of the correction mechanism under the Fiscal Compact (Fiscal Union) 21. Euro area Member States' commitment to supporting all the proposals or recommendations submitted by the Commission to the Council of the European Union unless a qualified majority of the Council members should object to the Commission's position (Fiscal Union) 22. Enhanced economic dialogue between the EU institutions, particularly between the European Parliament, the Council of the European Union and the European Commission, under the 'six-pack' (Fiscal Union and Economic Union)
European Parliament	1. Control of supervisory action by the ECB and the Supervisory Board and of activities of the Single Resolution Board (Banking Union) 2. Approval of the appointment by the Council of the European Union of the Chair and the Vice-Chair of the Supervisory Board (Banking Union) 3. Provision of opinions on employment guidelines in the euro area Member States under the European Semester procedure (Economic Union) 4. Organisation of European Parliament debates and the adoption of resolutions on the implementation by the EMU Member States of priorities for the fiscal year concerned under the European Semester procedure (Fiscal Union) 5. Receipt of reports by the President of the Euro Summit after each Euro Summit meeting under the Fiscal Compact (Fiscal Union) 6. Organisation of the Interparliamentary Committee Meetings for the relevant committees of the European Parliament and of national parliaments, addressing economic governance in the EU and held as part of the European Parliamentary Week coordinated with the European Semester cycle (Fiscal Union)

Institution	Powers
	7. Organisation of the Interparliamentary Conference on Stability, Economic Coordination and Governance in the EU, attended by representatives of the European Parliament and of particular national parliaments, established under the Fiscal Compact. The IPC SECG is held within the framework of the European Parliamentary Week, being coordinated with the European Semester cycle as well (Fiscal Union) 8. Enhanced economic dialogue between the EU institutions, particularly between the European Parliament, the Council of the European Union and the European Commission, under the 'six-pack' (Fiscal Union and Economic Union)
Court of Justice of the European Union	1. Jurisdiction in matters brought by one or more euro area Member States against other Member States having failed to transpose into their respective legal systems the provisions regarding the correction mechanism under the Fiscal Compact. If the Court of Justice should find failure by the Member State concerned to comply with its judgment, it might impose on it a lump sum or a penalty payment appropriate in the circumstances, up to 0.1% of its GDP (Fiscal Union).
Court of Auditors	1. Control of supervisory action by the ECB (Banking Union) 2. Audit of amounts spent by the beneficiaries of the Single Resolution Fund (Banking Union)
European Central Bank	1. Responsibility (in cooperation with the national competent authorities) for the effective and consistent functioning of the system of European banking supervision (Banking Union) 2. Carrying out of supervisory reviews, on-site inspections and investigations 3. Authorising banks and withdrawing authorisations of banks (in cooperation with the national competent authorities) as well as imposing fines on banks for failure to comply with the applicable provisions 4. Assessment of the acquisition and disposal of significant holdings in banks 5. Ensuring compliance with the EU's prudential requirements 6. Application of higher capital requirements (buffers) in order to handle financial threats 7. Monitoring of the supervision of smaller banks by the national supervisors, the power to independently take over direct supervision of any bank in a Member State participating in the Banking Union

Institution	Powers
	8. Informing the Single Resolution Board that a bank is failing or is likely to fail (Banking Union) 9. The President and the Vice-President of the ECB are members of the General Board of the European Systemic Risk Board
Euro Summit	1. Establishment of the Euro Summit as a new non-contractual body responsible for economic and budgetary governance in the euro area under the Fiscal Compact (Fiscal Union)
Eurogroup	1. Assessment of draft budgetary plans for the forthcoming year submitted by the euro area Member States under the 'two-pack' (Fiscal Union)
National Parliaments	1. The ECB and the Single Resolution Board submit annual reports on the performance of their respective supervisory tasks in the euro area (Banking Union) 2. Organisation of the Interparliamentary Committee Meetings for the relevant committees of the European Parliament and of national parliaments, addressing economic governance in the EU and held as part of the European Parliamentary Week coordinated with the European Semester cycle (Fiscal Union) 3. Interparliamentary Conference on Stability, Economic Coordination and Governance in the EU, attended by representatives of the European Parliament and of particular national parliaments, established under the Fiscal Compact. The IPC SECG is held within the framework of the European Parliamentary Week, being coordinated with the European Semester cycle as well (Fiscal Union)

Source: prepared by the author on the basis of: Council Regulation (EU) No 1024/2013, op. cit., pp. 1–45. Regulation (EU) No 806/2014 of the European Parliament and of the Council, op. cit., pp. 1–90. Directive 2014/49/EU of the European Parliament and of the Council, op. cit., pp. 150–163. Agreement on the transfer and mutualisation of contributions ..., op. cit., pp. 1–45. Regulation (EU) No 1176/2011 of the European Parliament and of the Council, op. cit., pp. 28–32. Regulation (EU) No 1174/2011 of the European Parliament and of the Council, op. cit., pp. 10–11. Council Regulation (EU) No 1177/2011, op. cit., pp. 33–40. Regulation (EU) No 1175/2011 of the European Parliament and of the Council, op. cit., pp. 12–24. Regulation (EU) No 1173/2011 of the European Parliament and of the Council, op. cit., pp. 1–7. Regulation (EU) No 472/2013 of the European Parliament and of the Council, op. cit., pp. 17–23. Regulation (EU) No 473/2013 of the European Parliament and of the Council, op. cit., pp. 1–10. Treaty on Stability, Coordination and Governance in the Economic and Monetary Union, op. cit., pp. 1–24. Single Resolution Mechanism, op. cit., pp. 1–3. European Council. Council of the European Union. Who does what in the European Semester, op. cit., p. 1. Europejski Tydzień Parlamentarny, op. cit., pp. 1–2. Konferencja Międzyparlamentarna ds. Stabilności, Koordynacji i Zarządzania Gospodarczego, op. cit., pp. 1–2. Spotkania Konferencji Międzyparlamentarnej ds. Stabilności, Koordynacji i Zarządzania Gospodarczego, op. cit., pp. 1–2. European Council, 24/25 March 2011, Conclusions..., Annex I, op. cit., pp. 13–20.

The successes of the system reform of the Economic and Monetary Union between 2010 and 2015 were quite impressive, but still insufficient for attaining all of its objectives. The period 2010–2012/13 witnessed considerable strengthening of economic and budgetary governance in the EMU through the introduction of the European Semester procedure, the adoption of the Euro Plus Pact, the 'six-pack' and the 'two-pack', the conclusion of the Fiscal Compact as well as the establishment of new crisis management instrument tools enhancing the financial stability of the euro area and of new instruments for the supervision of financial markets in the European Union. However, the above achievements failed to bring the expected results. In 2012, the debt crisis not only persisted, but it is still involved a real risk of spill-over effects on other euro area Member States. Such circumstances led to an idea of implementing a comprehensive system reform of the Economic and Monetary Union, launched in late 2012 and aimed at creating – in addition to the Monetary Union – the following three new structures: a Financial Union, a Fiscal Union and a genuine Economic Union. In 2012/13–2015, however, progress in that regard mostly concerned work on the legislative and international legal frameworks of the Banking Union as a component of the Financial Union. Although an incomplete Banking Union was established, three out of the four objectives of the reform with a deadline of mid-2015 remained unachieved. Thus, there was no third pillar of the Banking Union and no Common Backstop (CB) in the second pillar as the majority of the euro area Member States did not sign separate Loan Facility Agreements for the SRF[241]. Furthermore, among the 28 European Union Member States, despite significant

241 By 11 May 2016, such agreements had only been signed by eight out of the 19 euro area Member States obligatorily participating in the Banking Union, whereas another seven countries concluded them by 28 November 2016. Therefore, by the end of November 2016, the contributions transferred to the SRF amounted to EUR 10.8 billion. Cf. Rada Unii Europejskiej – Posiedzenie Rady Ecofin 12 lutego 2016 r. Wdrażanie Unii Bankowej [The Council of the European Union – Ecofin Council meeting of 12 February 2016. Implementation of the Banking Union], 'Przegląd Spraw Europejskich' 2016, no. 2, pp. 10–11. Rada Unii Europejskiej – Posiedzenie Rady Ecofin 25 maja 2016 r. Postępy we wdrażaniu Unii Bankowej [The Council of the European Union – Ecofin Council meeting of 25 May 2016. Progress on the implementation of the Banking Union], 'Przegląd Spraw Europejskich' 2016, no. 5, p. 13. Rada Unii Europejskiej. Posiedzenie Rady Ecofin 6 grudnia 2016 r. Postępy we wdrażaniu Unii Bankowej [The Council of the European Union – Ecofin Council meeting of 6 December 2016. Progress on the implementation of the Banking Union], 'Przegląd Spraw Europejskich' 2016, no. 12, p. 8.

delays in relation to the timeline set, many still had not transposed into their respective legal systems two legislative acts of relevance to the Banking Union: the BRRD and the DGSD. With an implementation deadline of 31 December 2014, the BRRD met with barriers to its transposition into national legislations as it was criticised in a number of EU Member States, mostly due to the provisions stipulating that in the event of a bank's failure deposits exceeding EUR 100,000 would be, in fact, subject to compulsory seizure. Therefore, particular Member States applied varying methods to implement the BRRD, i.e. their respective implementing acts introduced different orders of using debt instruments to absorb such a bank's losses. For example, the Polish Act of 10 June 2016 laid down certain preferential treatment of deposits in excess of EUR 100,000 held by individual clients or by small and medium-sized enterprises, stipulating that such deposits could only be used last to cover the resolution costs[242]. The transposition into national legal systems of the DGSD, with an implementation deadline of 3 July 2015, proved to be problematic as well. By the beginning of December 2015, as many as 10 EU Member States, including Poland, had not transposed the Directive; therefore, on 10 December of the same year, the European Commission issued 'reasoned opinions' requiring that the governments of the Member States concerned speed up work on the transposition of the legislative act in question. As some of the Member States, including Poland, still prolonged implementation work, the Commission brought the matter to the CJEU in May 2016[243]. Faced with judicial proceedings, the Member States accelerated their implementation procedures at a pace sufficient for the Slovak Presidency to announce, on 6 December 2016, based on the European Commission's data,

242 Bankowy Fundusz Gwarancyjny, Przymusowa restrukturyzacja w pytaniach i odpowiedziach [Bank Guarantee Fund. Resolution in questions and answers], https://www.bfg.pl/, pp. 1–5 [accessed: 22 July 2022]. In Poland, the Act in question was first used on 15 January 2020 when a bank likely to fail, Podkarpacki Bank Spółdzielczy, 'confiscated' tens of millions of zlotys from its clients. With a view to avoiding public panic, the 'confiscation' only concerned funds held by local authorities and large firms (having lost, respectively, 43.6% and less than 43% of their money), cf. Polski bank bezkarnie skonfiskował pieniądze klientów [A Polish bank confiscated its customers' money and got away with it], https://rekinfinansow.pl/, p. 1 [accessed: 20 July 2022].

243 Komisja Europejska – sprawa przeciwko Polsce w związku z niewdrożeniem przepisów unijnych dotyczących systemów gwarancji depozytów [The European Commission – Action against Poland for failure to implement EU provisions on deposit guarantee schemes], 'Przegląd Spraw Europejskich' 2016, no. 5, pp. 11–12.

successful implementation of the BRRD in all the EU Member States, whereas Belgium remained the only Member State not to transpose the DGSD into its legal system[244].

In addition, the work on other system changes to the EMU was also delayed in relation to the time-bound roadmap adopted by the European Council in December 2012. Efforts towards establishing a Fiscal Union were still in progress, whereas objections raised by certain Member States even precluded launching work or taking decisions on creating a separate budget or a separate budget line for the euro area within the EU's general budget, which was the most controversial objective of the whole reform at that time. Neither had endeavours to complete a genuine Economic Union resulted in putting in place a mechanism for economic policy coordination and harmonisation or in pursuing structural policies by the euro area Member States based on contractual arrangements comprising commitments to implement specific reforms. Finally, the euro area still showed signs of the debt crisis, such as significant economic performance discrepancies, nearly 18 million persons unemployed and serious risks of social exclusion in many Member States.

244 Cf. Rada Unii Europejskiej – Posiedzenie Rady Ecofin 12 lutego 2016 r., op. cit., pp. 10–11. Rada Unii Europejskiej – Posiedzenie Rady Ecofin 25 maja 2016 r., op. cit., p. 13. Rada Unii Europejskiej. Posiedzenie Rady Ecofin 6 grudnia 2016 r., op. cit., p. 8. The publication dates of the acts transposing the DGSD into the respective national legal systems were as follows: in Cyprus – 11 February, in Italy – 8 March, in Slovenia – 11 April, in Belgium – 12 May, in Poland – 8 July 2016. Cf. National transposition measures communicated by the Member States concerning: Directive 2014/49/EU of the European Parliament and of the Council of 16 April 2014 on deposit guarantee schemes (recast). Text with EEA relevance, https://eur-lex.europa.eu/legal-content/, pp. 1–5 [accessed: 21 October 2022].

Chapter III: The second stage of the reform of the Economic and Monetary Union in 2015–2022

1. The Five Presidents' Report of 22 June 2015. The system reforms proposed

In the first half of 2015, due to the limited success of the first stage of reforming the Economic and Monetary Union, the new President of the European Commission, Jean-Claude Juncker, submitted two extremely important documents intended to speed up work on the reform in question. On 12 February 2015, he put forward the Analytical Note *Preparing for Next Steps on Better Economic Governance in the Euro Area*[245]; later that year, on 22 June, he presented the report entitled *Completing Europe's Economic and Monetary Union*[246]. Both documents were prepared in close cooperation with the new President of the Euro Summit, Donald Tusk, the new President of the Eurogroup, Jeroen Dijsselbloem, the President of the European Central Bank, Mario Draghi, and the President of the European Parliament, Martin Schulz. The report of 22 June 2015, also referred to as the Five Presidents' Report, went much further than that presented by Van Rompuy two and a half years before. Whereas the latter outlined a clear direction for the system reform of the Economic and Monetary Union, the former set out very specific objectives, instruments, methods and a precise roadmap for implementing the reform. At the first stage of reforming the EMU system, the top

245 Preparing for Next Steps on Better Economic Governance in the Euro Area', Analytical Note by Jean-Claude Juncker in close cooperation with Donald Tusk, Jeroen Dijsselbloem and Mario Draghi, Informal European Council held on 12 February 2015, https://eur-lex.europa.eu/legal-content/EN/TXT/PDF/?uri=OJ:C: 2016:013: FULL&from=HR

246 European Commission. Completing Europe's Economic and Monetary Union. Report by: Jean-Claude Juncker in close cooperation with Donald Tusk, Jeroen Dijsselbloem, Mario Draghi and Martin Schulz, Brussels, 22 June 2015, p. 2. European Commission. Press release. Five Presidents' Report sets out plan for strengthening Europe's Economic and Monetary Union as of 1 July 2015, Brussels, 22 June 2015, pp. 1–4. For more on the subject cf. J.J. Węc, Dynamika reformy ustrojowej strefy euro, op. cit., pp. 181–194.

priority was to establish a Banking Union; the Five Presidents' Report shifted the focus to economic policy coordination and harmonisation in the euro area[247]. The common denominator of the two reports was moving towards a Financial Union, a Fiscal Union and a genuine Economic Union.

According to the Five Presidents' Report, the process towards a deeper Economic and Monetary Union was open to all the European Union Member States. 'It should be transparent and preserve the integrity of the Single Market in all its aspects'. The authors also indicated that – despite undeniable achievements – the Single European Market was still incomplete. It concerned the liberalisation of the movement of goods, services and capital. Therefore, 'completing and fully exploiting the Single Market in goods and services, digital, energy and capital markets should be part of a stronger boost towards economic union, as well as more jobs and higher growth'[248].

As highlighted in the Report, in spite of the most severe financial and economic crisis in 70 years, the euro remained the second most important currency in the world, accounting for nearly a quarter of global foreign exchange reserves, whereas almost 60 countries and territories worldwide either directly or indirectly pegged their currencies to it. Due to the system reform already implemented, the integrity of the euro area as a whole had been preserved, whereas the internal market remained strong[249]. On the other hand, the euro area was

---

247 It resulted from the Euro Summit decision of 24 October 2014, pointing out that closer coordination of economic policies was essential to ensure the smooth functioning of the Economic and Monetary Union. Therefore, the euro area Heads of State or Government invited the President of the European Commission, in cooperation with the President of the Euro Summit, the President of the Eurogroup and the President of the European Central Bank, to prepare a report on next steps to improve economic governance in the euro area, cf. Rada Europejska – oświadczenie przywódców państw strefy euro [The European Council – the Euro Summit statement], 'Przegląd Spraw Europejskich' 2014, no. 10, p. 11.

248 European Commission. Completing Europe's Economic and Monetary Union, op. cit., p. 2.

249 Ibidem, p. 4. Therefore, it was necessary to continue the system reform launched in 2012. According to the Report in question, the euro area Member States should be able to better prevent crises through sustainable fiscal and economic policies. They should also effectively respond to and absorb economic shocks 'through having suitably resilient economies and sufficient fiscal buffers over the economic cycle'. With a uniform monetary policy set for the euro area as a whole, national fiscal policies became pivotal in stabilising the economy experiencing a local shock. 'And with all countries sharing a single exchange rate, they need flexible economies that can react quickly to downturns. Otherwise they risk that recessions leave deep and permanent

still characterised by significant economic and social disproportions, destabilising the Economic and Monetary Union. The decision on establishing the Economic and Monetary Union under the Maastricht Treaty of 7 February 1992, on the sole basis of sharing a single currency but with no foundations for an economic union, was regarded as a wrong one, both politically and economically. The EMU was even compared to 'a house... only partially finished', but when 'the storm hit, its walls and roof had to be stabilised quickly'[250].

Therefore, the system reform should be based on the following four objectives – 'fronts': (1) establishing a genuine Economic Union ensuring that 'each economy has the structural features to prosper within the Monetary Union'; (2) establishing a Financial Union through completing the Banking Union and accelerating the Capital Markets Union; (3) establishing a Fiscal Union, to deliver 'both fiscal sustainability and fiscal stabilisation'; (4) making efforts 'towards a Political Union' that should provide 'the foundation for all of the above through genuine democratic accountability, legitimacy and institutional strengthening'[251]. The proposal for creating the foundations for a Political Union was another novelty in the Five Presidents' Report, differentiating it from the report by Van Rompuy. The former emphasised that all 'four Unions depend on each other. Therefore, they must develop in parallel and all euro area Member-States must participate in all Unions'[252].

The Five Presidents' Report laid out a plan for completing the Economic and Monetary Union in three stages. Stage 1 would last from 1 July 2015 to 30 June 2017. During the two years, the existing instruments and Treaties would be used for 'boosting competitiveness and structural convergence', conducting responsible fiscal policies at the national and euro area levels and enhancing democratic legitimacy for the reforms. The focus of Stage 2 should be on more far-reaching changes. It should also include the establishment of 'a set of commonly agreed benchmarks for convergence that could be given a legal nature' as well as of a

---

scars'. For all economies to permanently benefit from participating in the euro area, they should also 'be able to share the impact of shocks through risk-sharing' within the Economic and Monetary Union. In the short term, the risk-sharing 'can be achieved through integrated financial and capital markets (private risk-sharing) combined with the necessary common backstops, i.e. a last-resort financial safety net, to the Banking Union'. In the medium term, 'public risk-sharing should be enhanced through a mechanism of fiscal stabilisation for the euro area as a whole', cf. ibidem.

250 Ibidem, p. 4.

251 Ibidem, p. 5.

252 Ibidem, pp. 5–6.

euro area treasury. Stage 3 of the reform would lead to establishing a genuine Economic and Monetary Union by 2025[253].

The Report provided no concrete date for the transition from Stage 2 to Stage 3 of the system reform[254]. On the other hand, it announced the presentation of a White Paper by the European Commission in the spring of 2017, to set out detailed steps for completing Stage 1 and moving to Stage 2. In the document, the European Commission would assess progress made and indicate the necessary steps, 'including measures of a legal nature', to be taken in Stage 2. The White Paper should be prepared in consultation with the Presidents of the other European Union institutions[255].

1.1. The Financial Union

As underlined by the five Presidents, the Economic and Financial Unions should be 'complementary and mutually reinforcing'. Therefore, progress on their establishment 'must be a top priority' for Stage 1 of the planned reform. The Financial Union would make the financial system 'truly single or else the impulses from monetary policy decisions (e.g. changes in policy interest rates) will not be transmitted uniformly across its Member States'. That was the case during the debt crisis in the euro area, widening the economic differences between its Member States. The Financial Union should be composed of a Banking Union and a Capital Markets Union. Therefore, it was necessary to complete the Banking Union and to launch the Capital Markets Union. Both components of the Financial Union should be established in Stage 1 of the planned reform[256].

1.1.1. The Banking Union

The Report also called for completing the Banking Union. Anticipating that the Single Resolution Fund would become operational on 1 January 2016, the authors proposed taking four further measures. Firstly, the full transposition

---

253 Ibidem, p. 5.

254 Apparently, for the sake of official prudence, due to past failures to meet the time limits set for particular steps of the euro area reform, the document concerned was very vague about Stage 2, outlined in the medium and long term, and about Stage 3 as the final one, to end at the latest by 2025, cf. European Commission. Completing Europe's Economic and Monetary Union. (Annex 1: Roadmap Towards a Complete Economic and Monetary Union), op. cit., pp. 20–21.

255 Ibidem, pp. 5–6.

256 Ibidem, pp. 11–12.

into national law of the BRRD was vital for sharing risk with the private sector. Secondly, a common backstop for the SRF as a credit line from the European Stability Mechanism should be set up. Thirdly, all the Member States participating in the first and second pillars of the Banking Union should enter into an agreement on a bridge financing mechanism to ensure, in addition to the SRF in the eight-year transitional period, enough money to cover costs of the resolution or winding-up of failing banks where necessary. Fourthly, a new European Deposit Insurance Scheme (EDIS) should be established in place of the previously planned harmonisation of laws on national deposit guarantee schemes. A key element of the EDIS should be a common scheme of funding through *ex ante* risk-based fees paid by all the participating banks, as in the case of the Single Resolution Fund[257].

The proposal of the setting up of the EDIS was the most surprising novelty in the Five Presidents' Report as it implied changing the DGSD-based project already being put in place and moving away from the idea to harmonise Member States' laws on national deposit guarantee schemes towards their unification. As argued in the Report, although the DGSD would lead to more harmonisation of national deposit guarantee frameworks, particularly with regard to the pre-funding of national schemes, such a harmonised set-up would remain vulnerable to major local shocks. In contrast, the EDIS would make the Banking Union more resilient to future financial crises, all banks participating in the Banking Union would enjoy a level playing field, whereas responsibility for deposit guarantees would be shifted from Member States to the EU level[258]. Therefore, the Report proposed 'to devise the EDIS as a re-insurance system at the European level for the national deposit guarantee schemes'[259], which implied that the new project would draw on the DGSD solutions.

1.1.2. The Capital Markets Union

Alongside the completion of the Banking Union, launching the Capital Markets Union should also be a priority in the establishment of the Financial Union. The new structure should ensure more diversified sources of finance, enhance the

257 At the same time, the five Presidents indicated potential new risks in the banking sector, including risks related to the development of the shadow banking system. Therefore, they proposed to strengthen the EU's macro-prudential institutions, particularly the European Systemic Risk Board, cf. ibidem, p. 12.

258 Ibidem, pp. 13–14.

259 Ibidem, p. 11.

cross-border risk-sharing mechanism and constitute a *sui generis* buffer against systemic shocks in the financial sector. The Capital Markets Union would enable undertakings, including small and medium-sized enterprises, to access other sources of non-bank financing, in addition to bank loans. Further, it would 'strengthen cross-border risk-sharing through deepening integration of bond and equity markets, the latter of which is a key shock absorber'. A truly integrated capital market would serve as a buffer against systemic shocks in the financial sector and facilitate private sector risk-sharing across the Member States. However, according to the Report, 'as the closer integration of capital markets and gradual removal of remaining national barriers could create new risks to financial stability', it would be necessary to establish 'a single European capital markets supervisor'[260].

1.2. The Fiscal Union

One lesson to be learnt from euro area debt crisis was that fiscal policies were vital to all the Member States participating in the Monetary Union. A common monetary policy oriented towards price stability was no guarantee of smooth functioning of the Economic and Monetary Union. Unsustainable fiscal policies both undermined price stability in the European Union and harmed financial stability as they created 'contagion between Member States and financial fragmentation'. Therefore, as argued in the Report, responsible national fiscal policies pursued by the Member States should meet two conditions: firstly, they must guarantee the sustainability of public debt and the operation of fiscal automatic stabilisers to cushion country-specific economic shocks; secondly, the sum of national budget balances must lead to an appropriate fiscal stance at the euro area level[261]. It should be emphasised that the establishment of the Fiscal Union would not involve a full unification of the fiscal policies conducted by the euro area Member States. The euro area Member States would still freely shape their tax policies and decide on their preferred allocation of budgetary expenditure[262]. The target place for joint decision-making in that regard should be a newly planned euro area treasury, to ensure that the Member States' policies could be used countercyclically, with adequate financial buffers against country-specific economic shocks.

---

260 European Commission. Completing Europe's Economic and Monetary Union, op. cit., p. 12.

261 Ibidem, p. 14.

262 Ibidem.

1.2.1. The system of fiscal councils in the euro area

The packages of legal acts on economic governance adopted and implemented in the previous years, i.e. the 'six-pack', the 'two-pack' and the Fiscal Compact, had significantly improved the *ex ante* coordination of fiscal policies in the Economic and Monetary Union as a whole and enhanced the surveillance of the countries experiencing financial difficulties. However, all those measures proved to be insufficient. Therefore, the five Presidents advocated further strengthening of the coordination mechanism through establishing, already in Stage 1 of the reform, a new European Fiscal Board as an advisory entity. The Board would be composed of five members and provide assessments of the fiscal situation in the euro area as a whole. It should coordinate and support the network of national fiscal councils already proposed in the Fiscal Compact. According to the Report, such national fiscal councils should be strengthened by guaranteeing their freedom to provide independent assessments of the execution and performance of national budgets against the fiscal policy objectives set out for the euro area as a whole. Another benefit of establishing such a European Fiscal Board would be making the fiscal rules in the euro area more symmetric. During an economic upturn, the euro area Member States should use budget surpluses to create a financial buffer against a slowdown. The European Fiscal Board could also issue independent opinions on fiscal policy orientations at various times during an economic cycle and prepare adequate country-specific recommendations for the euro area Member States[263].

1.2.2. The fiscal stabilisation function

To better handle economic shocks whose mitigation could be impossible for individual countries, the Report also proposed establishing, in Stage 2 of the reform but in the longer term, a fiscal stabilisation function for the euro area, aimed to facilitate the cushioning of large macroeconomic shocks and, consequently, to improve the resilience of the whole Economic and Monetary Union to such shocks. Therefore, their proposal concerned the creation of a special expert group to exactly design such a function. It should be based on the following guiding principles: firstly, the fiscal stabilisation function, also called the Stabilisation Mechanism[264], should be established within the European Union's legal

263 For an interpretation of that part of the Report, cf. M. Gwóźdź-Lasoń, S. Miklaszewicz, K. Pujer, op. cit., pp. 52–53.

264 In the Five Presidents' Report, it was referred to as the fiscal stabilisation function; however, from President Jean-Claude Juncker's State of the Union Address of 13

framework rather than as an intergovernmental solution; secondly, it should be consistent with the existing EU fiscal framework and with procedures for economic policy coordination; thirdly, it should be open and transparent for all the European Union Member States; fourthly, it should not be an instrument for crisis management as that function was already performed by the European Stability Mechanism. The creation of such a Stabilisation Mechanism for the euro area should also be the culmination of the reform process, whereby achieving 'a significant degree of economic convergence, financial integration and further coordination and pooling of decision making on national budgets' should be seen as a precondition[265].

1.3. The Economic Union

Due to its intergovernmental and non-binding nature, the Euro Plus Pact failed to bring the expected results. Another weakness of that solution was the lack of an institution responsible for monitoring and enforcing compliance. Therefore, the Report recommended establishing a genuine Economic Union based on convergence, growth and jobs. To that end, within Stage 1 of the reform, the authors proposed the following measures: firstly, creating a euro area system of Competitiveness Authorities; secondly, improving and strengthening the Macroeconomic Imbalance Procedure; thirdly, placing greater emphasis on employment and social performance as well as on stronger coordination of economic policies, also within the European Semester; fourthly, reorganising and simplifying ('revamping') the European Semester procedure, through improved links between topics relevant to the euro area as a whole and country-specific issues. All those pillars should be implemented in line with the Community method, with their results reflected in the European Union law. Within Stage 2 of the reform, the convergence process should involve legally binding common standards regarding labour markets, competitiveness, the business environment, public administrations and certain aspects of tax policy[266].

September 2017, it was also called the Stabilisation Mechanism or the Stabilisation Function. Cf. European Commission. President Jean-Claude Juncker. State of the Union Address 2017, Brussels, 13 September 2017, SPEECH/17/3165, pp. 7–8.

265 European Commission. Completing Europe's Economic and Monetary Union, op. cit., pp. 14–15.

266 Ibidem, p. 7.

1.3.1. *A euro area system of Competitiveness Authorities*

Although previous reforms resulted in enhanced euro area governance for the coordination and surveillance of fiscal policies, it still needed improvement in terms of competitiveness. Therefore, as recommended by the five Presidents, each euro area Member State should create its own competitiveness authority. Such national authorities should be independent entities empowered to assess the development of wages in relation to labour productivity in the relevant Member States and to monitor progress made with economic reforms. Thus, they would contribute to economic convergence and increased sense of responsibility for implementing necessary reforms at the national level. Their combined efforts would help enhance the overall competitiveness in the euro area. Such a euro area system of Competitiveness Authorities should involve the national bodies and the European Commission. The latter would be responsible for the coordination of actions of the former. The outcome of the coordination could be taken into account in the European Commission's decisions to be made under the European Semester, in particular with regard to the Annual Growth Survey and the Macroeconomic Imbalance Procedure. Each Member State should independently decide on the organisational structure of its national Competitiveness Authority[267].

1.3.2. *Improving and strengthening the Macroeconomic Imbalance Procedure*

The Report recommended improving and strengthening the Macroeconomic Imbalance Procedure (MIP), constituting part of the European Semester. To that end, it proposed to use the MIP not only as a tool for detecting, preventing and correcting macroeconomic imbalances, but also for encouraging structural reforms to foster growth and jobs in line with the Europe 2020 strategy. Further, the MIP should serve to better monitor and overcome macroeconomic imbalances for the euro area as a whole rather than for particular Member States. Therefore, the focus should be both on the correction of harmful external deficits (e.g. 'sudden stops' of capital flows) and on reforms in euro area Member States such as Germany, running excessive and sustained current account surpluses due to limited domestic demand or low growth potential. Counteracting such

---

267 Ibidem, pp. 7–8. At that time, such competitiveness authorities were already in place in Belgium and the Netherlands.

developments would be important to ensuring effective rebalancing in the euro area as a whole[268].

1.3.3. *Employment and social performance*

As the successful completion of a 'genuine' Economic and Monetary Union required smooth functioning of labour markets and welfare systems in all the euro area Member States, it should be a priority for the European Semester procedure. Therefore, the Report highlighted that the main challenges related to euro area job markets included increasing the employment of people of all ages; preventing 'the divide between "insiders" with high protection and wages and "outsiders"'; reducing taxes on labour; providing tailored support for unemployed persons to re-enter the labour market; enhancing lifelong learning and education. With regard to issues beyond job markets, it was recommended to ensure access for every citizen to 'adequate education', to create an effective social protection system to primarily protect 'the most vulnerable in society, including a "social protection floor"', and to reform pension and health systems. Pension reforms should 'include aligning the retirement age with life expectancy'. The recommendations contained in the Report also concerned 'a deeper integration of national labour markets by facilitating geographic and professional mobility', also 'through better recognition of qualifications, easier access to public sector jobs for non-nationals and better coordination of social security systems'[269].

1.3.4. *A stronger coordination of economic policies*

Although the Report acknowledged the significant strengthening of the coordination of economic policies in the euro area through the European Semester, the five Presidents still saw room for simplifying and improving the procedure, with particular emphasis on four issues. Firstly, recommendations given to the Member States should focus on priority reforms aimed at stimulating economic growth, promoting job creation and exploiting the opportunities offered by the Single Market. On the other hand, such recommendations should 'remain "political", i.e. Member States should have a degree of freedom concerning the exact measures to be implemented', whereas the National Reform Programmes prepared annually by the Member States should 'serve as a basis for them to discuss their reform intentions'. Secondly, preparing periodic reports, regular peer

268 Ibidem.
269 Ibidem, pp. 8–9.

reviews and the 'comply-or-explain' approach should be used systematically, with a coordinating role in that regard played by the Eurogroup (Stage 1). It would also involve making full use of the Macroeconomic Imbalance Procedure. Thirdly, the European Semester procedure should be implemented in two successive stages: (1) for the euro area as a whole (from November of year *n-1* to February of year *n*); (2) at the national level (from March to July of year *n*)[270]. Therefore, euro area recommendations should be formulated first and followed by country-specific discussions and recommendations. The Report referred to those changes as 'revamping' the European Semester. Fourthly, the annual cycle of the European Semester should 'go together with a stronger multi-annual approach', resulting from the renewed convergence process[271].

1.4. Legitimacy

To ensure a democratically legitimate basis for the system changes to be implemented, the Report proposed the following steps for the euro area: (1) extending the powers conferred on the European Parliament and on the national parliaments; (2) consolidating the external representation of the European Union and of the euro area vis-à-vis international financial institutions; (3) integrating intergovernmental agreements regarding the euro area into the European Union's primary law; (4) strengthening the role of the Eurogroup, also through a reinforcement of its presidency; and (5) setting up a euro area treasury responsible for fiscal policy.

1.4.1. The European Parliament and the national parliaments

In connection with the above-mentioned reorganisation ('revamping') of the European Semester, the following three changes should take place already in Stage 1: firstly, parliamentary oversight in the revamped European Semester procedure should be strengthened; secondly, cooperation between the European Parliament and the national parliaments within the European Parliamentary Week should become closer; thirdly, the national parliaments should more systematically exercise the right to convene a Commissioner in accordance with the provisions of the 'two-pack'[272].

---

270 Year *n-1* means the previous year, whereas year *n* means the current year, cf. European Commission. Completing Europe's Economic and Monetary Union. (Annex 2: A More Integrated European Semester), op. cit., p. 22.

271 Ibidem, pp. 9–11.

272 Ibidem, p. 17.

With regard to the strengthening of parliamentary control as part of the revamped European Semester procedure, at the first stage of the Semester (from November of year *n-1* to February of year *n*) the European Commission could participate in a plenary debate at the European Parliament both before issuing the Annual Growth Survey and after its adoption. On the submission of the Annual Growth Survey, the European Commission would present the relevant euro area recommendations and a list of Member States considered to be in need of in-depth reviews under the Macroeconomic Imbalance Procedure. After the presentation by the European Commission of country-specific recommendations, a second plenary debate would take place, under the relevant economic dialogue provisions of the 'six-pack'. As foreseen in the 'six-pack' and 'two-pack' legislation, the dialogue should also involve the different formations of the Council of the European Union and the Eurogroup. The second stage of the European Semester procedure (from March to July of year *n*) would focus on reviews and assessments of the performance of and policies pursued by the Member States in the light of the priorities set. It would start with the publication of the European Commission's country reports and end with the adoption of country-specific recommendations. At that stage, the Member States should systematically involve their respective national parliaments in the discussion on national priorities[273].

The second proposal for strengthening legitimacy would concern more active involvement of representatives of the national parliaments in the discussion on economic policy priorities in the EMU. At the same time, representatives of the European Commission and of the Council of the European Union could take part in meetings held within the European Parliamentary Week, regarding national parliamentary debates both on country-specific recommendations and within the annual budgetary procedure. Furthermore, the national parliaments should be more closely involved in the adoption of the National Reform Programmes, the Stability and Convergence Programmes of the EMU Member States. Lastly, the national parliaments should be encouraged to more systematically exercise their right, enshrined in the 'two-pack', to convene a Commissioner for a presentation of the European Commission's opinion on a draft budgetary plan or of its recommendation to a Member State subject to an excessive deficit procedure[274].

---

273 European Commission. Completing Europe's Economic and Monetary Union. (Annex 2: A More Integrated European Semester), op. cit., p. 22.

274 Ibidem, p. 17.

1.4.2. The Eurogroup

As indicated by the Report, already in Stage 1 of the system reform it would be necessary to strengthen the Eurogroup presidency and to reinforce the means at its disposal. It would be fully justified due to the extended powers of the Eurogroup in the revamped European Semester procedure[275].

1.4.3. Consolidating the external representation of the euro area

Stage 1 of the planned system reform should already involve the launch and subsequent continuation of consolidating the external representation of the euro area in relations with international institutions. Due to the large economic and financial size of the European Union and the single monetary and exchange rate policy of the euro area Member States, the EU policy decisions and economic developments were increasingly relevant to the world economy. Nevertheless, the euro area still lacked a single representation to the international financial institutions. The EU could not fully use its political and economic power as each Member State spoke on its own behalf. According to the Report, the absence of a common representation of the euro area was particularly disadvantageous in relations with the International Monetary Fund; therefore, it should be the place to start changes in that regard[276].

1.4.4. Integrating intergovernmental solutions into EU law and the harmonisation of national laws

At the height of the debt crisis, certain far-reaching decisions needed to be taken under intergovernmental arrangements as such solutions allowed accelerating the decision-making process and overcoming opposition from the governments of some of the Member States. Specifically, it concerned the Fiscal Compact, the Euro Plus Pact, the Agreement on the Single Resolution Fund and the Treaty establishing the European Stability Mechanism. According to the Five Presidents, the time had come to incorporate, in Stage 2 of the reform but in the medium term, the provisions of those intergovernmental arrangements into EU law[277].

In the same period, through the harmonisation of national laws, it would be necessary to formalise the convergence process, aimed at creating more resilient

275 Ibidem, p. 18.
276 Ibidem, p. 17.
277 Ibidem, p. 18.

economic structures and reducing development differences in the euro area. Sovereignty over policies of common concern would then be shared by all the Member States. Therefore, some areas would need further harmonisation of national legislations; in other fields, where 'different policies can lead to similarly good performance', it would involve finding country-specific solutions. As mentioned before, the convergence process would entail binding standards for labour markets, competitiveness, business environment, public administration and certain aspects of tax policy (such as corporate tax base). Furthermore, the Macroeconomic Imbalance Procedure should also be used as a tool for supporting and monitoring progress towards reforms in particular euro area Member States rather than only for preventing and correcting such imbalances. Access to a shock absorption mechanism, to be established for the euro area as a whole, should be conditional on 'significant and sustained convergence towards similarly resilient economies'[278].

1.4.5. A European Fiscal Board and a euro area treasury

Ensuring democratic accountability and legitimacy would involve, already in Stage 1 of the reform, the establishment of the above-mentioned European Fiscal Board. It should coordinate and complement activities of the national fiscal councils and provide independent assessments of the performance and execution of the Member States' budgets in terms of objectives and recommendations specified within the EU fiscal governance framework. Opinions given by the European Fiscal Board would be taken into account by the European Commission in its decision-making on the European Semester procedure, but the Commission would be able to deviate from them in justified cases[279]. Stage 2 of establishing the Fiscal Union would involve the creation of a euro area treasury. It should serve as a platform for joint decision-making on fiscal policy in the euro area. As mentioned before, it would not imply the 'centralisation of all aspects of revenue and expenditure policy' since the euro area Member States would still decide on 'taxation and the allocation of budgetary expenditures'[280].

---

278 Ibidem, p. 9.
279 Ibidem, pp. 14, 23.
280 Ibidem, p. 18.

2. The implementation of the assumptions of the Five Presidents' Report in 2015–2017. The European Council decisions and the legislative initiatives by the European Commission

On 25–26 June 2015, the European Council took note of the Five Presidents' Report and asked the Council of the European Union to 'rapidly examine' the assumptions thereof[281]. Later that year, on 15 October, the European Council finally endorsed the report in question. After two months, in its Conclusions adopted on 17–18 December 2015, the European Council asked the Council of the European Union to 'swiftly examine the proposals put forward by the Commission as a follow-up to the report'. Further, it indicated three areas where work should advance particularly rapidly: (1) improving the effectiveness of economic and fiscal governance, to stimulate competitiveness, convergence and sustainability; (2) reinforcing the external representation of the euro area, 'to better reflect its weight in the world economy'; and (3) completing the Banking Union for enhanced financial stability of the euro area. The European Council also requested that the Council of the European Union prepare and submit a report on the progress on the reform by June 2016. Furthermore, it announced returning to the reform-related issues 'at the latest by the end of 2017'[282]. On 28 June 2016, in line with the announcement, the European Council took stock of the advancements in the work on the system reform. It positively evaluated the progress towards completing the Economic and Monetary Union, including the Banking Union, and called for work to be continued. The European Council also endorsed the recommendation by the Council of the European Union on the establishment of National Productivity Boards (previously referred to as National Competitiveness Boards) in the euro area[283].

On 28 January 2015, the European Commission started work on building a Capital Markets Union, intended as the other component – in addition to the Banking Union – of the Financial Union. The new structure would include all the European Union Member States. Its functioning should contribute to reducing

281 European Council meeting (25 and 26 June 2015), Conclusions, Brussels, 26 June 2015, EUCO 22/15, p. 8.

282 European Council meeting (15 October 2015), Conclusions, Brussels, 16 October 2015, EUCO 26/15, p. 6. European Council meeting (15 October 2015), Conclusions, Brussels, 18 December 2015, EUCO 28/15, p. 5.

283 European Council, 28 June 2016, Conclusions, Brussels, 28 June 2016, EUCO 26/16, p. 6.

borrowing costs, in particular for small and medium-sized enterprises, and to increasing the attractiveness of the European Union as an investment destination. On 30 September 2015, or around a dozen weeks after issuing the Five Presidents' Report, the European Commission published a communication to the European Parliament, the Council, the European Economic and Social Committee and to the Committee of the Regions. It set out the main priority areas for action to be taken towards establishing a Capital Markets Union by 2019[284]. Soon after the endorsement by the European Council of the Five Presidents' Report, on 21 October 2015, the European Commission published two more communications to the European Parliament, the Council and the European Central Bank. One concerned the implementation of Stage 1 of the reform and preparing for Stage 2; the other addressed steps for establishing a more consistent external representation of the euro area in international fora.

Among the actions to be undertaken in Stage 1 of the reform (by 30 June 2017), the European Commission pointed to the following five key issues: (1) revising the European Semester procedure in accordance with the timeline attached to the Communication in question (Economic Union)[285]; (2) introducing national Competitiveness Boards (Economic Union); (3) appointing an advisory European Fiscal Board (Fiscal Union); (4) reinforcing the external representation of the euro area (Legitimacy); (5) further steps towards a Financial Union, particularly via establishing a European Deposit Insurance Scheme (Financial

---

284 European Commission. Communication from the Commission to the European Parliament, the Council, the European Economic and Social Committee and the Committee of the Regions. Action Plan on Building a Capital Markets Union, Brussels, 30 September 2015, COM(2015) 468 final, pp. 1–30. For an analysis of the communication, cf. Komisja Europejska – publikacja *Planu działania na rzecz tworzenia unii rynków kapitałowych* [The European Commission – the publication of the *Action Plan on Building a Capital Markets Union*], 'Przegląd Spraw Europejskich' 2015, no. 8–9, pp. 7–9. Cf. also: Komisja Europejska – początek prac nad projektem unii rynków kapitałowych [The European Commission – the start of work on the proposed establishment of a Capital Markets Union], 'Przegląd Spraw Europejskich' 2015, no. 1, pp. 8–9.

285 In general, a revamped European Semester was to be based on the recommendations from the Five Presidents' Report, i.e. reorganising it in two consecutive stages and strengthening parliamentary control – the powers of the European Parliament and the national parliaments, cf. European Commission. Communication from the Commission to the European Parliament, the Council and the European Central Bank. On steps towards Completing Economic and Monetary Union, Brussels, 21 October 2015, COM(2015) 600 final, p. 17.

Union)[286]. With regard to the last element, the European Commission emphasised that it would make full use of the powers conferred on it under the Treaty to ensure the full transposition of the BRRD and the DGSD by the Member States. The Commission also urged the Member States participating in the Banking Union to ratify, by 30 November 2015, the Intergovernmental Agreement on the transfer and mutualisation of contributions to the SRF and invited them to agree on a Common Backstop for the Single Resolution Fund as a credit line from the European Stability Mechanism[287].

With regard to Stage 2 of the reform (from 1 July 2017), the European Commission mainly focused on the preparatory work. As emphasised by the Commission, 2016 would be of crucial importance to reaching an agreement on measures for completing the institutional framework of the Economic and Monetary Union. Therefore, the EU institutions and Member States should agree on and take measures for ensuring that the Competitiveness Boards and the European Fiscal Board would become operational by mid-2016. Further, the European Commission announced establishing, in mid-2016, an Expert Group 'to explore the legal, economic and political preconditions' for developing 'the more long-term proposals' described in the Five Presidents' Report[288].

The other Communication from the Commission of 21 October 2015 set out a detailed roadmap for reinforcing the external representation of the euro area, mostly in relations with the International Monetary Fund as a key international organisation in global economic governance. It seemed fully justified not only due to significant fragmentation of the external representation of the euro area in the IMF, but also in connection with the planned completion of a genuine Economic Union, Financial Union and Fiscal Union. It would also reflect the legitimacy of the system changes to the euro area[289].

In parallel to the above-mentioned Communications, on 21 October 2015, the European Commission issued three legislative initiatives, concerning the Economic Union, the Fiscal Union and the external representation of the euro area respectively.

---

286 Ibidem, p. 2. As complementary measures, the European Parliament would take steps to improve legitimacy, mostly democratic accountability of the economic governance system at the European Union level.

287 Ibidem, pp. 13–16.

288 Ibidem, pp. 15–17.

289 European Commission. Communication from the Commission to the European Parliament, the Council and the European Central Bank. A roadmap for moving towards a more consistent external representation of the euro area in international fora, Brussels, 21 October 2015, COM(2015) 602 final, pp. 1–11.

The first initiative was the Commission's Recommendation for a Council Recommendation on the establishment of National Competitiveness Boards within the Euro Area. Although it was addressed to the euro area Member States, the other Member States of the European Union were also invited to establish similar bodies. Each Member State should set up one Competitiveness Board. Such National Competitiveness Boards should cooperate with the European Commission within the European Semester procedure as well as with competitiveness boards of other Member States to coordinate their views. They should publish their analysis and advice in an annual report[290]. The second initiative concerned the adoption by the European Commission of a decision establishing an advisory European Fiscal Board. It was solely addressed to the euro area Member States. The European Fiscal Board should be an independent body working with the European Commission. Its tasks would be to contribute in an advisory capacity to the exercise of the Commission's functions in the multilateral fiscal surveillance in the euro area and to closely cooperate with the national fiscal councils set up in the Member States[291]. The third legislative initiative concerned a Council decision laying down measures in view of progressively establishing, by 2025 at the latest, unified representation of the euro area in the International Monetary Fund pursuant to Article 138 TFEU. The representation should be based on the following principles: firstly, in the Board of Governors and in the International Monetary and Financial Committee of the IMF, the views of the euro area should be presented by the President of the Eurogroup; secondly, in the IMF Executive Board, the euro area should be directly represented by the Executive Director of a euro area constituency, following the establishment of one or several constituencies composed only of euro area Member States, whereby the Executive Director should be elected upon proposal of the President of the Eurogroup and in accordance with the procedure provided for in Article 2 of Protocol No 14 on the Euro Group, annexed to the TEU and TFEU[292].

---

290 European Commission. Recommendation for a Council Recommendation. On the establishment of National Competitiveness Boards within the Euro Area, Brussels, 21 October 2015, COM(2015) 601 final, pp. 1–6.

291 European Commission. Commission Decision (EU) 2015/1937 of 21 October 2015 establishing an independent advisory European Fiscal Board, Official Journal of the European Union, L 282, 28.10.2015, pp. 37–40.

292 European Commission. Proposal for a Council decision laying down measures in view of progressively establishing unified representation of the euro area in the International Monetary Fund, Brussels, 21 October 2015, COM(2015) 603 final, pp. 1–10. In its Communication preceding the proposal in question, the European Commission mentioned the possibility of submitting further legal proposals with a view to

On 24 November 2015, the European Commission put forward a new legislative proposal on the establishment of a European Deposit Insurance Scheme. The initiative concerned amending Regulation (EU) 806/2014 of the European Parliament and of the Council of 15 July 2014 establishing the Single Resolution Mechanism and the Single Resolution Fund[293]. Since the creation of the EDIS required amendments to the above-mentioned Regulation, it reflected very close relationships between the financing mechanisms within the Banking Union, i.e. the Single Resolution Fund, the Common Backstop and the European Deposit Insurance Scheme. However, not only Regulation (EU) No 806/2014 of the European Parliament and of the Council but also the BRRD – establishing a recovery and resolution framework – contained provisions allowing the use of funds from deposit guarantee schemes for the resolution of credit institutions, including banks. According to Marcin Borsuk and Kamil Klupa, the establishment of an EU scheme for deposit insurance was a logical next step towards completing the Banking Union. In spite of the changes introduced under the DGSD, due to the lack of a centralised deposit guarantee scheme, depositors in particular Member States were still exposed to significant local shocks whose scale could be too large for national deposit guarantee schemes to handle, whereas the solvency of the relevant national deposit guarantee scheme was still closely related to the fiscal situation of the Member State concerned; in an crisis, it could be a threat to public finance, thus to banks. The debt crisis had shown, especially in Cyprus, the dependence of national deposit guarantee schemes on the country's solvency. Furthermore, the introduction of the EDIS would also logically complement shifting responsibility for banking supervision and resolution to the supranational level[294].

Bearing in mind that the provisions on the establishment and functioning of the EDIS should be directly applicable in the Member States and with a view to avoiding

---

reinforcing the external representation of the euro area in other international fora as well, cf. European Commission. Communication from the Commission to the European Parliament, the Council and the European Central Bank. A roadmap for moving towards a more consistent external representation of the euro area..., op. cit., pp. 1–11.

293 European Commission. Proposal for a regulation of the European Parliament and of the Council amending Regulation (EU) 806/2014..., op. cit., pp. 1–69. The proposal was accompanied by the Communication from the Commission envisaging the introduction of measures to further reduce risks remaining in the banking system, in parallel with efforts to establish the EDIS, cf. European Commission. Communication from the Commission to the European Parliament, the Council, the European Central Bank, the European Economic and Social Committee and the Committee of the Regions. "Towards the completion of the Banking Union", Strasbourg, 24 November 2015, COM(2015) 587 final, pp. 1–11.

294 For more on the subject, cf. M. Borsuk, K. Klupa, op. cit., pp. 21–24.

divergent interpretations across countries, the European Commission proposed adopting a regulation as the appropriate legal instrument[295]. The EDIS would only concern the Member States participating in the Banking Union. It should be based on the existing harmonisation of national deposit guarantee schemes managed under the DGSD, but it should also ultimately lead to unifying them. The European Deposit Insurance Scheme would be established in three successive stages: (1) the reinsurance period (2017–2020): the EDIS would provide additional funds to national deposit guarantee schemes in the performance of their mandatory functions, i.e. payouts to depositors and contributions to resolution; (2) the co-insurance period (2020–2024): the functioning of the EDIS would gradually increase the degree of the mutualisation of depositor risk across national deposit guarantee schemes; (3) the full insurance period: the EDIS would provide full funding of the liquidity need and cover all losses of national DGSs (from 2024). As the main difference between the reinsurance and co-insurance periods, in the latter payouts to depositors would be shared by the relevant national deposit guarantee scheme and the EDIS from the first losses. The funding would be immediately accessible for the relevant national deposit guarantee scheme to cover losses arising from a payout event or a request to contribute to resolution. Initially, the EDIS share would be 20% of the liability need of the participating DGS concerned. It would increase each subsequent year by 20 percentage points and reach 80% in the last year of co-insurance[296]. The non-euro area Member States joining the Banking Union would be required to participate in all the three pillars.

To facilitate the performance of the tasks of the European Deposit Insurance Scheme, the proposal for a regulation also provided for establishing a Deposit Insurance Fund (DIF), separate from the Single Resolution Fund and filled by *ex-ante* contributions owed by banks to the Single Resolution Board. The proposal also envisaged the attribution to the Board of the powers and obligations related to the management of the EDIS and the DIF. Therefore, the existing Single Resolution Board would be transformed into a Single Resolution and Deposit Insurance Board.

295 European Commission. Proposal for a regulation of the European Parliament and of the Council amending Regulation (EU) 806/2014 in order to establish a European Deposit Insurance Scheme, Strasbourg, 24 November 2015, COM(2015) 586 final, pp. 6–7.

296 For more on the subject, cf. M. Borsuk, K. Klupa, op. cit., pp. 26–27. Cf. also: European Commission. Proposal for a regulation of the European Parliament and of the Council amending Regulation (EU) 806/2014..., op. cit., pp. 8, 14–15, 27–28.

It should perform decision-making, monitoring and enforcement functions in the second and third pillars of the Banking Union (cf. Figure 8)[297].

The implementation of the assumptions of the Five Presidents' Report was not very impressive in 2015–2017. Commission Decision (EU) 2015/1937 of 21 October 2015 establishing an independent advisory European Fiscal Board entered into force on 1 November 2015, whereas the Council of the European Union adopted its recommendation on the establishment of National Productivity (Competitiveness) Boards on 20 September 2016[298]. But the legislative work on two very important proposals was still in progress. Those were as follows: the proposal for a regulation of the European Parliament and of the Council amending Regulation (EU) 806/2014 in order to establish a European Deposit Insurance Scheme and the proposal for a Council decision laying down measures in view of progressively establishing unified representation of the euro area in the International Monetary Fund, by 2025 at the latest.

GOVERNING BODY	FUND
Single Resolution and Deposit Insurance Board 1. Composition similar to that of the Single Resolution Board 2. Decision-making, monitoring and enforcement powers 3. Representatives of the national resolution authorities (1 for each participating Member State)	**Deposit Insurance Fund** 1. To be established until 2024 2. Contributions from banks located in the Member States (EUR 43 billion from 2024)

Figure 8: The European Deposit Insurance Scheme according to the proposal from the European Commission

Source: prepared by the author on the basis of: European Commission. Proposal for a regulation of the European Parliament and of the Council amending Regulation (EU) 806/2014..., op. cit., pp. 6–8, 14–15, 20, 27–28.

Whereas the created European Fiscal Board performed an advisory function under the multilateral surveillance procedure in the euro area and closely

297 European Commission. Proposal for a regulation of the European Parliament and of the Council amending Regulation (EU) 806/2014..., op. cit., pp. 4, 20.

298 During the legislative process, the Council of the European Union renamed the bodies concerned to National Productivity Boards, hence the name used hereinafter.

cooperated with the national fiscal councils in that regard[299], the National Productivity Boards as advisory bodies should analyse developments and policies concerning productivity and competitiveness in the euro area Member States[300]. The non-euro area Member States were also encouraged to establish their national productivity boards. Specifically, such productivity boards were tasked with producing expert opinions and annual reports, including diagnosis and analysis of changes in the field of productivity and competitiveness in the euro area Member States concerned. They should consider 'the long-term drivers and enablers of productivity and competitiveness, including innovation, and the capacity to attract investment, businesses and human capital' as well as of cost and non-cost factors affecting prices and quality of goods and services in the short term[301]. Such independent expert analyses, e.g. annual reports, should be used by the Member States and the European Commission in the context of the European Semester and the Macroeconomic Imbalance Procedure[302]. The Council Recommendation of 20 September 2016 was supposed to be implemented in each euro area Member State's legal system by 20 March 2018; however, by the end of December of that year, the requirement was only met by 10 euro area Member States and several other countries had advanced transposition measures in place.

Furthermore, on 23 November 2016, the European Commission put forward a proposal for amending the BRRD. On 12 December 2017, the European Parliament and the Council of the European Union adopted Directive (EU) 2017/2399, amending Directive 2014/59/EU as regards the ranking of unsecured debt instruments in insolvency hierarchy. The new Directive, hereinafter referred to as BRRD II, introduced measures to additionally strengthen the recovery and resolution framework and the loss-absorbing and recapitalisation capacity of the competent authorities, with a view to effectively protecting financial stability and public funds[303]. BRRD II entered into force on 28 December 2017. All the EU

---

299 Commission Decision (EU) 2015/1937 of 21 October 2015, op. cit., pp. 37–40.

300 Council Recommendation of 20 September 2016 on the establishment of National Productivity Boards, Official Journal of the European Union, C 349, 24.9.2016, pp. 1–4.

301 Ibidem, p. 3.

302 Ibidem.

303 Directive (EU) 2017/2399 of the European Parliament and of the Council of 12 December 2017 amending Directive 2014/59/EU as regards the ranking of unsecured debt instruments in insolvency hierarchy, Official Journal of the European Union, L 345, 27.12.2017, pp. 96–101.

Member States except for Portugal implemented the Directive in question before 4 June 2021[304].

3. The implementation of the assumptions of the Five Presidents' Report in 2017–2022. Divergent views of the European Commission and of the euro area Member States

3.1. The initiatives by the European Commission

3.1.1. The White Paper of 1 March 2017

As announced before, the European Commission prepared and published its White Paper on the Future of Europe on 1 March 2017[305]. The document comprised five scenarios for the further development of Europe by 2025. Scenario 1 assumed that the EU would carry on with its reform agenda in accordance with the European Commission's Political Guidelines 'A New Start for Europe' of 15 July 2014[306] and with the Bratislava Declaration adopted by the Heads of State or Government on 16 September 2016[307]. It would involve strengthening the single market, including in the energy and digital sectors; gradual advancements in the functioning of the euro area; closer cooperation in the management of the EU's external borders and progress towards a common European asylum system; as well as reinforced cooperation in the field of common security and defence policy (CSDP)[308]. Scenario 2 envisaged that the single market would only develop with regard to the movement of goods and capital, whereas the free movement

304 Cf. European Commission BRRD Transposition status, https://ec.europa.eu/en/, pp. 1–2 [accessed: 22 July 2022].

305 The submission of the document was announced by the President of the European Commission, Jean-Claude Juncker, as early as his State of the Union Address given on 14 September 2016, cf. European Commission. State of the Union Address 2016: Towards a better Europe – a Europe that protects, empowers and defends, Strasbourg, 14 September 2016, Speech/16/3043, p. 2.

306 A new start for Europe: My agenda for Jobs, Growth, Fairness and Democratic Change, https://ec.europa.eu/commission/presscorner/detail/en/SPEECH_14_546, pp. 1–2.

307 Informal meeting of the 27 heads of state or government. Bratislava Declaration. Bratislava, 16 September 2016, pp. 1–6, https://www.informal+meeting+of+the+27+head s+of+state+or+government.+Bratislava+.

308 European Commission. White Paper on the Future of Europe. Reflections and scenarios for the EU27 by 2025, Brussels, 1 March 2017, COM(2017) 2025, pp. 7–8.

of services and labour would not be fully guaranteed. In addition, it assumed that no more common solutions would be introduced in fields such as cooperation in the euro area, migration and asylum policy, external border controls or CSDP[309]. The idea of Scenario 3 was strengthening cooperation within one or more groups of Member States ('coalitions of the willing') in specific areas on the one hand and the other EU Member States' sticking to the previous course, as in Scenario 1, on the other hand. Closer cooperation in the scenario in question would entail pursuing integration goals in accordance with the concept of two or more integration speeds, thus *de facto* enhanced cooperation[310], in the following fields: taxation and social matters in the euro area, migration, the management of external borders and asylum policy of the European Union as well as CSDP (military coordination and joint equipment)[311].

Scenario 4 assumed closer cooperation and more effective enforcement of initiatives only in areas such as minimum common standards for the single market, innovation, common commercial policy, strengthening and stabilising the euro area, the management of external borders, asylum policy, counter-terrorism matters, deeper integration in the field of CSDP, including the creation of a European Defence Union. On the other hand, the scenario assumed withdrawal from or limiting cooperation concerning regional policy, public health, social and employment policy, although only to the extent not related to functioning of the single market[312]. Lastly, Scenario 5 envisaged deeper integration (through the reinforcement of the Community method and the establishment of new norms, standards and instruments) in all policy areas, based on joint decisions made by the Member States' governments. On the one hand, it implied the harmonisation of standards within the framework of the single market, the establishment of the Financial Union and a genuine Economic Union within the EMU as envisaged in the Five Presidents' Report of 22 June 2015; on the other hand, as in Scenario 4, the EU Member States would cooperate more closely in the management of external borders, asylum policy and counter-terrorism matters as well as in the

309 Ibidem, pp. 9–10.

310 According to the provisions on enhanced cooperation, if at least nine Member States wish to establish enhanced cooperation and as a last resort only, they may adopt legal acts solely binding on the Member States participating in such enhanced cooperation. The governing rules for and limitations on enhanced cooperation are laid down in Article 20(1) to (4) TEU, Article 329(1) and (2), Article 330 and Article 331(1) and (2) TFEU.

311 European Commission. White Paper, op. cit., pp. 11–12.

312 Ibidem, pp. 13–14.

common security and defence policy, including the creation of a European Defence Union[313].

3.1.2. *The Reflection Paper on the deepening of the Economic and Monetary Union of 31 May 2017*

The White Paper was widely discussed in the context of further development of the European Union, by the European Commission, the European Parliament, the national parliaments and interested Member States. From April to June 2017, the European Commission published five documents called 'reflection papers'. The first reflection paper concerned establishing the social dimension of the Economic Union (26 April); the second one addressed harnessing globalisation (10 May); the third one concerned deepening the Economic and Monetary Union (31 May); the fourth one outlined further development of the common security and defence policy of the European Union (7 June); the fifth one opened a debate on the future of EU finances (28 June). Each document contained proposals rather than decisions on the development of the European Union by 2025[314]. It is worth emphasising that the reflection papers significantly differed in compatibility with the five scenarios presented in the White Paper. The Reflection Paper on the deepening of the Economic and Monetary Union assumed the European Union should develop along the lines described in Scenarios 3 and 5. The Reflection Paper on the social dimension of the European Union contained three scenarios, consistent with the assumptions of Scenarios 2, 3 and 5 from the White Paper. The Reflection Paper on the future of the common security and defence policy also envisaged three scenarios of reforming the area in line with elements of Scenarios 1, 4 and 5 from the White Paper. The Reflection Paper on the further development of EU finances was the most strongly linked with the five scenarios. The Reflection Paper on globalisation concerned the analysis of the benefits and losses arising from the process in question, being the most loosely tied to the scenarios.

Announced on 31 May 2017, the Reflection Paper on the deepening of the Economic and Monetary Union confirmed, but also revised the assumptions

313 Ibidem, pp. 15–16. Cf. also: European Commission. Press release, Brussels, 1 March 2017, IP/17/385, pp. 1–3. For an analysis of the White Paper, cf. Komisja Europejska. Biała Księga dotycząca przyszłości UE [The European Commission. The White Paper on the Future of Europe], 'Przegląd Spraw Europejskich' 2017, no. 3, pp. 5–6.

314 European Commission. White Paper, op. cit., p. 26.

of the Five Presidents' Report of 22 June 2015. It legitimised the overall direction of the system reform of the Economic and Monetary Union, including the establishment of the Financial Union, the Fiscal Union and a genuine Economic Union. However, some of the main objectives and tasks as well as the roadmap towards them were changed[315]. In efforts to establish the designed Financial Union, the top priority would be to complete the Banking Union and to create the Capital Markets Union. With regard to the Banking Union, the Reflection Paper indicated two missing components of key importance: a Common Backstop for the Single Resolution Fund, part of the second pillar of the Banking Union, and a European Deposit Insurance Scheme, or the third pillar of the Banking Union. The Common Backstop would be the last of several instruments supporting the process of the resolution of credit institutions, including banks. It could be used if the funds from banks' shareholders, creditors and the SRF itself should prove insufficient. Its financing sources were still open to discussion. In its Reflection Paper, the European Commission proposed two alternatives: a credit line from the European Stability Mechanism (after necessary amendments to the existing legislation); loans or guarantees for the SRF granted by the euro area Member States. In contrast to the Five Presidents' Report, having foreseen that the new structures would be established by mid-2017, the document concerned extended the period to 2019, or even to 2025. As a possible way forward, the Common Backstop should be set up by the end of 2019, whereas the European Deposit Insurance Scheme – by the end of 2025. The Capital Markets Union, to form the Financial Union together with the Banking Union, should be put in place by 2025[316].

One measure of paramount importance to establishing the planned Fiscal Union was creating a stabilisation function for the euro area. Another option still explored, although as a rather vague concept in the document in question, was the idea of establishing a separate euro area budget (fiscal capacity)[317]. With regard to completing a genuine Economic Union, the following medium- and long-term objectives should be achieved as a matter of priority: (1)

315 Cf. also: J.J. Węc, Dynamika reformy ustrojowej, op. cit., pp. 174–181. J. Koleśnik, op. cit., pp. 101–103. A. Jurkowska-Zeidler, Fundamentalne zmiany…, op. cit., pp. 189–192.

316 European Commission. Reflection Paper on the deepening of the Economic and Monetary Union, Brussels, 31 May 2017, COM(2017) 291 final, pp. 19–23, 31.

317 European Commission. Reflection Paper on the deepening of the Economic and Monetary Union, op. cit., pp. 23–27, 31.

fostering social convergence in the EMU through the establishment of a European Pillar of Social Rights to guarantee minimum social standards to those employed in the EU (by the end of 2017); (2) deepening economic and social convergence in the EMU through further reinforcement of the European Semester procedure, thus enhancing the coordination of the economic policies of the Member States (by the end of 2019); (3) using the existing or planned EU structures to deepen economic and social convergence (the single market, including the Digital Single Market, the Energy Union, the Financial Union and the Fiscal Union) (by the end of 2025); (4) facilitating access for the EMU Member States undertaking structural reforms of their economies to the European Structural and Investment (ESI) Funds (by the end of 2025)[318].

In contrast to the Five Presidents' Report, in the document concerned the European Commission made no mention of the necessity to establish even the foundations of a Political Union, only noting the need for stronger institutional legitimacy. It would be achieved through measures such as extending the powers of the European Parliament and of the national parliaments in the euro area and in the Economic and Monetary Union, in particular under the European Semester procedure; consolidating the external representation of the euro area in the International Monetary Fund, in accordance with the European Commission's proposal of 21 October 2015; establishing the European Monetary Fund (EMF) based on the European Stability Mechanism; as well as integrating the Fiscal Compact and other intergovernmental agreements concerning the Economic and Monetary Union into European Union law (cf. Figures 9 and 10)[319].

---

318 Until 31 December 2020, the European Structural and Investment Funds included the following: the European Regional Development Fund, the European Social Fund, the Cohesion Fund, the European Agricultural Fund for Rural Development and the European Maritime and Fisheries Fund. From 1 January 2021, the European Structural and Investment Funds comprise the following: the Just Transition Fund, the European Social Fund Plus (ESF+), the European Regional Development Fund, the Cohesion Fund and the European Maritime, Fisheries and Aquaculture Fund. The common agricultural policy is funded by the following: the European Agricultural Fund for Rural Development and the European Agricultural Guarantee Fund, both outside the ESI Funds. European Commission. Reflection Paper on the deepening of the Economic and Monetary Union, op. cit., pp. 23–26.

319 Ibidem, pp. 27–28.

Stage 1: 2017–2019	
FINANCIAL UNION	**ECONOMIC AND FISCAL UNION**
BANKING UNION 1. **Setting up a Common Backstop for the SRF** 2. **Establishing a European Deposit Insurance Scheme** 3. **Agreement on legislative proposals concerning the Capital Markets Union**	**ECONOMIC AND SOCIAL CONVERGENCE** • **Further strengthening the European Semester of economic policy coordination** **PREPARATION OF THE NEW EU MULTIANNUAL FINANCIAL FRAMEWORK** • **Stronger focus on support to reforms and greater links with euro area priorities** **COMMISSION'S PROPOSAL FOR A EURO AREA STABILISATION FUNCTION** **SEPARATE EURO AREA BUDGET LINE WITHIN THE EU'S GENERAL BUDGET (plan)**

Figure 9: Roadmap towards the completion of the Economic and Monetary Union by 2025. Stage 1 (the European Commission's concept)

Source: prepared by the author on the basis of: European Commission. Reflection Paper on the deepening of the Economic and Monetary Union, op. cit., pp. 1–31.

The proclamation of the European Pillar of Social Rights by the European Parliament, the Council of the European Union and the European Commission in Göteborg on 17 November 2017 was followed by early work on its implementation. The document set out 20 rights and principles to govern equal opportunities and access to employment, fair working conditions and social protection and inclusion, thus to provide the basis for well-functioning labour markets and welfare systems[320]. More than three years later, on 4 March 2021, the European Commission presented its European Pillar of Social Rights Action Plan. As recommended in the Communication, the European Union should strive for attaining three social objectives in the areas of employment, skills and social protection. Those headline targets to be achieved by 2030 were as follows: (1) at least 78% of the population aged 20 to 64 should be in employment; (2) at least 60% of all

320 For information on the 20 rights and principles set out by the European Pillar of Social Rights, cf. Council of the European Union. European Pillar of Social Rights. Press release, Brussels, 17 November 2017, 673/17, p. 1. The European Pillar of Social Rights in 20 principles, https://commission.europa.eu/strategy-and-policy/priorities-2019-2024/economy-works-people/jobs-growth-and-investment/european-pillar-social-rights/european-pillar-social-rights-20-principles_en, pp. 1–5.

Stage 2: 2020–2025	
FINANCIAL UNION	**ECONOMIC AND FISCAL UNION**
1. **Roll-out of the European Deposit Insurance Scheme** 2. **Establishment of the Capital Markets Union (to help provide access to funding for businesses and households and to reduce reliance on banks)**	**ECONOMIC AND SOCIAL CONVERGENCE** • **Further strengthening of the European Semester** • **Easier access for the euro area and EU Member States (conducting structural reforms) to the European Structural and Investment Funds** • **Guarantee of minimum social standards (European Pillar of Social Rights of 17 November 2017)** **IMPLEMENTATION OF THE NEW EU MULTIANNUAL FINANCIAL FRAMEWORK** **CREATION OF A SEPARATE EURO AREA BUDGET LINE** • **Support for structural reforms in the euro area Member States** • **Financing expenditure under the euro area stabilisation function** • **Guarantee of financing the Common Backstop for the Single Resolution Fund** • **Pre-accession assistance for future members of the euro area (pre-accession instrument)** **ESTABLISHMENT OF A EURO AREA STABILISATION FUNCTION**

Figure 10: Roadmap towards the completion of the Economic and Monetary Union by 2025. Stage 2 (the European Commission's concept)

Source: prepared by the author on the basis of: European Commission. Reflection Paper on the deepening of the Economic and Monetary Union, op. cit., pp. 1–31.

adults should participate in training every year; (3) the number of people at risk of poverty or social exclusion should be reduced by at least 15 million. Therefore, the EU social targets set out in the European Commission's Action Plan should be consistent with the UN Sustainable Development Goals[321].

321 European Commission. Communication from the Commission to the European Parliament, the Council, the European Economic and Social Committee and the Committee of the Regions. The European Pillar of Social Rights Action Plan, Brussels, 4 March 2021, COM(2021) 102 final, pp. 1–36.

3.1.3. Jean-Claude Juncker's address of 13 September 2017

On 13 September 2017, the President of the European Commission, Jean-Claude Juncker, gave his annual State of the Union Address presenting a roadmap outlining of the existing and new system reforms of the EU. Those to be continued primarily concerned the Economic and Monetary Union, the common security and defence policy, migration, the protection of external borders and the asylum policy of the European Union.

With regard to the Economic and Monetary Union, Juncker stressed the necessity to complete the Banking Union, to be based on the European Deposit Insurance Scheme, an issue raising much controversy, especially in Germany. To encourage Member States to join the euro area, he proposed to create a special Euro-accession Instrument, providing technical and financial assistance to the candidates. The most important institutional changes in the Economic and Monetary Union would concern transforming the European Stability Mechanism into a European Monetary Fund and appointing a European Minister of Economy and Finance, to also perform the function of the European Commission Vice-President and preside the Eurogroup. Such a new position would combine the roles of the Commissioner for economic and financial affairs and of the Eurogroup President. The European Economy and Finance Minister would be accountable to the European Parliament. His or her powers would include promoting and supporting structural reforms as well as coordinating all EU financial instruments to be deployed for Member States experiencing a financial or economic crisis.

The President of the European Commission also announced that the Commission would not pursue too far-reaching and extremely controversial, especially for the non-euro area Member States, French proposals for introducing institutional changes, primarily the establishment of a separate euro area parliament or a budget for the euro area. Therefore, Juncker proposed that, instead, there should be a strong euro area budget line within the EU budget[322]. It should perform four functions: (1) support structural reforms in the euro area Member States; (2) finance the euro area stabilisation function; (3) guarantee the funding of the Common Backstop for the SRF; and (4) provide pre-accession assistance to Member States wishing to join the euro area[323]. The proposal for establishing

322 European Commission. President Jean-Claude Juncker's State of the Union Address 2017, Brussels, 13 September 2017, SPEECH/17/3165, pp. 7–8.

323 European Commission. State of the Union Address 2017. Roadmap for a more united, stronger and more democratic union, Brussels, 13 September 2017, pp. 1–2.

a special euro area budget line could be seen as a breakthrough decision as it resolved the disputes having arisen in the European Union in 2011 over the idea of creating a separate euro area budget[324]; further, it was also an answer to the question about the functioning of the Common Backstop for the SRF. Creating a 'genuine' Economic and Monetary Union should be complemented by changes in the Member States' social policies. Therefore, with reference to the above-mentioned Reflection Paper of 26 April 2017, the President of the European Commission advocated the establishment of the European Pillar of Social Rights to guarantee minimum social policy standards, but without prejudice to the existing competences of the Member States in the area concerned. He also announced the creation of a common European Labour Authority, responsible for monitoring the labour market[325].

3.1.4. The legislative package of 6 December 2017

As a follow-up to Juncker's address, on 6 December 2017, the European Commission submitted a legislative package (also called the 'roadmap') setting out further directions of the system reform of the Economic and Monetary Union for eighteen months. It referred to the Five Presidents' Report of 22 June 2015, the European Commission's Reflection Papers on the deepening of the Economic and Monetary Union of 31 May 2017 and on the future of EU finances of 28 June 2017 as well as to Juncker's address of 13 September of the same year[326]. The package comprised four proposals for legal acts and three communications[327].

---

324 The opinion remained unchanged regardless of the proposal put forward by French President Emmanuel Macron on the establishment of a separate euro area budget, as discussed below. The majority of the EU Member States, including Germany – France's closest ally – did not support the initiative.

325 European Commission. President Jean-Claude Juncker's State of the Union Address 2017, op. cit., pp. 6–7.

326 For more on the subject, cf. J.J. Węc, Prospects for the System Reform of the European Union by 2025: Implications for Poland, 'Przegląd Zachodni' 2019, Special Issue, pp. 7–23.

327 For more on the subject, cf. J.J. Węc, The European Union at a historic turning point. Current challenges and scenarios of overcoming them, [in:] European Integration – Polish Perspective, Z. Czachór, T.G. Grosse, W. Paruch (eds.), Warszawa 2020, pp. 173–183. Cf. also: J.J. Węc, Perspektywy zmian ustrojowych w Unii Europejskiej do 2025 r. Implikacje dla Polski [Prospects for the System Reform of the European Union by 2025: Implications for Poland], 'Przegląd Zachodni' 2018, no. 1, pp. 7–13, 21–24.

The legislative initiatives included: (1) a proposal for a Regulation on the establishment of the European Monetary Fund; (2) a proposal for a Directive laying down provisions for strengthening fiscal responsibility and the medium-term budgetary orientation in the Member States (providing for, *inter alia*, the integration of the Fiscal Compact into the EU legal framework under Article 126(14) TFEU); (3) a proposal for a Regulation amending Regulation (EU) 2017/825 of 17 May 2017 on the establishment of the Structural Reform Support Programme for the period 2017 to 2020 (also by using funds from the Flexibility Instrument for the Member States preparing to join the euro area); and (4) a proposal for a Regulation amending Regulation (EU) No 1303/2013 of 17 December 2013, laying down common provisions on the European Structural and Investment Funds.

The first proposal for a regulation assumed the establishment of the European Monetary Fund in place of the European Stability Mechanism under Article 352 TFEU (the flexibility clause), thus without revising the Treaties. The EMF would be the successor to the ESM, replacing it in its legal position and assuming all its rights and obligations (Article 2 of the proposed Regulation)[328]. The establishment of the EMF would also mean that the ESM, as an international financial institution, would be incorporated into the framework of the European Union. The EMF would be a new European Union body, having legal personality and an autonomous budget (Article 1 and Article 29(1) and (2) of the proposed Statute)[329]. The EMF Members should be the euro area Member States (Article 2 of the proposed Statute). Just as the ESM, it should be financed from the contributions by the euro area Member States, whereas the voting rights of each EMF Member should be equal to the number of shares allocated to it in the authorised capital stock of the EMF (Article 4(7) of the proposed Statute)[330]. The proposed Directive on strengthening fiscal responsibility and the medium-term budgetary orientation was aimed to integrate the Fiscal Compact into the EU legal framework under Article 126(14) TFEU and to further strengthen the excessive deficit procedure. The Directive would ensure 'compliance with obligations relating

328 European Commission. Proposal for a Council Regulation on the establishment of the European Monetary Fund, Brussels, 6 December 2017, COM(2017) 827 final, pp. 26–27.

329 European Commission. Statute of the European Monetary Fund. Annex to the Proposal for a Council Regulation on the establishment of the European Monetary Fund, Brussels, 6 December 2017, COM(2017) 827 final, p. 1.

330 Ibidem.

to the avoidance of excessive government deficits' (Article 1(1) of the proposed Directive). Its provisions would apply to all the euro area Member States and to the non-euro area Member States having notified the European Commission of their decisions to that effect (Article 1(1) and (2), Article 4(1) of the proposed Directive)[331].

The proposal for a Regulation amending Regulation (EU) 2017/825 of 17 May 2017 concerned the establishment of the Structural Reform Support Programme for the period 2017 to 2020. It provided for increasing funds available for the technical assistance component of the Programme from EUR 142.8 billion to EUR 222.8 billion under the current Multiannual Financial Framework, specifically by using the Flexibility Instrument. The funds should be allocated – which was the essential amendment to be introduced under the Regulation – to implementing structural reforms in the non-euro area Member States intending to join the euro area in the future (Article 4, Article 5a, Article 10(1) of the proposed Regulation)[332]. As regards the proposal for a Regulation amending Regulation (EU) No 1303/2013 of 17 December 2013, laying down common provisions on the five European Structural and Investment Funds, its objective was to strengthen the links between the European Union's general budget and the European Semester procedure through the use of the performance reserve[333]. The funds would be allocated to supporting structural reforms on the basis of reform commitments undertaken by the Member States in their National Reform Programmes (Article 1 of the proposed Regulation)[334].

331 European Commission. Proposal for a Council Directive laying down provisions for strengthening fiscal responsibility and the medium-term budgetary orientation in the Member States, Brussels, 6 December 2017, COM(2017) 824 final, pp. 11–13.

332 European Commission. Proposal for a Regulation of the European Parliament and of the Council amending Regulation (EU) 2017/825 to increase the financial envelope of the Structural Reform Support Programme and adapt its general objective, Brussels, 6 December 2017, COM(2017) 825 final, pp. 8–9.

333 The national performance reserve is the part of the resources available within the European Structural and Investment Funds and allocated to a Member State, at the end of the programming period (in that case, in 2019), to support the best performing programmes in terms of achieving milestones, management quality and implementation progress, cf. Komisja Europejska. Pakiet dokumentów dotyczących pogłębiania unii gospodarczej i walutowej [The European Commission. The package of documents on the deepening of the Economic and Monetary Union], 'Przegląd Spraw Europejskich', grudzień 2017 r. – styczeń 2018 r. [December 2017 – January 2018], p. 7.

334 European Commission. Proposal for a Regulation of the European Parliament and of the Council amending Regulation (EU) No 1303/2013 of the European Parliament and of the Council of 17 December 2013 laying down common provisions on the European Regional Development Fund, the European Social Fund, the Cohesion Fund,

The package of the above-mentioned legislative proposals was accompanied by three communications from the European Commission, the first of which concerned the creation of the post of a European Minister of Economy and Finance. The document set out the Minister's key functions to be performed in the governance architecture of the Economic and Monetary Union, the institutional framework of operation and the effects of the setting up of the new position, combining the roles of the Commissioner for economic and financial affairs and of the Eurogroup President[335]. In the second communication, the European Commission announced introducing new budgetary instruments for the euro area, in particular: (1) budgetary and technical support for structural reforms (post-2020)[336]; (2) a convergence instrument to provide pre-accession (technical and financial) assistance for the Member States interested in joining the euro area (post-2020); (3) a Common Backstop in the form of a credit line or guarantee for the SRF; and (4) a euro area Stabilisation Function[337].

The third communication from the European Commission contained a detailed plan – 'roadmap' – for completing the Economic and Monetary Union[338]. Thus,

---

the European Agricultural Fund for Rural Development and the European Maritime and Fisheries Fund and laying down general provisions on the European Regional Development Fund, the European Social Fund, the Cohesion Fund and the European Maritime and Fisheries Fund and repealing Council Regulation (EC) No 1083/2006 as regards support to structural reforms in Member States, Brussels, 6 December 2017, COM(2017) 826 final, pp. 6–8.

335 European Commission. Communication from the Commission to the European Parliament, the European Council, the Council and the European Central Bank. A European Minister of Economy and Finance, Brussels, 6 December 2017, COM(2017) 823 final, pp. 6–8.

336 Among other objectives, the new budgetary and technical instruments should provide the continuation of assistance provided for in the proposed Regulation of 6 December 2017, granted under the Structural Reform Support Programme in 2017–2020. Established for that purpose in 2015, the Structural Reform Support Service was tasked with providing, as requested by the Member States concerned, technical assistance in implementing reforms and strengthening their public administrations. It assisted 15 Member States in carrying out more than 150 projects by late 2017.

337 European Commission. Communication from the Commission to the European Parliament, the European Council, the Council and the European Central Bank. New budgetary instruments for a stable euro area within the Union framework, Brussels, 6 December 2017, COM(2017) 822 final, pp. 2–4, 10.

338 European Commission. Communication from the Commission to the European Parliament, the European Council, the Council and the European Central Bank. Further steps towards completing Europe's economic and monetary union: a roadmap, Brussels, 6 December 2017, COM(2017) 821 final, pp. 1–16. It corresponded both to the

as the top priorities in efforts to establish the Financial Union, the Commission pointed to the creation, by mid-2019, of two new structures: the Common Backstop for the SRF and the European Deposit Insurance Scheme[339]. The Common Backstop should be financed from the European Monetary Fund, filled by contributions from the Member States. It would only be used if the funds from banks' shareholders, creditors and the SRF itself should prove insufficient. The establishment by the end of 2025 of the Capital Markets Union, a component – in addition to the Banking Union – of the Financial Union, would be equally important. As argued by the Commission, the Capital Markets Union should improve access to finance for companies and households, thus reducing the burden on banks or even competing with them in that regard. Acknowledging the work of the European Systemic Risk Board, the European Commission also announced – somewhat revising its position from the Reflection Paper – that it would put forward a legislative proposal for an enabling framework for European Sovereign Bond-backed Securities in 2018[340]. A task regarded as crucial for establishing the Fiscal Union was creating a euro area Stabilisation Function, to become operational by the end of 2025[341]. Therefore, the Commission announced publishing the relevant legislative proposal by mid-2019. The work on completing a genuine Economic Union should focus on deepening the economic and social convergence in the euro area and across the European Union. The European Commission proposed to execute three tasks: firstly, further strengthening of the European Semester, thus of economic policy coordination; secondly, providing more flexible access for the euro area and EU Member States (undertaking structural reforms of their economies) to the European Structural and

---

European Commission's Reflection Paper of 31 May 2017 and to the Communication from the Commission of 11 October of the same year. Cf. European Commission. Communication from the Commission to the European Parliament, the Council, the European Central Bank, the European Economic and Social Committee and the Committee of the Regions on completing the Banking Union, Brussels, 11 October 2017, COM (2017) 592 final, pp. 1–20. Cf. also: European Commission. Reflection Paper on the deepening of the Economic and Monetary Union, op. cit., pp. 1–44.

339 The roadmap envisaged in the Commission's Reflection Paper of 31 May 2017 assumed later dates for establishing the new structures: the Common Backstop would be created by the end of 2019 and the European Deposit Insurance Scheme – by the end of 2025, cf. European Commission. Reflection Paper on the deepening of the Economic and Monetary Union, op. cit., p. 31.

340 European Commission. Communication from the Commission to the European Parliament, the European Council, the Council and the European Central Bank. Further steps towards completing Europe's economic and monetary union: a roadmap, Brussels, 6 December 2017, COM(2017) 821 final, pp. 11–12, 16.

341 Ibidem, p. 17.

Investment Funds; thirdly, guaranteeing the minimum social standards set out in the European Pillar of Social Rights of 17 November 2017. Furthermore, the European Commission announced publishing legislative proposals for the new multiannual financial framework (by May 2018), followed by submitting proposals concerning support for the euro area Member States in implementing their structural reforms in the post-2020 period and establishing a dedicated convergence facility for the Member States preparing to join the euro area (by mid-2019)[342].

3.1.4.1. The European Monetary Fund

The organisational structure of the European Monetary Fund would be similar to that of the European Stability Mechanism. As the main governing bodies, the EMF should have a Board of Governors, a Board of Directors and a Managing Director (Article 4(1) of the proposed Statute). The Board of Governors would be composed of Governors and alternate Governors, one from each EMF Member, whereby the Governor should be a member of the government of that EMF Member with responsibility for financial affairs, thus in practice the Finance Minister. The Chairperson of the Board of Governors should be the Eurogroup President (Article 5(1) and (2) of the proposed Statute). Therefore, it must be noted that the composition of the Board of Governors would be identical with that of the Eurogroup (cf. Figure 11). The Board of Directors would be composed of Directors and alternate Directors appointed by the Governors from among persons of high competence in economic and financial matters (Article 6(1) of the proposed Statute). In comparison with the European Stability Mechanism, the scope of tasks entrusted to the European Monetary Fund would be much broader.

The EMF would not only grant financial assistance to indebted economies, but also function as a Common Backstop in the form of credit lines or guarantees for the SRF (Article 3(1) and (2) of the proposed Statute)[343]; in the future, it could also be conferred new financial instruments, e.g. with a view to supporting the Stabilisation Function for the euro area[344].

---

342 European Commission. Communication from the Commission to the European Parliament, the European Council, the Council and the European Central Bank. Further steps towards completing Europe's economic and monetary union: a roadmap, COM(2017) 821 final, op. cit., pp. 12–15.

343 European Commission. Statute of the European Monetary Fund, op. cit., p. 1.

344 European Commission. Proposal for a Council Regulation on the establishment of the European Monetary Fund. op. cit., pp. 25–26.

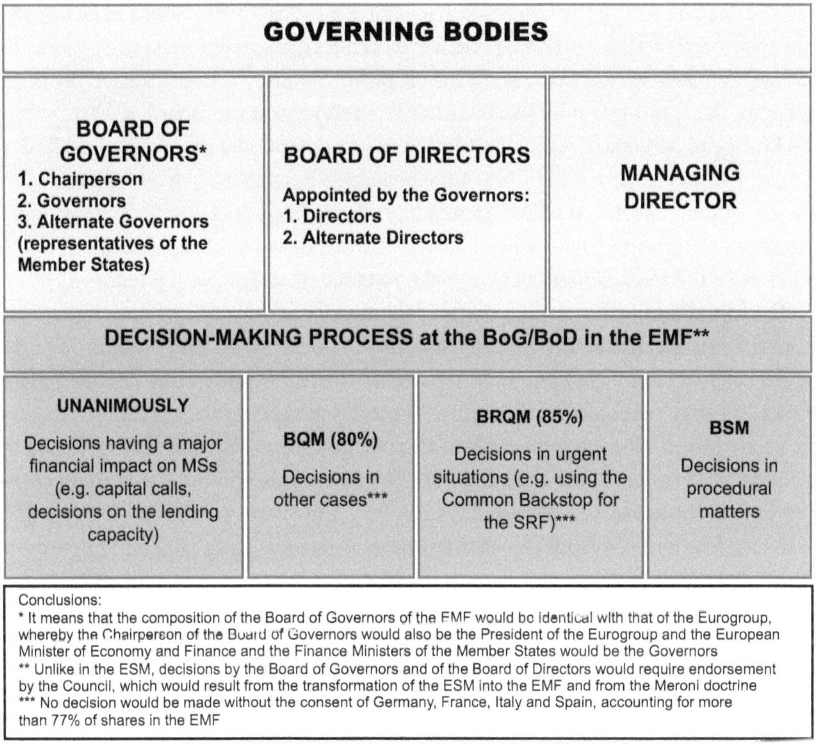

Figure 11: The organisational structure of and the decision-making process in the European Monetary Fund as proposed by the European Commission

Source: prepared by the author on the basis of: European Commission. Proposal for a Council Regulation on the establishment of the European Monetary Fund. op. cit., pp. 25–26. European Commission. Statute of the European Monetary Fund, op. cit., pp. 2–5.

Both the Board of Governors and the Board of Directors would take decisions in accordance with the following four procedures: by unanimity, reinforced qualified majority (85%), qualified majority (80%) or simple majority of the votes cast (Article 4(2) to (6) of the proposed Statute). However, the decision-making process in the European Monetary Fund would be much more flexible than that in the ESM. The requirement of unanimity would only apply to decisions of the Board of Governors and of the Board of Directors having a major financial impact on the Member States but not urgently needed (e.g. making capital calls, increasing or decreasing the minimum lending capacity) (Article 5(6) of the proposed Statute). But in urgent situations where the lack of a decision should threaten the economic or financial stability of the euro area (with regard to decisions on stability support, disbursements and the deployment of the Common Backstop for the SRF), the Board of Governors and the Board of Directors would decide by reinforced qualified majority requiring 85% of the votes cast (Article 5(7) of the proposed Statute)[345]. In contrast to the ESM, however, decisions taken by the Board of Governors and the Board of Directors of the European Monetary Fund would need to be approved by the Council of the European Union (Article 3(1) to (2) of the proposed Regulation), due to the transformation of the ESM into the EMF as well as to the Meroni doctrine[346]. The European Monetary Fund would also be more directly involved, alongside the European Commission, in the management of financial assistance programmes (cf. Figure 12).

The initial authorised capital stock of the European Monetary Fund, taken over from the European Stability Mechanism, should be EUR 704,798.7 million. But the Board of Governors would be able to increase the initial authorised capital stock if it should prove necessary in the future. The rules governing the creation of the key for subscription, or contributions by particular euro area Member States, should be identical with those for the ECB and the ESM. Therefore, without the consent of the four largest countries, i.e. Germany, France, Italy and Spain, accounting for over 77% of shares, it would be impossible to take any decision requiring qualified majority or reinforced qualified majority.

---

345 European Commission. Statute of the European Monetary Fund, op. cit., pp. 2–5. Cf. also J.J. Węc, Pierwsza polska prezydencja, op. cit., p. 149.

346 Having arisen from the case-law of the Court of Justice, the Meroni doctrine relates to the extent of the delegation by EU institutions and bodies of their powers and tasks to other bodies, in particular to EU agencies. In its judgment of 13 June 1958, the Court of Justice ruled that the delegation of powers by the High Authority was not possible (but if it should be, it would be subject to very restrictive criteria); however, according to the judgment of 22 January 2014, the prohibition on delegating powers to agencies solely concerned discretionary powers, cf. M. Będkowski-Kozioł, Status i zadania Europejskiej Agencji Kolejowej – stan obecny i perspektywy w świetle projektu IV pakietu kolejowego UE [The status and tasks of the European Railway Agency – the current state and prospects in the light of the legislative proposals for a fourth railway package], 'internetowy Kwartalnik Antymonopolowy i Regulacyjny', 2014, no. 7, www.ikar.wz.uw.edu.pl, pp. 40–41 [accessed: 22 July 2022]. J. Ruszkowski, L. Wojnicz (eds.), Multi-Level Governance w Unii Europejskiej [Multi-Level Governance in the European Union], Szczecin-Warszawa 2013, p. 46. M. Chamon, The empowerment of agencies under the Meroni doctrine and article 114 TFEU: comment on United Kingdom v. Parliament and Council (short-selling) and the proposed Single Resolution Mechanism, 'European Law Review' 2014, no. 3, p. 383. M. Chamon, EU Agencies: Legal and Political Limits to the Transformation of the EU Administration, Oxford 2016.

Initially, the lending capacity of the European Monetary Fund (EMF) would be at least EUR 500 billion, reflecting the lending capacity of the ESM. In the future, however, the Board of Governors would be able to also increase the EMF's lending capacity as appropriate[347].

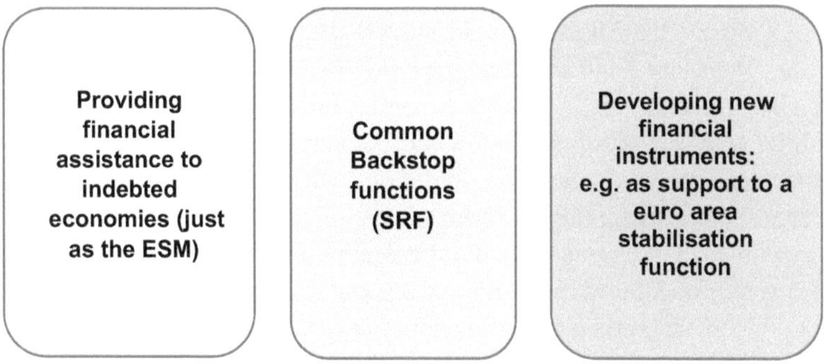

Figure 12: The powers of the European Monetary Fund as proposed by the European Commission

Source: prepared by the author on the basis of: European Commission. Proposal for a Council Regulation on the establishment of the European Monetary Fund. op. cit., pp. 25–26. European Commission. Statute of the European Monetary Fund, op. cit., pp. 2–5.

3.1.4.2. *The European Minister of Economy and Finance*

The new position of a European Minister of Economy and Finance would be created under Article 2 of Protocol No 14 on the Euro Group, i.e. without the need to revise the Treaties. Pursuant to the provision in question, the Ministers of the Member States whose currency is the euro elect a president for two and a half years, by a majority of the votes cast[348]. The European Minister of Economy and Finance would not impinge on national competences of the Member States. The Minister would be accountable towards the European Parliament on all matters related to its functions. Furthermore, the Minister should be available for regular dialogue with the European Parliament as well as for dialogues with the national parliaments[349].

347 European Commission. Statute of the European Monetary Fund, op. cit., pp. 22–23.
348 Protocol (No 14) on the Euro Group, [in:] Treaty of Lisbon, op. cit., p. 283.
349 European Commission. Communication from the Commission to the European Parliament, the European Council, the Council and the European Central Bank. A European Minister of Economy and Finance, Brussels, 6 December 2017, COM(2017) 823 final, pp. 6–8.

The term of office of the Minister would be two and a half years; however, the Eurogroup could agree to elect the Minister for five years (two consecutive mandates), thus aligning its mandate with the mandate of the Commission. Therefore, such a change would not require a Treaty revision either.

The European Minister of Economy and Finance should have the following six key tasks. Firstly, the Minister would oversee the work of the newly established European Monetary Fund in which – as mentioned before – he or she would *ex officio* chair the Board of Governors. Secondly, the Minister would pursue the general interest of the European Union and euro area economy; the task would be of importance due to the fact that only monetary policy fell within the exclusive competence of the EU in the euro area, whereas financial, budgetary and economic policies remained decentralised and individually conducted by the Member States. Therefore, the function of the European Minister of Economy and Finance would allow to further strengthen economic policy coordination, or even harmonisation. Thirdly, the Minister should ensure better external and internal representation of the euro area, i.e. its more efficient and consistent representation in relations with the EU institutions and bodies as well as with the Member States, third countries and international organisations. That function was divided between the European Commission, the European Central Bank, the President of the Eurogroup and the EU Council Presidency. Fourthly, the Minister would further strengthen economic policy coordination in the euro area and oversee economic, fiscal and financial rules, also with a view to implementing structural reforms in the Member States. Fifthly, the Minister would coordinate the surveillance of the euro area Member States' fiscal policies, in cooperation with the European Fiscal Board and national fiscal councils. The task would serve to ensure fiscal sustainability and the application of the Stability and Growth Pact. Sixthly and lastly, the Minister would enhance the oversight of the use of relevant funds from the European Union's general budget and other financial and budgetary instruments (the EIB and the ESM) in support of structural reforms, macroeconomic stabilisation (the euro area) and convergence (the non-participating Member States) (cf. Figure 13)[350].

3.1.4.3. The Stabilisation Function

The creation of a stabilisation function was already envisaged in the Five Presidents' Report of 22 June 2015 and subsequently in the European Commission's Reflection

---

350 One goal would be to establish a stronger link between the European Semester procedure and the use of the funding available under the five European Structural and Investment Funds of the European Union, ibidem, pp. 3–5.

Paper on the deepening of the Economic and Monetary Union of 31 May 2017. Whereas the former document only outlined framework conditions for establishing such a function (e.g. the legal coordination procedures)[351], the latter defined its basic powers and possible financing sources.

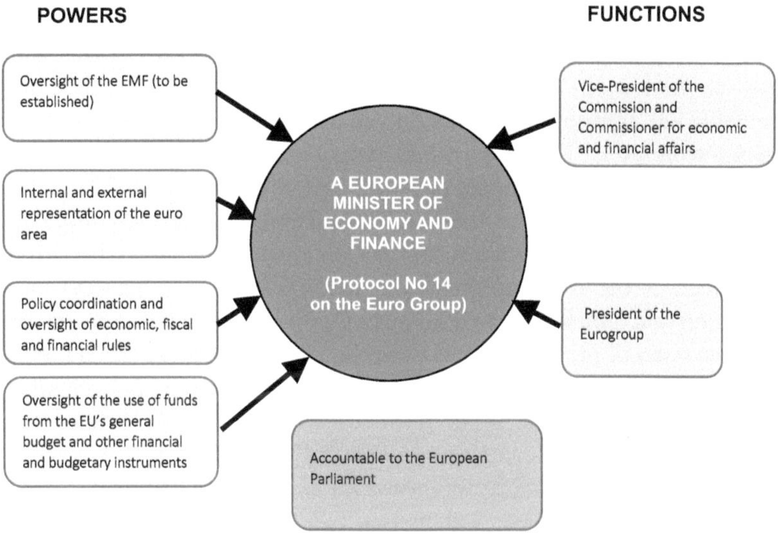

Figure 13: The powers and functions of the European Minister of Economy and Finance as proposed by the European Commission

Source: prepared by the author on the basis of: European Commission. Communication from the Commission to the European Parliament, the European Council, the Council and the European Central Bank. A European Minister of Economy and Finance, Brussels, 6 December 2017, COM(2017) 823 final, p. 2.

In its Reflection Paper, the European Commission argued that the Stabilisation Function should 'complement the national budget stabilisers in the event of severe asymmetric shocks' and 'allow running smoother aggregate fiscal policies for the euro area in unusual circumstances' when monetary policy should

351 European Commission. Completing Europe's Economic and Monetary Union, op. cit., pp. 14–15.

reach its limits[352]. Such a stabilisation function would be explored in two main areas: investment protection and an unemployment insurance scheme. Whereas the former would be aimed at protecting public investment from the consequences of an economic slump, the latter would be in place for cases of a sudden increase in unemployment rates. The Stabilisation Function should be financed from the European Stability Mechanism or the general budget of the European Union (provided that the function should be integrated into the EU Multiannual Financial Framework), or from an entirely new instrument, to be filled by the Member States' contributions based on a share of GDP or a share of VAT, or by revenues from excise duties, corporate taxes or other levies. The Stabilisation Function for the euro area should be established by the end of 2025.[353]

The financing rules for the Stabilisation Function were set out in more detail in the relevant Communication from the Commission of 6 December 2017, as a component of the 'roadmap'. According to the document in question, such a stabilisation function, to be managed by the European Commission, would combine three types of funds: (1) loans from the European Union's general budget and the European Monetary Fund[354]; (2) grants from the EU budget; and (3) a dedicated fund – referred to an 'insurance mechanism' – to be filled by the Member States' voluntary contributions or rather vague 'dedicated resources' (cf. Figure 14)[355]. The common denominator for all the three documents was the assumption that the euro area Stabilisation Function should crown the process of system reforms implemented in the EMU and constitute a special instrument combining the European Union's public finances, to guarantee preserving appropriate investment levels in the event of asymmetric shocks in the euro area Member States.

It must be emphasised that – in terms of system reform – the most far-reaching changes proposed by the European Commission in its 'roadmap' of 6 December 2017 were the initiatives aimed at establishing the European Monetary Fund, the

352 European Commission. Reflection Paper on the deepening of the Economic and Monetary Union, op. cit., pp. 23–27, 33.

353 Ibidem, pp. 23–27, 33.

354 An alternative to EMF loans would be a precautionary credit line through the EMF, provided as short-term liquidity support to a euro area Member State facing an asymmetric shock. Cf. European Commission. Communication from the Commission to the European Parliament, the European Council, the Council and the European Central Bank. New budgetary instruments for a stable euro area within the Union framework, op. cit., pp. 14–16.

355 Ibidem, pp. 5–16.

European Deposit Insurance Scheme, the Stabilisation Function and the position of a European Minister of Economy and Finance.

The transformation of the intergovernmental European Stability Mechanism into the European Monetary Fund, to be integrated into the institutional and legal framework of the European Union, would involve not only shifting the relevant competences of the Member States' governments to the EU level but also extending the powers of the European Monetary Fund and changing the decision-making process. However, as a decisive element, the creation of the Common Backstop as a credit line for the SRF but based on the European Stability Mechanism seemed, at least for the time being, to be sufficient[356]. With regard to fiscal risk-sharing instruments, i.e. the designed mutualisation of debt and creation of a euro area Stabilisation Function, both the issuance of EU bonds and the establishment of such a function would rely not only on the successful completion of the Fiscal Union, but also, to a significant extent, on broad political support in the EMU and euro area Member States, perhaps even on a Treaty revision, depending on the scope of the innovation proposed[357]. Whereas a European Minister of Economy and Finance could be appointed under the existing Treaties (pursuant to Article 2 of Protocol No 14 on the Euro Group), the solution in question would still entail shifting certain competences of the Member States in economic, financial and fiscal policies to the EU level, as a consequence of strengthened coordination, or even harmonisation of national laws in the areas concerned.

---

356 According to Anna Trzcińska, in the event of a system-wide financial crisis, the European Stability Mechanism would be able to handle it or at least the ESM could deliver much more effective support for the recovery of the banking sector than the Single Resolution Fund. As indicated by studies of previous crises conducted by the European Commission and the Bruegel Institute, the approximate costs of a system-wide banking crisis could be EUR 350 billion, which – considering the ESM lending capacity of EUR 500 billion – allowed concluding that the European Stability Mechanism itself would be effective as a common fiscal backstop for the Banking Union. For more on the subject, cf. A. Trzcińska, op. cit., pp. 53–57.

357 For more on the subject, cf. M. Gwóźdź-Lasoń, S. Miklaszewicz, K. Pujer, op. cit., pp. 54–64.

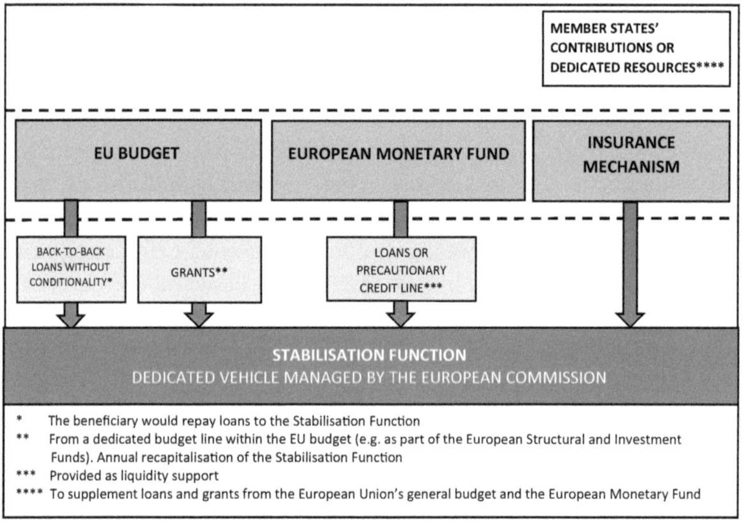

Figure 14: Stabilisation function as proposed by the European Commission

Source: prepared by the author on the basis of: European Commission. Communication from the Commission to the European Parliament, the European Council, the Council and the European Central Bank. New budgetary instruments for a stable euro area within the Union framework, Brussels, 6 December 2017, COM(2017) 822 final, p. 16.

As a separate issue, it remains open to question whether establishing the Fiscal Union would enhance the competitiveness of the euro area Member States having lost it in the aftermath of the debt crisis. According to economists such as Stefan Kawalec and Ernest Pytlarczyk, any attempt at increasing the competitiveness of an uncompetitive region within a single currency area through fiscal transfers would be a contradiction in terms[358]. As demonstrated by them on the basis of studies conducted by the European Central Bank as well as by German and Italian experts, both fiscal transfers to the EU Member States benefiting from the European Structural and Investment Funds and transfers to southern Italy or eastern Germany failed to be effective as a method for stimulating the competitiveness of economically weak regions of the EU[359]. The inflow of funds to countries attempting to regain

358 Ibidem, pp. 131–132.
359 For more on the subject, cf. S. Kawalec, E. Pytlarczyk, op. cit., pp. 119–131.

competitiveness through internal devaluation policies undermines such policies. Whereas internal devaluation aims to drive down domestic demand, prices and wages, such incoming fiscal transfers boost demand and fuel price and wage growth, thus hindering efforts to regain competitiveness[360]. The conclusion drawn by Stefan Kawalec and Ernest Pytlarczyk from their analysis is thoroughly pessimistic: the Fiscal Union may lead to solidifying the divide of the euro area into competitive countries, generating current account surpluses, and Member States running deficits, in need of continuous support[361]. The risk is all the more real since such uncompetitive euro area economies are unable to use the most effective tool for increasing competitiveness, i.e. adjusting the exchange rate by weakening the national currency, as they have none[362]. On the other hand, it must be pointed out that other economists, e.g. Jerzy Rymarczyk and Sławomir Miklaszewicz, see the establishment of the Fiscal Union as a possible driver of the stability and sustainability of the euro area, but subject to a significant increase in the EU's general budget[363]. Based on the example of the US federal budget, they argue – and the view is shared by Stefan Kawalec and Ernest Pytlarczyk – that the larger the EU budget or a separate euro area budget would be, the greater role it would play in its euro area stabilisation function[364].

360 Ibidem, p. 132.
361 Ibidem.
362 Ibidem, p. 43.
363 Cf. M. Gwóźdź-Lasoń, S. Miklaszewicz, K. Pujer, op. cit., p. 64. For a similar view, cf. J. Rymarczyk, Antykryzysowe reformy w Europejskiej Unii Gospodarczej i Walutowej [Anti-crisis reforms in the European Economic and Monetary Union], 'Prace Naukowe Uniwersytetu Ekonomicznego we Wrocławiu', 2017, no. 498, p. 305.
364 The general budget of the European Union is approx. 1% of EU GDP, whereas the US federal budget accounts for around 20% of the GDP of the United States of America, cf. M. Gwóźdź-Lasoń, S. Miklaszewicz, K. Pujer, op. cit., pp. 64–66. S. Kawalec, E. Pytlarczyk, op. cit., pp. 129–131. The stabilisation function of the US federal budget is additionally strengthened by automatic stabilisers: if GDP should contract in a state, 25% to 40% of such a fall would be compensated for by the federal budget, cf. S. Kawalec, E. Pytlarczyk, op. cit., p. 130.

3.2. The euro area Member States' positions towards the proposals from the European Commission

3.2.1. France's Initiative for Europe of 26 September 2017

On 26 September 2017, less than two weeks after Juncker's address, French President Emmanuel Macron gave his speech entitled 'Initiative for Europe' at the Sorbonne University. In the part concerning the reform of the Economic and Monetary Union, the French President – unlike Juncker – still advocated the establishment of a separate euro area budget, to be managed by a 'common minister' and subject to parliamentary control at the European level (*contrôle parlementaire au niveau européen*). Such a budget would be filled by two new sources: the taxation of digital companies and a European carbon tax related to CO_2 emissions. If necessary, an additional source of budgetary revenue would be corporate income tax, subject to a prior harmonisation of the relevant national laws[365]. Bearing in mind the economic and social challenges facing the euro area, Macron also proposed developing a long-term economic and political strategy for the Economic and Monetary Union. It was an extremely important proposal as the absence of such a strategy constituted a major weakness of the EMU. Macron considered fight against youth unemployment to be equally vital since the average unemployment rate in the age group concerned across the euro area continued to be high, at as much as 20%[366]. With reference to Juncker's address, the French President proposed taking action for strengthening tax and social convergence in the Economic and Monetary Union. Tax convergence would primarily consist in the harmonisation of national laws on corporate taxation, whereas social convergence would involve the establishment of the European Pillar of Social Rights[367].

---

365 Initiative pour l'Europe – Discours d'Emmanuel Macron pour une Europe souveraine, unie, démocratique, Paris, 26 septembre 2017, http://www.elysee.fr/, p. 12 [accessed: 19 May 2018]. Tax on digital corporations would mainly come from the taxation of US Internet companies (Facebook, Amazon, Google) in the EU Member States where they earn income, cf. M. Strzałkowski, Emmanuel Macron przedstawił swój pomysł na UE [Emmanuel Macron has presented his idea for the EU], EURACTIV, 26 September 2017, pp. 1–2.

366 Initiative pour l'Europe, op. cit., p. 11.

367 Sharing Juncker's view, the French President confirmed France's stance on revising Directive 96/71 on the posting of workers and supported the relevant legislative proposal from the European Commission, cf. ibidem, pp. 13–14. For information on the position taken by Juncker and the European Commission on the issue, cf. European Commission. President Jean-Claude Juncker's State of the Union Address 2017, op.

Although the proposals put forward by the French President with regard to a separate budget and parliamentary control for the euro area still differed from the position taken by Juncker and the European Commission, as well as by nearly all the EU Member States, they constituted significant concessions in relation to France's previous initiatives, i.e. Macron having advocated not only a large euro area budget, accounting for several per cent of GDP, but also the adoption of such a budget by a separate parliament. The revision of the French proposals on those issues was largely due to the results of the German federal (Bundestag) election of 24 September 2017, with surprisingly successful performance of FDP and AfD, firmly opposed to deep system reforms of the Economic and Monetary Union[368].

3.2.2. The euro area Member States' positions on the proposed establishment of a European Deposit Insurance Scheme

Following the publication of the Five Presidents' Report on 22 June 2015, some of its assumptions met with criticism from certain Member States of the EU.

---

cit., pp. 6–7. Having rejected opposition from eleven Member States: Poland, Bulgaria, the Czech Republic, Denmark, Estonia, Croatia, Hungary, Latvia, Lithuania, Romania and Slovakia, on 20 July 2016, the European Commission maintained its position on the matter. According to the revision, a worker posted by their employer to another European Union Member State should be entitled to receive the same remuneration as a local worker rather than only to earn the minimum wage; after two years, the labour law of the host Member State should fully apply to such a posted worker.

368 The results of the federal election in question were as follows: CDU/CSU – 33% of the vote, SPD – 20.5%, AfD – 12.6%, FDP – 10.7%, The Left – 9.2%, Alliance 90/The Greens – 8.9% of the vote, cf. Bundestagswahl 2017. Das Endergebnis und die Ergebnisse in jedem Bundesland, https://www.merkur.de/, [accessed: 18 May 2018], p. 1. Macron gave his speech two days after the Bundestag election, but its content was sent to Chancellor Merkel shortly after the announcement of the election results, cf. J. Bielecki, Po wyborach w Niemczech reforma strefy euro Macrona jest martwa [Following the federal election in Germany, Macron's reform of the euro area is dead], 25 September 2017, http://www.rp.pl, pp. 1–2 [accessed: 22 July 2022]. When Macron received the Charlemagne Prize in Aachen on 10 May 2018, he made another attempt to persuade Merkel to efficiently work together on reforming the euro area. They reached an agreement that before the European Council meeting to be held in June 2018 France and Germany would present a joint proposal for system changes, cf. K. Janoś, J. Kubera, W stronę kompromisu? Stan francusko-niemieckich rozmów o strefie euro [Towards a compromise? The status of Franco–German talks on the euro area], 'Biuletyn Instytutu Zachodniego', 2018, no. 345, pp. 1–5.

Representatives of the German Government, previously among the strongest advocates of the DGSD, proved to be the fiercest opponents. On 4 November 2015, at the request of the parliamentary groups of CDU/CSU and SPD, forming the government coalition, the Bundestag adopted a resolution expressing its firm disapproval of the proposal for establishing the EDIS. It considered the mutualisation of national Deposit Guarantee Schemes to be off the mark and only result in 'false incentives'. Such a design would neither contribute to increasing confidence in banks nor create any significant conditions for the stability of the banking sector in the euro area. According to the Bundestag, instead of pursuing the idea of establishing the EDIS, the European Commission should focus on the implementation of the DGSD. Therefore, the Bundestag urged the Federal Government to take action aimed at blocking the proposed establishment of the EDIS and at effectively introducing in all the Member States, as well as at the European Union level, the existing measures towards completing the third pillar of the Banking Union, i.e. the implementation of the DGSD[369].

The submission by the European Commission of its proposal for a Regulation establishing the EDIS[370] on 24 November 2015 was immediately and sharply criticised by the German Finance Minister, Wolfgang Schäuble. During the 2016 draft budget debate at the Bundestag, he elaborated on the above-mentioned opinion of the parliamentary groups of CDU/CSU and SPD that the European Commission's proposal created 'false incentives', allowing some euro area

---

369 Deutscher Bundestag, Verhandlungen des Deutschen Bundestages. Anlagen zu den Stenographischen Berichten (Drucksachen). 18. Wahlperiode. Antrag der Fraktionen der CDU/CSU und SPD. Zu den Überlegungen der Europäischen Kommission zur Schaffung einer Europäischen Einlagensicherung. Drucksache 18/6548, 4. November 2015, pp. 1–3 https://www.bundestag.de/ [accessed: 22 July 2022]. For Franz C. Mayer's speech given at a meeting of the Committee on European Union Affairs of the Bundestag, cf. F. C. Mayer, Stellungnahme zu dem Bericht „Die Wirtschafts- und Währungsunion Europas vollenden" (Bericht der fünf Präsidenten) für die öffentliche Anhörung im Deutschen Bundestag, Ausschuss für die Angelegenheiten der Europäischen Union, Montag, 2. November 2015, pp. 1–10 https://www.bundestag.de/ [accessed: 22 July 2022].

370 European Commission. Proposal for a regulation of the European Parliament and of the Council amending Regulation (EU) 806/2014 in order to establish a European Deposit Insurance Scheme, Strasbourg, 24 November 2015, COM(2015) 586 final, pp. 1–69.

Member States to run into debt at the expense of other countries[371]. Schäuble's critical attitude to the idea of establishing a joint Deposit Insurance Fund for the euro area as a whole had already been known during the legislative negotiations regarding the proposal for the DGSD and it returned with new force. Whereas in his presentation of the proposal the Commissioner responsible for financial affairs, Jonathan Hill (the European Commission), spoke of the necessity to establish an EDIS as 'unfinished business on the Banking Union', by no means as a 'free ride' for banks facing financial difficulties, Schäuble warned that the proposal was premature and risky for customers of German banks, to be forced to guarantee deposits held by bank customers in other euro area Member States[372]. According to Schäuble, it would be necessary, therefore, to first complete the Banking Union based on the already adopted legal regulations, i.e. the DGSD, to verify the functioning of such a new structure in practice and subsequently to consider further strengthening its third pillar. As also expressed by certain German banks, Schäuble even prophesied that the establishment of an EDIS could be the first step towards transforming the Banking Union into a 'transfer union'[373].

The view taken by the German Finance Minister was shared by the President of Deutsche Bank, Jens Weidmann, who pointed out that there were no reasons or conditions for creating an EDIS. The national banking systems were still highly dependent on the Member States' financial and economic policies (e.g. corporate insolvency procedures varied between countries). Furthermore, the establishment of such a scheme would involve the risk that the consequences of erroneous political decisions taken by particular governments would be suffered by all bank customers in the euro area[374]. Schäuble's position was supported by savings banks (*Deutsche Sparkassen*) and cooperative banks

---

371 Deutscher Bundestag, Verhandlungen des Deutschen Bundestages. Stenographische Berichte. 18. Wahlperiode. 138. Sitzung am 24. November 2015, p. 13508, http://dip21.bundestag.de/ [accessed: 22 July 2022].

372 EU riskiert bei Einlagensicherung offenen Streit mit Berlin, Euractiv, 25. November 2015, pp. 1–2. Schäuble warnt vor "falschen Anreizen" durch EU-Einlagensicherung, 'Handelsblatt', 24. November 2015, p. 1, https://www.handelsblatt.com/de/ [accessed: 20 July 2022]. M. Kröger, Europäische Einlagensicherung: Haften deutsche Sparer nun für die Banken der Krisenländer?, 25. November 2015, http://www.spiegel.de/. pp. 1–2 [accessed: 18 May 2022].

373 Europäische Einlagensicherung. Schäuble will Sparer nicht versichern, 'Die Tageszeitung' 25. November 2015, p. 1, https://taz.de/ [accessed: 20 July 2022].

374 EU riskiert, op. cit., p. 2.

(*Genossenschaftsbanken*), previously counting on special provisions basically excluding them from the EDIS. However, as it turned out that the European Commission's proposal of 24 November 2015 provided for no 'opt-out' regulations, they raised a clamour[375].

In other euro area Member States – except for Austria, Sweden, Denmark and the Netherlands – the proposal from the European Commission gave rise to no such controversies. France and most of the southern countries of the euro area were particularly enthusiastic about it. As stressed by representatives of those governments, it was pointless to maintain national deposit guarantee schemes in the single currency area. The EDIS should strengthen customer confidence in banks, thus preventing future panic runs on banks to withdraw deposits in crisis situations, as in the case of Greece – short-term withdrawals of as much as EUR 45 billion by bank customers destabilised the whole Greek financial system[376].

As a result of the sharp criticism of the European Commission's proposal in Germany, the German Federal Government was able to postpone final decisions on the matter. Under pressure from Germany, the intended fragment relating to the EDIS was deleted from the draft conclusions of the December 2015 European Council. On the other hand, it must be emphasised that the issue of the Banking Union was only marginally discussed by the European Council as other problems came to the fore, e.g. the migration crisis facing the European Union and combating terrorism[377]. However, after less than two months, on 25 February 2016, the Bundestag adopted a firm resolution, mostly addressed to the European Commission. Not only did it repeat all the doubts already contained in the declaration of 4 November 2015, but it also raised new objections. First and foremost, the resolution challenged the legal basis for the European Commission's proposal of 24 November 2015, i.e. Article 114 TFEU, providing for the harmonisation rather than unification of the provisions laid down by law, regulation or administrative action in Member States and aimed at the establishment and functioning of the internal market. According to the Bundestag, the provisions in question did not allow the mutualisation of national deposit

---

375 M. Kröger, op. cit., pp. 1–2. Bundesverband deutscher Banken, Europäische Einlagensicherung, 25. November 2015, https://bankenverband.de/, pp. 1–2 [accessed: 18 May 2022].

376 M. Kröger, op. cit., pp. 1–2. Europäische Einlagensicherung, op. cit., p. 1.

377 European Council, 17/18 December 2015, Conclusions, Brussels, 18 December 2015, EUCO 28/15, op. cit., pp. 1–8. W. Mussler, Währungsunion: Juncker sucht Konflikt mit Schäuble, 15. Dezember 2015, http://www.faz.net/de/, pp. 1–2 [accessed: 22 July 2022].

guarantee schemes. Furthermore, the proposal from the European Commission envisaged the establishment of a Deposit Insurance Fund which would serve – in the opinion of the Bundestag – to '(re)finance national deposit guarantee schemes'. Therefore, the proposal assumed the creation of a new source of revenue for the European Union, whereas the still applicable Treaties clearly stated that the financing of new tasks of the Union would require the unanimity of all the Member States. Further in the resolution, the Bundestag stated that the European Commission's proposal might also infringe the principle of subsidiarity and the principle of proportionality. The argument was that the Commission had failed – despite the requirements laid down in Protocol No 2 on the application of the principles of subsidiarity and proportionality, annexed to the TEU and the TFEU – to 'consult widely' on the draft legislative act concerned (Article 2 of the Protocol) and to justify it with a statement containing some assessment of the proposal's financial impact (Article 5 of the Protocol). Finally, the resolution formulated the same conditions addressed to the European Commission as those set for the German Federal Government on 4 November 2015. The Bundestag urged the Commission to withdraw from the intention to establish an EDIS and to ensure effective entry into force of the already adopted measures aimed at completing the Banking Union[378].

3.2.3. *The stance of the Euro Summit and of the Eurogroup on the European Commission's 'roadmap'*

The European Commission prepared its 'roadmap' of 6 December 2017 contrary to clear indications that the euro area leaders would not endorse such radical system changes. Therefore, the document did not meet with their approval. A few days after the publication of the 'roadmap' by the European Commission, the President of the European Council, also serving as President of the Euro Summit,

378 Deutscher Bundestag, Verhandlungen des Deutschen Bundestages. Anlagen zu den Stenographischen Berichten (Drucksachen). 18. Wahlperiode. Antrag der Fraktionen der CDU/CSU und SPD zu dem Vorschlag für eine Verordnung des Europäischen Parlaments und des Rates zur Änderung der Verordnung (EU) Nr. 806/2014 im Hinblick auf die Schaffung eines europäischen Einlagensicherungssystems KOM(2015) 586 endg.: Ratsdok. 14649/15, Drucksache 18/7644, 23. February 2016, pp. 1–4, https://www.bundestag.de/ [accessed: 22 July 2022]. CSU-Landesgruppe im Bundestag, Union lehnt gemeinsame europäische Einlagensicherung ab. Regulatorische Sonderbehandlung von Staatsanleihen überprüfen, https://www.csu-landesgruppe.de/, p. 1 [accessed: 20 July 2020].

Donald Tusk, sent all leaders a diplomatic note containing competitive, but primarily more cautious, reform proposals and requesting their responses at the forthcoming meeting. Consequently, according to the Leaders' Agenda prepared for the December 2017 Euro Summit, 'there is consensus on the overall goal' of the system reform of the Economic and Monetary Union, but 'Member States differ in their assessment of what needs to be done, as well as in the urgency they attach to this task. In the absence of market pressure, the collective political will to make further progress has weakened'[379]. The Leaders' Agenda also expressed the opinion that there was 'broad convergence' among the euro area governments on further directions of the reform with regard to the following three issues: (1) putting into operation a common backstop for the Single Resolution Fund in the form of a 'credit line from the European Stability Mechanism' (sic!); (2) considering the possibility for the European Stability Mechanism to 'become a so-called European Monetary Fund'; (3) further developing the Council Roadmap of 17 June 2016, providing for measures such as the gradual introduction of a European Deposit Insurance Scheme[380].

On the other hand, the Leaders' Agenda in question contained a statement that '[o]n a number of other issues ... discussions have not led to broad convergence'; those included streamlining the fiscal rules to simplify the existing framework or strengthen their implementation and enforcement, setting up a euro area stabilisation function and establishing the post of a European Minister of Economy and Finance. At the same time, the euro area leaders were asked to

379 Euro Summit. Leaders' Agenda, Brussels, December 2017, www.consilium.europa.eu, p. 1 [accessed: 22 July 2022].

380 On 17 June 2016, the Council of the European Union adopted its political conclusions containing, *inter alia*, a roadmap to complete the Banking Union. The roadmap was based on three main issues: (1) establishing the Common Backstop; (2) creating the European Deposit Insurance Scheme; and (3) regulations aimed at reducing and sharing risks in the banking sector (e.g. additional prudential requirements for banks, more harmonised application of the Banking Union framework in particular Member States, etc.), cf. Council of the European Union. Council Conclusions, Brussels, 17 June 2016, https://www.consilium.europa.eu/ en/press/press-releases/2016/06/17/ conclusions-on-banking-union/, p. 1 [accessed: 22 July 2022]. On 17 October 2017, in response to both Juncker's address and Macron's proposals and on the margin of the European Council meeting, the Heads of State or Government adopted the Leaders' Agenda containing an overall timeline for further work on the system reform of the EMU for the following 18 months, or until mid-2019, cf. European Council. Leaders' Agenda, Brussels, October 2017, www.consilium.europa.eu, pp. 1–3 [accessed: 22 July 2022].

mandate the Eurogroup or the Council of the European Union, as appropriate, to continue work on the systemic solutions addressed, especially those characterised by the largest degree of convergence[381].

As a result, on 15 December 2017, the Euro Summit formally approved Tusk's proposal that in the following six months work should only concentrate on progress towards establishing the Common Backstop, the European Deposit Insurance Scheme and reforming the European Stability Mechanism, 'possibly to become a so-called European Monetary Fund'[382]. On the other hand, however, on 6 March 2018 in Brussels, the governments of eight euro area Member States – the Netherlands, Sweden, Finland, Denmark, Ireland, Lithuania, Latvia and Estonia – issued their joint statement of opposition to such far-reaching transfers of competence to the European level as the target model for reforming the euro area. The joint statement was prepared and made public at the initiative of Dutch Prime Minister Mark Rutte, who had informed German Chancellor Merkel of his plan four days before. Although the signatories to the new initiative agreed to establishing the Banking Union and the Capital Markets Union as well as to transforming the European Stability Mechanism into the European Monetary Fund, but to little more. At the same time, they were critical of other proposals contained in the most recent address by Juncker and in Macron's Sorbonne speech. They also took the opportunity to urge the French and German governments not to impose their concepts for reforming the EMU on medium-sized and smaller Member States[383].

In such a climate, after less than two weeks, Tusk issued another diplomatic note to the euro area Heads of State or Government. According to his proposal, the following Euro Summit should seek answers to several questions. Firstly, should a stabilisation function/fiscal capacity for the euro area be set up? If yes, what would be its main purposes? Secondly, should it be aimed at macroeconomic stabilisation, support to investment and employment, promotion of structural reforms? Thirdly, should such a new structure be part and parcel of the EU budget or an instrument outside the EU budget? Fourthly, should more be done

381 Euro Summit. Leaders' Agenda, Brussels, December 2017, op. cit., pp. 1–2.

382 Euro Summit. Statement, Brussels, 15 December 2017, https://www.consilium.europa.eu/en/meetings/euro-summit/2017/12/15/, p. 1 [accessed: 22 July 2022].

383 Ministry of Finance, Finland, Finance ministers from Denmark, Estonia, Finland, Ireland, Latvia, Lithuania, the Netherlands and Sweden underline their shared views and values in the discussion on the architecture of the EMU, https://vm.fi/documents/10623/6305483/Position+EMU+Denmark+Estonia+Finland+Ireland+Latvia+Lithuania+ the+Netherlands+and+Sweden.pdf [accessed: 22 July 2022], p. 1.

at the European level to promote competitiveness- and growth-enhancing structural reforms, reduce imbalances and ensure sustained convergence? Fifthly, which instruments should be used to that effect?[384]

In response to Tusk's diplomatic note, at the Euro Summit held on 23 March 2018, the euro area Heads of State or Government took a surprising decision implying withdrawal from the arrangements made on 15 December 2017 and the return to the idea of establishing a credit line for the SRF within a revised European Stability Mechanism. It involved abandoning the concept of creating a European Monetary Fund in the foreseeable future. But the list of the most pressing priority actions still included the following: (1) generally understood strengthening of the Banking Union; and (2) the reform of the European Stability Mechanism. Although the discussion covered other long-term aspects of the system reform, including the proposed creation of a euro area stabilisation function, no compromise was reached. No written conclusions from the debate were adopted[385]. Those decisions were reaffirmed by the following Euro Summit held on 14 December 2018. The euro area Heads of State or Government approved the Eurogroup report; specifically, they endorsed the terms of reference of the Common Backstop to the Single Resolution Fund and the related term sheet on the European Stability Mechanism reform, mandated the Eurogroup to work on the model of a budgetary instrument for convergence and competitiveness for the euro area, i.e. a separate euro area budget line, and called to advance work on establishing a European Deposit Insurance Scheme. The Eurogroup was also asked to prepare the necessary amendments to the Treaty establishing the European Stability Mechanism by June 2019 (cf. Figures 15 and 16)[386].

On 14 June 2019, in connection with the need to prepare a draft Council Regulation on a new Multiannual Financial Framework for 2021–2027, the

384 Euro Summit. Leaders' Agenda, Brussels, March 2018, www.consilium.europa.eu, p. 1 [accessed: 22 July 2022].

385 Euro Summit. Statement, Brussels, 23 March 2018, www.consilium.europa.eu, p. 1 [accessed: 22 July 2022].

386 Council of the EU, Press release, 4 December 2018, Eurogroup report to Leaders on EMU deepening, https://www.consilium.europa.eu/en/, pp. 1–2 [accessed: 22 July 2022]. Euro Summit, Statement, Brussels, 14 December 2018, EURO 503/18, p. 1. European Commission. Communication from the Commission to the European Parliament, the European Council, the Council and the European Central Bank. Deepening Europe's Economic and Monetary Union: Taking stock four years after the Five Presidents' Report. European Commission's contribution to the Euro Summit on 21 June 2019, Brussels, 12 June 2019, COM(2019) 279 final, p. 2.

Eurogroup agreed on the main features, a 'term sheet', of the Budgetary Instrument for Convergence and Competitiveness (BICC), or a separate budget line for the euro area. It would be part of the EU's general budget and Multiannual Financial Framework. However, no agreement could be reached on additional financing sources for the BICC, although two new taxes were considered: financial transaction tax and the taxation of digital companies. Furthermore, the Eurogroup agreed on the revision of the Treaty establishing the European Stability Mechanism with a view to creating a Common Backstop and, in its context, a flexible credit line for the Single Resolution Fund. At the same time, the Finance Ministers reached no agreement on the establishment of the European Deposit Insurance Scheme. On 21 June 2019, the Heads of State or Government of the euro area approved all proposals from the Eurogroup. They agreed to the creation of the BICC, the revision of the ESM Treaty, including extended surveillance powers of the European Union over euro area Member States having economic imbalances, as well as to the establishment of the Common Backstop for the SRF in the form of a credit line based on the European Stability Mechanism[387].

<table>
<tr><th colspan="2">PERIOD 2017–2018</th></tr>
<tr><th>FINANCIAL UNION</th><th>ECONOMIC AND FISCAL UNION</th></tr>
<tr><td>BANKING UNION
1. Establishing a Common Backstop for the Single Resolution Fund in the form of a credit line from the European Monetary Fund
2. Establishing a European Deposit Insurance Scheme</td><td>NEW EU MULTIANNUAL FINANCIAL FRAMEWORK (no consensus)
EURO AREA STABILISATION FUNCTION (no consensus)
SEPARATE EURO AREA BUDGET LINE WITHIN THE EU'S GENERAL BUDGET (no consensus)</td></tr>
<tr><th colspan="2">DEMOCRATIC ACCOUNTABILITY AND EFFECTIVE GOVERNANCE</th></tr>
</table>

Figure 15: Action plan towards completing the Economic and Monetary Union. Stage I: 2017–2018 (Euro Summit design)

Source: prepared by the author on the basis of: European Council. Euro Summit. Leaders' Agenda, Brussels, October 2017, op. cit., pp. 1–3. Euro Summit. Leaders' Agenda, Brussels, December 2017,

387 Euro Summit, Statement, Brussels, 21 June 2019, https://www.consilium.europa.eu/, p. 1 [accessed: 22 July 2022].

op. cit., p. 1. Euro Summit. Statement, Brussels, 15 December 2017, op. cit., p. 1. Ministry of Finance, Finland, Finance ministers from Denmark, Estonia, Finland, Ireland, Latvia, Lithuania, the Netherlands and Sweden underline their shared views and values in the discussion on the architecture of the EMU, op. cit. p. 1. Euro Summit. Statement, Brussels, 23 March 2018, op. cit., p. 1. Council of the EU, Press release, 4 December 2018, Eurogroup report to Leaders on EMU deepening, op. cit., pp. 1–2. Euro Summit, Statement, Brussels, 14 December 2018, EURO 503/18, p. 1. Euro Summit, Statement, Brussels, 21 June 2019, op. cit., p. 1. Euro Summit. Statement, Brussels, 23 March 2018, op. cit., p. 1. Council of the EU, Press release, 30 November 2020, Statement of the Eurogroup in inclusive format on the ESM reform and the early introduction of the backstop to the Single Resolution Fund, op. cit., pp. 1–3. Council of the EU. Statement by the Eurogroup President, Paschal Donohoe, op. cit., p. 1. Euro Summit. Statement, Brussels, 11 December 2020, op. cit., p. 1.

PERIOD 2018–2022	
FINANCIAL UNION	ECONOMIC AND FISCAL UNION
BANKING UNION 1. **Establishing a Common Backstop for the Single Resolution Fund in the form of a credit line from the European Stability Mechanism** 2. **Establishing a European Deposit Insurance Scheme**	**NEW EU MULTIANNUAL FINANCIAL FRAMEWORK** **EURO AREA STABILISATION FUNCTION (no consensus)** **SEPARATE BUDGET LINE FOR THE EURO AREA WITHIN THE EU'S GENERAL BUDGET (agreement in 2018–2020, no consensus from May 2020)**
DEMOCRATIC ACCOUNTABILITY AND EFFECTIVE GOVERNANCE	

Figure 16: Action plan towards completing the Economic and Monetary Union. Stage II: 2018–2022 (Euro Summit design)

Source: prepared by the author on the basis of: European Council. Euro Summit. Leaders' Agenda, Brussels, October 2017, op. cit., pp. 1–3. Euro Summit. Leaders' Agenda, Brussels, December 2017, op. cit., p. 1. Euro Summit. Statement, Brussels, 15 December 2017, op. cit., p. 1. Ministry of Finance, Finland, Finance ministers from Denmark, Estonia, Finland, Ireland, Latvia, Lithuania, the Netherlands and Sweden underline their shared views and values in the discussion on the architecture of the EMU, op. cit. p. 1. Euro Summit. Leaders' Agenda, March 2018, op. cit., p. 1. Euro Summit. Statement, Brussels, 23 March 2018, op. cit., p. 1. Council of the EU, Press release, 4 December 2018, Eurogroup report to Leaders on EMU deepening, op. cit., pp. 1–2. Euro Summit, Statement, Brussels, 14 December 2018, op. cit., p. 1. Euro Summit, Statement, Brussels, 21 June 2019, op. cit., p. 1. Euro Summit. Statement, Brussels, 23 March 2018, op. cit., p. 1. Euro Summit. Statement, Brussels, 14 December 2018, op. cit., p. 1. Council of the EU, Press release, 30 November 2020, Statement of the Eurogroup, op. cit., pp. 1–3. Council of the EU. Statement by the Eurogroup President, Paschal Donohoe, op. cit., p. 1. Euro Summit. Statement, Brussels, 11 December 2020, op. cit., p. 1.

On 24 July 2019, as part of preparations for the commencement of negotiations on the Multiannual Financial Framework for 2021–2027, the European Commission put forward a proposal for a Regulation of the European Parliament and of the Council on establishing the BICC[388]. Together with the Commission's proposal for a Regulation of the European Parliament and of the Council on the establishment of the Reform Support Programme, already published on 31 May 2018, it would be a component of the legislative package laying down the Multiannual Financial Framework[389].

However, due to the outbreak of the pandemic in 2020 and the ensuing economic, social and political consequences, the European Union institutions and Member States were forced to revise their previous plans for reforming the Economic and Monetary Union. Combating and mitigating the pandemic became a top priority. Therefore, in May 2020, the European Commission decided to withdraw the two above-mentioned legislative proposals [COM(2018) 391 final and COM(2019) 354 final]. Instead, on 28 May 2020, the Commission published a proposal for a new Regulation of the European Parliament and of the Council establishing a Recovery and Resilience Facility (RRF)[390]. It was also legally connected with the proposal for a Council Regulation laying down the multiannual financial framework for the years 2021 to 2027 and with four other draft legislative acts. As a result of legislative negotiations regarding the legislative proposals in question, between December 2020 and February 2021, the EU legislature adopted a total of six legal (legislative and non-legislative) acts.

The whole legislative package included the following: (1) Council Regulation (EU) 2020/2094 of 14 December 2020 establishing a European Union Recovery Instrument (Next Generation EU); (2) Council Decision (EU, Euratom) 2020/2053 of 14 December 2020 on the system of own resources of the EU; (3) Regulation (EU, Euratom) 2020/2092 of the European Parliament and of the Council of 16 December 2020 on a general regime of conditionality for the protection

388 European Commission. Proposal for a Regulation of the European Parliament and of the Council on a governance framework for the budgetary instrument for convergence and competitiveness for the euro area, Brussels, 24 July 2019, COM(2019) 354 final, pp. 1–14.

389 European Commission. Proposal for a Regulation of the European Parliament and of the Council on the establishment of the Reform Support Programme, Brussels, 31 May 2018, COM(2018) 391 final, pp. 1–42.

390 European Commission. Proposal for a Regulation of the European Parliament and of the Council establishing a Recovery and Resilience Facility, Brussels, 28 May 2020, COM(2020) 408 final, p. 2.

of the Union budget (making the protection of the EU budget and Next Generation EU funds conditional on respecting the principles of the rule of law); (4) Interinstitutional Agreement of 16 December 2020 between the European Parliament, the Council of the European Union and the European Commission on budgetary discipline, cooperation, sound financial management and own resources; (5) Council Regulation (EU, Euratom) 2020/2093 of 17 December 2020 laying down the multiannual financial framework for the years 2021 to 2027; (6) Regulation (EU) 2021/241 of the European Parliament and of the Council of 12 February 2021 establishing the Recovery and Resilience Facility[391].

The emergency recovery fund for economies affected by the pandemic, or 'Next Generation EU', also called the Recovery Fund, would be filled through the issuance of bonds by the European Commission, worth a total of EUR 750 billion in 2018 prices. Approx. 90% (EUR 672.5 billion) of the funds were allocated to one of its key programmes, i.e. the RRF. Under the RRF, the Member States would receive support in the form of grants (up to EUR 312.5 billion) and loans (up to EUR 360 billion). The remaining approx. 10% (EUR 77.5 billion) of Next Generation EU funds were assigned to reinforcing six other programmes: (1) REACT-EU under the Cohesion Fund, to address the adverse economic consequences of the pandemic in the first years of recovery (EUR 47.5 billion); (2) the Just Transition Fund (EUR 10 billion); (3) rural development (EUR 7.5 billion);

---

391 Council Regulation (EU) 2020/2094 of 14 December 2020 establishing a European Union Recovery Instrument to support the recovery in the aftermath of the COVID-19 crisis, Official Journal of the European Union, L 433I, 22.12.2020, pp. 23–27. Council Decision (EU, Euratom) 2020/2053 of 14 December 2020 on the system of own resources of the European Union and repealing Decision 2014/335/EU, Euratom, Official Journal of the European Union, L 424, 15.12.2020, pp. 1–10. Regulation (EU, Euratom) 2020/2092 of the European Parliament and of the Council of 16 December 2020 on a general regime of conditionality for the protection of the Union budget, Official Journal of the European Union, L 433I, 22.12.2020, pp. 1–10. Interinstitutional Agreement of 16 December 2020 between the European Parliament, the Council of the European Union and the European Commission on budgetary discipline, on cooperation in budgetary matters and on sound financial management, as well as on new own resources, including a roadmap towards the introduction of new own resources, Official Journal of the European Union, L 433I, 22.12.2020, pp. 28–46. Council Regulation (EU, Euratom) 2020/2093 of 17 December 2020 laying down the multiannual financial framework for the years 2021 to 2027, Official Journal of the European Union, L 433I, 22.12.2020, pp. 11–22. Regulation (EU) 2021/241 of the European Parliament and of the Council of 12 February 2021 establishing the Recovery and Resilience Facility, Official Journal of the European Union, L 57, 18.2.2021, pp. 17–75.

(4) InvestEU (EUR 5.6 billion); (5) the Union Civil Protection Mechanism, under the RescEU (EUR 1.9 billion); (6) Horizon Europe (EUR 5 billion). Given the size of the Multiannual Financial Framework (2021–2027) at EUR 1,074.3 billion, the total commitment appropriations of the European Union reached an unprecedented amount of EUR 1,824.3 billion[392].

The legislative package in question, setting out the financial framework for the European Union's seven-year budget for the period 2021–2027, introduced three novelties in comparison with the previous multiannual budgets. Firstly, all the European Union Member States agreed to the financing of the European Union Recovery Instrument (Next Generation EU) from the issuance of multiannual bonds by the European Commission. Thus, for the first time in the history of the European Union, all the Member States gave their consent to the mutualisation of debt. The debt would be repaid between 2028 and 2058, from newly established sources of the EU budget revenue, i.e. a plastic tax, a digital levy (from the taxation of digital giants), a financial transaction tax and a carbon border adjustment mechanism. The creation of the above-mentioned new categories of own resources was another novelty; the plastic tax was supposed to be introduced as early as 1 January 2021, whereas the European Commission would submit its proposals for the other taxes by the end of June 2024. Lastly, the use by the European Union Member States of funds available under the Multiannual Financial Framework and the Recovery Fund would be subject to respecting the rule of law.

It must be emphasised that the approval by Germany, Austria, the Netherlands, Denmark and Sweden of debt mutualisation was supposed to be a one-off event. The above-mentioned countries had previously objected to issuing EU bonds, being concerned about their assuming financial responsibility for debts incurred by other EU Member States, which would allow weaker and less disciplined

392 Cf. Council of the European Union. Multiannual Financial Framework 2021–2027 and Next Generation EU (commitments, in 2018 prices), https://www.consilium.europa.eu/en/press/press-releases/2020/12/17/multiannual-financial-framework-for-2021-2027-adopted/, pp. 1–3. Council of the European Union. Press release. Multiannual financial framework for 2021–2027 adopted, Brussels, 17 December 2020, https://www.consilium.europa.eu/en/infographics/mff2021-2027-ngeu-final/, pp. 1–2. The activation of the Recovery Fund depended on all the EU Member States having ratified the Council Decision of 14 December 2020 on the system of own resources. The ratification process lasted until May 2021. It is worth noting that – for the first time in the history of the European Union – the MFF also included the European Development Fund, previously outside the EU budget.

economies to undeservedly use cheap financing by wealthier northern countries[393]. But the pandemic crisis of 2020–2021 contributed to the reorientation of their approach. It shook the foundations of the European Union's internal market due to closed borders and involved a serious risk of further deepening of the South–North divide in the euro area. As noted by Marek Prawda, the benefits derived by those countries from their membership of the internal market, and additionally of the euro area for Germany, Austria and the Netherlands, became more important to the governments in question than any possible financial and economic losses arising from the mutualisation of bonds[394].

As mentioned before, on 23 March 2018, the euro area Heads of State or Government made a decision implying the return to the idea of establishing a credit line for the SRF within a revised European Stability Mechanism. They asked the Eurogroup to prepare the necessary amendments to the ESM Treaty in connection with the planned creation of the Common Backstop[395]. Nine months later, on 14 December 2018, the Euro Summit in inclusive format, i.e. attended by the Heads of State or Government of all the EU Member States, endorsed the terms of reference of the Common Backstop and the term sheet on the European Stability Mechanism reform[396]. On 30 November 2020, the Eurogroup in inclusive format, i.e. including the Finance Ministers of all the EU Member States, made a statement announcing that the revised ESM Treaty would be signed in January 2021 and ratified by the beginning of 2022. Therefore, the Common Backstop to the Single Resolution Fund in the form of a credit line from the European Stability Mechanism would be established two years ahead of schedule[397].

---

393 For more on the subject, cf. J.J. Węc, Perspektywy reformy ustrojowej strefy euro do 2025 r. Aspekty instytucjonalno-prawne [Prospects for the system reform of the euro area by 2025. The institutional and legal aspects], [in:] Unia Europejska w turbulentnym świecie: 30 lat Traktatu z Maastricht [The European Union in a turbulent world: 30 years after the Maastricht Treaty], J. M. Fiszer, T. Stępniewski (eds.), Lublin – Warszawa 2022, pp. 111–112.

394 M. Prawda, Iść wolniej, a w każdym razie inaczej. Jak zbudować opowieść o Unii po pandemii? [Proceeding at a slower pace or, in any event, following a different path. How to build a tale of the Union after the pandemic?], 'Rocznik Integracji Europejskiej' 2021, pp. 31–32.

395 Euro Summit. Statement, Brussels, 23 March 2018, www.consilium.europa.eu.

396 Euro Summit. Statement, Brussels, 14 December 2018, EURO 503/18, p. 1.

397 Council of the EU, Press release, 30 November 2020, Statement of the Eurogroup in inclusive format on the ESM reform and the early introduction of the backstop to the Single Resolution Fund, https://www.consilium.europa.eu/. pp. 1–3 [accessed: 22 July 2022]. Council of the EU. Statement by the Eurogroup President, Paschal Donohoe, on

The above-mentioned Eurogroup statement was endorsed on 11 December 2020, at the Euro Summit in inclusive format[398]; on 27 January 2021, all the euro area Member States except for Estonia signed two intergovernmental agreements: (1) the Agreement amending the Treaty establishing the European Stability Mechanism; and (2) the Agreement amending the Agreement on the transfer and mutualisation of contributions to the Single Resolution Fund[399]. With a delay resulting from temporary difficulties due to change of government, Estonia signed both Agreements on 8 February of the same year[400].

The Agreement amending the Treaty establishing the European Stability Mechanism extended the mandate of the international organisation concerned to new tasks and responsibilities. Having at its disposal a more accessible precautionary credit line, the ESM should play a greater role in financial assistance programmes and crisis management and prevention. Under the revised Treaty, the European Stability Mechanism should provide the Common Backstop to the SRF, whereas recourse to loans for the resolution cases at hand should be 'of last resort', i.e. where the financial means of the SRF should be depleted. The non-euro area Member States should also provide financing to the SRF through parallel credit lines. The nominal cap for ESM loans to the SRF was set at EUR 68 billion. If the ESM Common Backstop credit line should be used, the Single Resolution Fund would repay the ESM loan with funds from bank contributions within three years, although the period could be extended to the total maturity of up to five years. The Common Backstop should be used as a last resort only, that is, with the SRF depleted and the SRB unable to raise sufficient contributions or to borrow funds from other sources at acceptable interest rates. The Agreement amending the ESM Treaty was to enter into force after its ratification by all the euro area Member States[401].

---

the signature of ESM Treaty and the Single Resolution Fund Amending Agreements, 27 January 2021, https://www.consilium.europa.eu/en/, p. 1 [accessed: 22 July 2022].

398 Euro Summit. Statement, Brussels, 11 December 2020, EURO 502/20, p. 1.

399 State of play of ESM treaty ratification. Agreement Amending the Treaty Establishing the European Stability Mechanism, https://www.consilium.europa.eu/en/, p. 1 [accessed: 22 July 2022]. State of play, Agreement amending the Agreement on the transfer and mutualisation of contributions to the Single Resolution Fund, https://www.consilium.europa.eu/en/, p. 1 [accessed: 22 July 2022].

400 State of play of ESM treaty ratification, op. cit., p. 1. State of play, Agreement amending the Agreement on the transfer..., op. cit., p. 1.

401 Agreement amending the Treaty establishing the European Stability Mechanism between the Kingdom of Belgium, the Federal Republic of Germany, the Republic of Estonia, Ireland, the Hellenic Republic, the Kingdom of Spain, the French Republic,

As regards the Agreement amending the Agreement on the Single Resolution Fund, it envisaged the creation of a Common Backstop in the form of a credit line to the SRF as early as 2022. It should be funded by contributions from the banking sector rather than from taxpayer money, which should loosen the relationship between banks and the Member States participating in the Banking Union. Before the entry into force of the Agreement in question, it was open for accession by the European Union Member States having signed the Agreement on the transfer and mutualisation of contributions to the Single Resolution Fund on 21 May 2015, i.e. all the non-euro area Member States except for Sweden[402]. Thus, the Agreement amending the Agreement on the Single Resolution Fund should enter into force on the date 'when the instruments of ratification, approval or acceptance have been deposited by all the Signatories participating' in the Single Supervisory Mechanism and in the Single Resolution Mechanism[403]. In the Joint Declaration annexed to both Agreements, the signatories undertook to complete the process of their ratification 'at the same time... and, in any event, as soon as necessary' for the establishment of the Common Backstop in accordance with the political decision made before, i.e. at the beginning of 2022[404].

On 16 December 2021, the Euro Summit held in inclusive format announced the continuation of work on completing the Banking Union and the Capital Markets Union, which should be key to implementing other system reforms in

---

the Italian Republic, the Republic of Cyprus, the Republic of Latvia, the Republic of Lithuania, the Grand Duchy of Luxembourg, the Republic of Malta, the Kingdom of the Netherlands, the Republic of Austria, the Portuguese Republic, the Republic of Slovenia, the Slovak Republic and the Republic of Finland, 27 January 2021, https://www.consilium.europa.eu/, pp. 1–41 [accessed: 22 July 2022].

402 Agreement amending the Agreement on the transfer and mutualisation of contributions to the Single Resolution Fund between the Kingdom of Belgium, the Republic of Bulgaria, the Czech Republic, the Kingdom of Denmark, the Federal Republic of Germany, the Republic of Estonia, Ireland, the Hellenic Republic, the Kingdom of Spain, the French Republic, the Republic of Croatia, the Italian Republic, the Republic of Cyprus, the Republic of Latvia, the Republic of Lithuania, the Grand Duchy of Luxembourg, Hungary, the Republic of Malta, the Kingdom of the Netherlands, the Republic of Austria, the Republic of Poland, the Portuguese Republic, the Republic of Slovenia, the Slovak Republic and the Republic of Finland, 27 January 2021, https://www.consilium.europa.eu/, pp. 1–12 [accessed: 22 July 2022].

403 Ibidem, p. 10.

404 Joint Declaration, 27 January 2021, https://www.consilium.europa.eu/, p. 1 [accessed: 22 July 2022].

the European Union, including the 'green and digital transitions'[405]. Therefore, the EU leaders stated that they looked forward to the entry into force of the Agreement amending the ESM Treaty and the launch of the Common Backstop to the Single Resolution Fund as early as possible[406]. As at February 2022, the Agreement amending the Treaty establishing the European Stability Mechanism was ratified by all the euro area Member States except for Germany and Italy[407], whereas the Agreement amending the Agreement on the transfer and mutualisation of contributions to the Single Resolution Fund was ratified by all the euro area Member States except for Germany and Italy and by all the Member States participating in the Single Supervisory Mechanism and the Single Resolution Mechanism except for Poland, the Czech Republic and Denmark[408].

On 3 May 2022, the Irish Finance Minister and the President of the Eurogroup, Paschal Donohoe, at the Eurogroup meeting in inclusive format, submitted a two-phase work plan for establishing a European Deposit Insurance Scheme. In the first phase, between 2024 and 2027, it would be necessary to include participating national DGSs in a reinsurance scheme ensuring voluntary borrowing between financing arrangements and to establish the foundations for a common insurance fund, to be filled by contributions owed and paid by banks in the participating Member States and calculated depending on the risks existing in national banking systems[409]. In the second phase, i.e. in 2028,

405 An act of vital importance to the establishment of the Capital Markets Union was Directive (EU) 2019/1023 of the European Parliament and of the Council of 20 June 2019 on preventive restructuring frameworks, on discharge of debt and disqualifications, and on measures to increase the efficiency of procedures concerning restructuring, insolvency and discharge of debt, and amending Directive (EU) 2017/1132 (Directive on restructuring and insolvency). Its adoption enabled failed entrepreneurs to make a fresh start and increased the effectiveness of restructuring and insolvency procedures. Cf. Directive (EU) 2019/1023 of the European Parliament and of the Council of 20 June 2019 on preventive restructuring frameworks, on discharge of debt and disqualifications, and on measures to increase the efficiency of procedures concerning restructuring, insolvency and discharge of debt, and amending Directive (EU) 2017/1132 (Directive on restructuring and insolvency), Official Journal of the European Union, L 172, 26.6.2019, pp. 18–55.

406 Szczyt państw strefy euro, Bruksela, 16 grudnia 2021 r. [Euro Summit, Brussels, 16 December 2021], 'Przegląd Spraw Europejskich' December 2021, p. 9.

407 State of play of ESM treaty ratification, op. cit., p. 1.

408 State of play, Agreement amending the Agreement..., op. cit., p. 1.

409 The first phase would also include special tests for banks in terms of stability and risk exposure (testing would cover the level of bad loans and the degree of the

a European Deposit Insurance Scheme would be set up. Where necessary, the EDIS would grant loans to banks in Member States for indispensable interventions[410]. Although the proposal was specifically designed to take into account the opinions and doubts previously submitted and raised by the governments of all the Member States[411], it again met, quite unexpectedly, with opposition from both smaller countries concerned about the growing influence of large banks in their respective markets and from large Member States, traditionally critical of the idea of debt mutualisation (Germany) or of the intention to limit the role of sovereign bonds in balance sheets of banks (Italy)[412].
As demonstrated by the outcome of the Eurogroup meeting, the euro area governments' views diverged much more strongly than expected (cf. Figure 17)[413]. As failure of Donohoe's work plan of 3 May 2022 would probably put an end to many years' efforts by the euro area Member States to establish a European Deposit Insurance Scheme[414], it would mean that within four years, i.e. from March 2018, or the abandonment of the plan to create a European Monetary Fund, the euro area governments had withdrawn from another fundamental project aimed at completing the Banking Union. Should those hypotheses materialise, the Banking Union would remain an incomplete structure in the sense that the principles of the functioning of the third pillar would be confined to the harmonisation rather than unification of deposit guarantee rules. Thus, responsibility for handling any financial shocks would still lie, first and foremost, with the European Central Bank and the euro area national central banks which – as in 2010–2018 – would be forced to make *ad hoc* decisions in an arduous process of political negotiations[415]. The Eurogroup decision of 3 May 2022 also indicated

---

concentration of sovereign bonds in balance sheets of banks), the introduction of provisions harmonising the functioning of national DGSs and specifying regulations on bank insolvency and State aid. For more on the subject, cf. S. Płóciennik, Granice integracji. Niemiecka blokada finalizacji unii bankowej [The limits of integration. Germany's blocking the completion of the banking union], Analizy OSW, 24 June 2022, https://www.osw.waw.pl/, p. 2 [accessed: 22 July 2022].

410 Ibidem.

411 Eurogroup meeting, Brussels, 3 May 2022, https://www.consilium.europa.eu/en/, p. 1 [accessed: 22 July 2022].

412 S. Płóciennik, Granice integracji. Niemiecka blokada finalizacji unii bankowej, op. cit. pp. 2–4.

413 J.J. Węc, Wpływ rządów Merkel…, op. cit., p. 51. M. Prawda, op. cit., pp. 31–32.

414 S. Płóciennik, op. cit., pp. 2–4.

415 Ibidem, p. 3.

very clearly that the limit of economic integration in the euro area was the scope of 'financial solidarity' in responding to economic shocks. Whereas the South, led by France and Italy, considered that the solidarity should be understood in the broadest sense of the word, i.e. it should also cover the mutualisation of debt and the establishment of a European Deposit Insurance Scheme, the North, primarily Germany, objected to the idea, being concerned that the EDIS would be an ordinary 'transfer union'. It also meant that the reorientation of the approach by the governments of Germany, Austria, the Netherlands, Denmark and Sweden to the mutualisation of debt in 2020–2021, reflected in the example of the above-mentioned Recovery Fund, did not pave the way for resolving the dispute over the creation of a European Deposit Insurance Scheme. According to some economists, the absence of full mutualisation of the third pillar of the Banking Union precluded Member States from deriving the Banking Union's benefits assumed[416].

During another meeting held on 16 June 2022, the Eurogroup in inclusive format made four important decisions indicating a change in the direction of reforming the Banking Union: firstly, strengthening 'the framework for the management of failing banks in the EU'; secondly, creating 'a more robust common protection for depositors'; thirdly, facilitating 'a more integrated single market for banking services'; fourthly, encouraging 'greater diversification of banks' sovereign bond holdings in the EU'[417]. The EU leaders also agreed that, 'as an immediate step, work on the Banking Union' should only be limited to 'strengthening the common framework for bank crisis management and national deposit guarantee schemes'. The common framework for crisis management should be strengthened by the following measures: (1) broader application of the existing resolution tools in crisis management at the level of the EU and of the Member States, 'including for smaller and medium-sized banks'; (2) further harmonisation of laws governing the use of national deposit guarantee schemes 'in crisis management, while ensuring appropriate flexibility for facilitating market exit

416 K. Waliszewski, Unia bankowa i unia rynków kapitałowych – analiza porównawcza europejskich projektów integracyjnych w obszarze finansowym [The banking union and the capital markets union – a comparative analysis of European integration proposals for the financial sector], 'Nauki o Finansach. Financial Sciences', 2015, no. 2, pp. 100–101. Cf. also D. Schoenmaker, Banking union: Where we're going wrong, [in:] T. Beck (ed.), Banking Union for Europe. Risks and Challenges, Centre for Economic Policy Research, London 2012.

417 Eurogroup statement on the future of the Banking Union of 16 June 2022, Brussels, 16 June 2022, https://www.consilium.europa.eu/en/, p. 1 [accessed: 22 July 2022].

Views taken by the European Commission and the Euro Summit	Consensus	Divergence
Phase I: 2017–2018	1. European Monetary Fund 2. Common Backstop as a credit line from the EMF 3. European Deposit Insurance Scheme	1. European Minister of Economy and Finance 2. Separate budget line for the euro area 3. Stabilisation Function 4. Foundations of Political Union
Phase II: 2018–2020	1. Common Backstop as a credit line from the ESM 2. European Deposit Insurance Scheme 3. Budgetary Instrument for Convergence and Competitiveness	1. European Minister of Economy and Finance 2. Separate budget line for the euro area 3. European Monetary Fund 4. Stabilisation Function 5. Foundations of Political Union
Phase III: 2020–2022	1. Common Backstop as a credit line from the ESM 2. European Deposit Insurance Scheme 3. EU Multiannual Financial Framework for 2021–2027 4. Implementation of the European Pillar of Social Rights	1. European Minister of Economy and Finance 2. Separate budget line for the euro area 3. European Monetary Fund 4. Stabilisation Function 5. Budgetary Instrument for Convergence and Competitiveness 6. Foundations of Political Union
Phase IV: from May 2022	1. Common Backstop as a credit line from the ESM 2. Harmonisation of national laws on deposit guarantee schemes (DGSD) 3. EU Multiannual Financial Framework for 2021–2027 4. Implementation of the European Pillar of Social Rights	1. European Minister of Economy and Finance 2. Separate budget line for the euro area 3. European Monetary Fund 4. Stabilisation Function 5. Budgetary Instrument for Convergence and Competitiveness 6. European Deposit Insurance Scheme 7. Foundations of Political Union

Figure 17: Consensus and divergence of views taken by the European Commission and the Euro Summit in 2017–2022

Source: prepared by the author on the basis of: Euro Summit. Statement, Brussels, 15 December 2017, op. cit., p. 1. Euro Summit. Statement, Brussels, 23 March 2018, op. cit., p. 1. Euro Summit. Statement, Brussels, 14 December 2018, op. cit., p. 1. Euro Summit. Statement, 21 June 2019, op. cit., p. 1. European Commission. Proposal for a Regulation of the European Parliament and of the Council establishing a Recovery and Resilience Facility, op. cit., p. 2. Council of the EU. Statement by the Eurogroup President, Paschal Donohoe, on the signature of ESM Treaty and the Single Resolution Fund Amending Agreements, 27 January 2021, op. cit., p. 1.

of failing banks in a manner that preserves the value of the bank's assets'; (3) the harmonisation of national bank insolvency laws with a view to ensuring consistency with the EU principles: the Crisis Management and Deposit Insurance (CMDI) framework. It meant *de facto* reinforcement of the DGSD provisions. On an indefinite future date, the state of the Banking Union would be reviewed and the Eurogroup would 'identify in a consensual manner possible further measures... to strengthen and complete' it[418].

Therefore, on the same day, the Eurogroup in inclusive format asked the European Commission, 'in full respect of its powers under the Treaties', to consider preparing legislative proposals regarding a reinforced CMDI framework, also inviting 'the co-legislators [the EU] to complete any legislative work during this institutional cycle until early-2024'. Further, work towards establishing the Capital Markets Union was regarded as a matter of priority as it should complement the Banking Union and constitute an indispensable element ensuring 'a larger and more diversified pool of resources to support our economies and foster the single market in financial services'[419].

On 24 June 2022, the Euro Summit in inclusive format approved all the above-mentioned decisions by the Eurogroup and also invited the European Commission 'to table legislative proposals so as to complete the reinforcement of the [CMDI] framework before the end of the current institutional cycle'. Furthermore, the Euro Summit urged the EU legislators to step up efforts in establishing the Capital Markets Union as the other – in addition to the Banking Union – component of the planned Financial Union. The Heads of State or Government also welcomed the progress made in that regard, including 'in the legislative work with a view to fostering long-term investment in the European Union, adapting banking and insurance prudential regulations, protecting financial transactions against cyber and criminal threats, regulating digital finance and combating money laundering'[420].

Apart from decisions concerning the completion of the Banking Union and the creation of the Capital Markets Union, an important role in the process of the system reform of 2017–2022 was played by efforts aimed at establishing a genuine Economic Union. On 7–8 May 2021, at the Porto Social Summit, the EU leaders, European institutions, social partners and non-governmental organisations committed to the three above-mentioned main social objectives (headline

418 Ibidem, p. 2.
419 Ibidem, pp. 2–3.
420 Euro Summit. Statement, Brussels, 24 June 2022, EURO 502/22, pp. 1–2.

targets) proposed in the European Commission's European Pillar of Social Rights Action Plan of 4 March 2021. The Porto Social Commitment was signed by the EU institutions, social partners and civil society representatives on 7 May and by the EU Heads of State or Government on the following day; the latter group also adopted a special political declaration on a 'Social Europe', referred to as the Porto Declaration. Subsequently, on 25 June 2021, the European Council approved the headline targets concerned, thus paving the way for their practical implementation. By mid-2022, most of the measures envisaged in the European Pillar of Social Rights Action Plan had been adopted or launched[421]. Their implementation would be financed under the Multiannual Financial Framework for 2021–2027 (mostly the ESF+) and from the Recovery Fund[422].

The system reform developments in 2015–2022 must be assessed ambivalently. On the one hand, Commission Decision (EU) 2015/1937 of 21 October 2015 establishing an independent advisory European Fiscal Board entered into force on 1 November 2015, whereas the Council of the European Union adopted its recommendation on the establishment of National Productivity (Competitiveness) Boards on 20 September 2016. The Structural Reform Support Service was established in June 2015 and transformed into the Directorate-General for Structural Reform Support in January 2020. On 27 January and 8 February 2021, the euro area Member States signed the Agreement amending the Treaty establishing the European Stability Mechanism and the Agreement amending the Agreement on the transfer and mutualisation of contributions to the Single Resolution Fund. It paved the way for establishing a Common Backstop for the SRF as a credit line from the European Stability Mechanism. In June 2022, the Eurogroup made and the Euro Summit approved political decisions on the directions of further harmonisation of laws governing the use of national deposit guarantee schemes in crisis management and the CMDI framework. The legislative procedure concerning the proposal for a Council decision laying down measures in view of progressively establishing unified representation of the euro area in the International Monetary Fund, by 2025 at the latest, was still in progress.

421 European Commission. Press release. European Pillar of Social Rights five years on: from principles to concrete action for a strong social Europe, Brussels, 17 November 2022, pp. 1–3.

422 European Commission. Communication from the Commission to the European Parliament, the Council, the European Economic and Social Committee and the Committee of the Regions. The European Pillar of Social Rights Action Plan, op. cit., pp. 5–6.

Furthermore, on 25 June 2021, the European Council approved the EU headline targets whose implementation would be a first step towards guaranteeing the minimum social standards set out in the European Pillar of Social Rights.

On the other hand, however, the lack of political will and disputes among the euro area Member States over the limits of financial solidarity basically resulted in the abandonment of the idea to establish a European Deposit Insurance Scheme and a European Monetary Fund, i.e. the two fundamental projects aimed at completing the Banking Union. For the same reason, work on the proposals for creating a euro area Stabilisation Function and the position of a European Minister of Economy and Finance was discontinued. Furthermore, the need to mobilise enormous funds to overcome the economic and social consequences of the pandemic stopped the legislative procedures regarding two draft regulations intended as significant components of the legislative package to lay down the Multiannual Financial Framework for 2021–2027: the proposals aimed at establishing the Budgetary Instrument for Convergence and Competitiveness as a separate budget line for the euro area and the Reform Support Programme for 2021–2027.

Conclusions

The system reform of the Economic and Monetary Union, having started in 2010, was one of the European Union's four instruments aimed at fighting the euro area debt crisis – in addition to financial assistance programmes for the indebted economies, recovery programmes for the Member States affected by the crisis and Eurosystem projects to enhance economic growth in the euro area. Due to taking all those measures and overcoming the debt crisis, the euro remained the world's second most important legal tender, accounting for nearly a fourth of global foreign-exchange reserves, whereas the integrity of the euro area was maintained.

It must be emphasised that the two research hypotheses put forward in the introductory remarks were fully confirmed by the source materials under examination. As demonstrated by the exegesis of EU primary and secondary law, the *acquis* relating to the Economic and Monetary Union reflected various compromises, frequently forced by the Member States' conflicting national interests. Some regulations were agreed during intergovernmental conferences (1990–1991, 1996–1997, 2000, 2007) and caused deficiencies in Treaty (primary) law, whereas other provisions resulted from the legislative process in the European Union, which led to shortcomings in EU secondary law. The euro area debt crisis exposed the systemic weaknesses of the Economic and Monetary Union, thus pushing the Member States' governments towards reforming the EMU system. Initially, it seemed sufficient to simply strengthen economic and budgetary governance (2010–2012), but subsequent debt crisis developments made the Member States' governments decide to implement a comprehensive system reform of the Economic and Monetary Union (2012).

The search for an answer to the first research question led to formulating the opinion that the euro area debt crisis had only been partially overcome, due to failures of some Member States in the implementation of their recovery programmes, excessively restrictive fiscal requirements, mostly imposed by Germany on the indebted economies, but also owing to unimpressive progress in the system reform of the Economic and Monetary Union. Having exited their respective assistance programmes, carried out corrective and recovery measures and implemented various Eurosystem projects, all the crisis-ridden Member States (Greece, Italy, Cyprus, Spain, Portugal and Ireland) entered growth paths, reduced their budget deficits and pushed down unemployment rates, but the debt crisis and the pandemic crisis cost them their economic competitiveness (except for Ireland) and they continued to face high public debt levels (except for Ireland); for some, the struggle has not ended.

With regard to the second research question, it must be emphasised that the creation of the Fiscal Union is unlikely to contribute to strengthening the competitiveness of the euro area economies weakened by the debt crisis (Greece, Italy, Cyprus, Spain and Portugal); on the contrary, it might even solidify the divide of the euro area into competitive and uncompetitive countries. As shown by past experience, fiscal transfers in the European Union have turned out to be an ineffective tool for boosting the competitiveness of economically weak Member States or regions in the EU. It is a lesson to be learnt from various studies by the European Central Bank as well as by German, Italian, Polish and other economists. The research has demonstrated that neither fiscal transfers to the EU Member States benefiting from the European Structural and Investment Funds nor transfers to southern Italy or eastern Germany have contributed to improving the competitiveness of economically weak regions in the Central and Eastern European countries or of eastern German or southern Italian regions. On the other hand, even if the Fiscal Union should be established, its creation would not result in full unification of the fiscal policies of the euro area Member States. The euro area governments would still freely shape their tax policies and decide on their preferred allocation of budgetary expenditure.

In answering the third and fourth research questions, it must be stated that the decision by the European Union Member States of 14 December 2020 on the mutualisation of debt as the basis for the functioning of the European Union Recovery Instrument *Next Generation EU* was treated by Germany, Austria, the Netherlands, Denmark and Sweden as a one-off event. Therefore, it could not serve as a point of reference for the proposed European Deposit Insurance Scheme. It was very clear in the failure of Donohoe's plan (3 May 2022). Furthermore, it showed that the limit of economic integration in the euro area was the scope of 'financial solidarity' for particular Member States in responding to economic shocks. Whereas the southern countries, such as Greece, Italy, Cyprus, Spain and Portugal, having lost much of their economic competitiveness to the debt crisis and the pandemic crisis, or France and Belgium, struggling with high public debt levels, took the stance that the solidarity should be understood in the broadest sense of the word, i.e. it should also cover the mutualisation of debt and the establishment of the European Deposit Insurance Scheme, the North, led by Germany, Austria and the Netherlands, objected to the idea, being concerned that debt mutualisation would involve transformation into a 'transfer union'. But efforts to arrive at a compromise on the matter were primarily hindered by the northern countries' economic interests. In that sense, disputes over the scope of financial solidarity determined the direction of system changes in the EMU.

The main successes of the system reform of the Economic and Monetary Union in 2010–2022 – which answers the fifth research question – are described below. Firstly, measures aimed at establishing the Financial Union encompassed the creation of the Banking Union composed of three pillars: the first pillar carrying out micro-prudential supervision of the most important credit institutions, including banks; the second pillar responsible for insolvency procedures concerning the institutions in question; and the third pillar, yet to be determined and still debated by the EMU Member States, most probably to be based on the harmonisation rather than unification of laws on national deposit guarantee schemes. Whereas tasks related to the micro-prudential supervision and insolvency procedures have been shifted to the EU level (the first and second pillars of the Banking Union), responsibility for deposit guarantee schemes will apparently remain with the Member States (the third pillar of the Banking Union). The planned creation of the European Monetary Fund was also replaced by a revision of the European Stability Mechanism, set up in 2012, by establishing an ESM-based Common Backstop for the Single Resolution Fund. As regards ongoing work on the establishment of the Capital Markets Union, one of the most important legislative acts was Directive (EU) 2019/1023 of the European Parliament and of the Council of 20 June 2019 on restructuring and insolvency. Its adoption enabled failed entrepreneurs to make a fresh start and increased the effectiveness of restructuring and insolvency procedures.

Secondly, the execution of the plan to establish the Fiscal Union comprised putting in place the European Semester (2011), the 'six-pack' (2011), the Fiscal Compact (2012) and the 'two-pack' (2013), which led to enhanced fiscal and macroeconomic surveillance of particular Member States of the euro area and the whole EMU. Macroeconomic and fiscal surveillance was developed by establishing the European Semester and then considerably deepened through the introduction of the Macroeconomic Imbalance Procedure, improvements in national budgetary frameworks and the reform of the Stability and Growth Pact, or a set of principles and rules for appropriate fiscal policy-making by the Member States. The Fiscal Compact strengthened the surveillance and coordination of economic policies and improved economic governance in the euro area. It also introduced the 'golden rule' – according to which the annual structural balance (deficit) of the general government of a euro area Member State must not exceed 0.5% of GDP – and established an automatic correction mechanism to ensure compliance. With a view to strengthening fiscal policy coordination, the European Fiscal Board was set up on 1 November 2015. The second Regulation from the 'two-pack' of 2013 established closer monitoring and coordination of budgetary policies in the euro area. Furthermore, the European Commission issued guidance on making use of the flexibility provided for in the Stability and Growth Pact to foster economic growth, facilitate reforms and accommodate investment.

Thirdly, efforts to establish a genuine Economic Union included the adoption of the Euro Plus Pact (2011) under which the signatory Member States committed to stronger economic policy coordination for improving the competitiveness of their economies, increasing employment and enhancing public finance and budgetary sustainability. The provisions of the 'six-pack' and the 'two-pack' were also crucial for completing a genuine Economic Union. Whereas the 'six-pack' reinforced the preventive arm of the Stability and Growth Pact, placing greater emphasis on the public debt criterion and increasing automatism in decision-making on sanctions, the 'two-pack' strengthened the European Union's economic and budgetary surveillance of the euro area Member States (the first Regulation of the 'two-pack'). With a view to promoting the process of structural reforms at the national level, the Structural Reform Support Service was established by the European Commission in June 2015 and transformed into the Directorate-General for Structural Reform Support on 1 January 2020. Its functions comprise providing assistance to all the European Union Member States in the preparation, design and implementation of structural reforms, included in their measures for job creation and sustainable economic growth. On 20 September 2016, the Council of the European Union decided to establish National Productivity Boards, tasked with producing expert analyses and annual reports to be used by the European Commission in the context of the European Semester and the Macroeconomic Imbalance Procedure for euro area Member States. Furthermore, on 25 June 2021, the European Council approved the EU social objectives (headline targets) for implementing the principles of the European Pillar of Social Rights of 17 November 2017.

Fourthly, to legitimise the system changes introduced to the Economic and Monetary Union, the powers of the European Union's institutions and bodies as well as of the national parliaments were extended. Under the Banking Union, new powers were mostly conferred on the European Central Bank and the Council of the European Union as well as – to a lesser degree – on the European Commission, the European Parliament, the Court of Auditors and the national parliaments. Simultaneously, in the ongoing process of establishing the Fiscal Union and completing a genuine Economic Union, new powers were mainly conferred on the European Commission and the Council of the European Union and, to a lesser extent, on the European Council, the European Parliament, the Court of Justice of the EU and the Eurogroup. But it must be emphasised that nearly all the changes aimed to ensure democratic accountability and legitimacy for the system reform of the EMU were introduced in 2010–2015, with only few of them implemented in 2015–2022. The latter period witnessed the introduction of the following institutional changes, already mentioned above: (1) the establishment of the Structural Reform Support Service, replaced by the Directorate-General for Structural Reform Support in January 2020; (2) the creation of the European Fiscal Board to perform an advisory function for the European Commission under the multilateral surveillance procedure in the euro area; (3) the setting up by the Council of the European Union of National Productivity Boards as advisory bodies to provide expert analyses and support for the European Commission in the context of the European Semester and the Macroeconomic Imbalance Procedure in the euro area Member States; (4) the adoption by the European Parliament and the Council of the European Union of BRRD II, aimed to further strengthen the recovery and resolution framework for credit institutions, including banks. On the other hand, failed initiatives encompassed consolidating the external representation of the European Union and of the euro area vis-à-vis international financial institutions; integrating the Fiscal Compact and other intergovernmental agreements into the European Union's primary law; strengthening the role of the Eurogroup, also through a reinforcement of its presidency; setting up a euro area treasury responsible for fiscal policy-making; and establishing the European Monetary Fund.

In addition to the conferral of new powers on the above-mentioned institutions and bodies of the European Union, already in Stage 1 of the system reform of the Economic and Monetary Union, i.e. in 2010–2015, the EU framework was reinforced with three new crisis management tools and centralised supervision of financial markets at the macro- and micro-prudential levels. Thus, between 2010 and 2012, changes aimed at strengthening economic and budgetary governance in the euro area included the establishment of the European Financial Stabilisation Mechanism (2010) and the European Financial Stability Facility (2010) as temporary crisis instruments, followed by the creation of the European Stability Mechanism (2012) as a permanent international organisation for the euro area as a whole. All the three crisis management tools served to reinforce the financial stability of the euro area Member States experiencing a crisis or economic difficulties. However, the European Financial Stabilisation Mechanism and the European Financial Stability Facility only provided assistance to three euro area Member States, i.e. Greece, Portugal and Ireland, the hardest hit countries at that time and experiencing the most serious economic difficulties, whereas the European Stability Mechanism was supposed to financially support all the euro area Member States. With regard to centralised supervision of financial markets, 2011 saw the setting up of the European System of Financial Supervision. Within the ESFS framework, the European Systemic Risk Board was tasked with macro-prudential oversight of the whole financial system of the European Union. At the same time, the sectoral supervisory authorities, i.e. the European Banking Authority, the European Securities and Markets Authority and the European Insurance and Occupational Pensions Authority, were established to supervise the banking, capital and insurance sectors respectively (micro-prudential supervision).

In an attempt to answer the sixth research question, it must be concluded that Stage 1 of the reform (2010–2015) showed rather impressive progress on system changes to the EMU, even though not all objectives of the reform could be achieved as and when planned, but in Stage 2 (2015–2022), particularly from late 2017, the euro area governments' drive for implementing the designed system changes gradually diminished because – as expressly stated in the Leaders' Agenda prepared for the December 2017 Euro Summit – '[i]n the absence of market pressure, the collective political will to make further progress has weakened'. Therefore, the main reasons for the relatively modest successes of Stage 2 of the system reform of the EMU were as follows: (1) the lack of sufficient political will of the euro area governments to implement it; (2) various difficulties and barriers arising from the Member States' conflicting national interests; and (3) the aggregate impact of several very severe crises facing the European Union during the reform. The absence of political will and disputes among the Member States about the limits of financial solidarity resulted in the abandonment of ideas such as the creation of a supranational European Deposit Insurance Scheme, the establishment of the European Monetary Fund, the appointment of a European Minister of Economy and Finance, whereas further work on developing a Stabilisation Function for the euro area was discontinued. Moreover, the need to mobilise enormous funds to overcome the economic and social consequences of the pandemic stopped the legislative procedures regarding two draft regulations, primarily the proposal for an act establishing a Budgetary Instrument for Convergence and Competitiveness, i.e. a separate budget line for the euro area. Nevertheless – as mentioned before – the period 2015–2022 saw the completion of the implementation of three key directives (the BRRD, BRRD II and DGSD) in the EU Member States' legal systems (Banking Union), political decisions on strengthening national CMDI frameworks and creating a Common Backstop in the form of a credit line for the SRF from the European Stability Mechanism (Banking Union), the establishment of the European Fiscal Board and national fiscal councils (Fiscal Union), the setting up of the Structural Reform Support

Service/Directorate-General for Structural Reform Support, the adoption of the Council Recommendation on the establishment of National Productivity Boards and the European Council's approval of the social objectives (headline targets) whose implementation would be a first step towards guaranteeing the minimum social standards set out in the European Pillar of Social Rights (Economic Union).

The dynamics of the system reform of the Economic and Monetary Union could also be observed in the course of legislative work on the proposals submitted by the European Commission, especially in 2015–2022, the period to witness crucial decisions in that regard. Thus, between 2015 and 2022, there were as many as thirty debates at the Council of the European Union and its preparatory bodies on the proposal for a regulation of the European Parliament and of the Council amending Regulation (EU) No 806/2014 in order to establish a European Deposit Insurance Scheme. The Council's last meeting on the matter, held on 3 February 2022, was unsuccessful since the draft regulation met with strong opposition from Germany, Austria, the Netherlands, Denmark and Sweden. Eventually, in spite of such a large number of meetings of the Council, the proposal for establishing an EDIS did not even reach the stage of first reading in the European Parliament[423]. In 2017–2018, the Council of the European Union debated five times about the draft Council Directive laying down provisions for strengthening fiscal responsibility and the medium-term budgetary orientation in the Member States (e.g. the incorporation of the Fiscal Compact into EU law). The last meeting of the Council addressing that issue took place on 16 May 2018, i.e. more than four years before the end of the period under review[424]. In 2018–2019, the Council of the European Union also had five meetings on the proposal for a Regulation of the European Parliament and of the Council on the establishment of the Reform Support Programme, to be included in the Multiannual Financial Framework for 2021–2027, but the project was subsequently withdrawn due to the pandemic[425]. In 2019, the Council of the European Union met four times to discuss the draft regulation of the European Parliament and of the Council on a governance framework for the budgetary instrument for convergence and competitiveness for the euro area, but the proposal concerned was also withdrawn due to the pandemic[426]. In 2017–2018, three debates at the

---

423 Procedure COM(2015) 586, p. 1.
424 Procedure COM(2017) 824, p. 1.
425 Procedure COM(2018) 391, p. 1.
426 Procedure COM(2019) 354, p. 1.

Council of the European Union addressed the draft Council Regulation on the establishment of the European Monetary Fund, with the last one held on 23 February 2018, i.e. more than four years before the end of the period under review[427]. The year 2015 saw the only debate of the Council of the European Union on the proposal for a Council decision laying down measures in view of progressively establishing unified representation of the euro area in the International Monetary Fund[428].

The above analysis substantiates the opinion that the stock of the twelve-year period of implementing the system reform of the Economic and Monetary Union must be very ambivalently assessed. Although a number of changes were successfully introduced, many projects were delayed or abandoned. With regard to the three new structures designed for the EMU, i.e. the Financial Union, the Fiscal Union and the Economic Union, the only successes included creating an incomplete Banking Union as a component of the Financial Union and the foundations of the Fiscal Union and a genuine Economic Union. The economic and financial consequences of the coronavirus pandemic and of Russia's aggression against Ukraine in 2022 will significantly hinder further implementation of the reform. Therefore, the following questions have yet to be answered: will the EU institutions and the Member States' governments responsible for the system reform of the EMU be sufficiently committed to implementing it as and when planned (by the end of 2025) or will its completion be postponed?

427 Procedure COM(2017) 827, p. 1.
428 Procedure COM(2015) 603, p. 1.

List of Tables, Charts and Figures

Tables

Table 1: Economic growth rates, budget deficit and public debt as a percentage of GDP in the Member States affected by the euro area debt crisis in 2009–2018 35
Table 2: Total transfers of external and internal funds allocated to overcoming the euro area crisis in 2010–2018 (EUR billion) 64
Table 3: Germany's financial contribution to the fight against the crisis (EUR billion) 66
Table 4: Economic growth rates, deficit-to-GDP and debt-to-GDP ratios in selected euro area Member States in 2019–2021 70
Table 5: New powers conferred on the European Union's institutions, bodies and authorities as well as on the national parliaments at the first stage of the system reform of the Economic and Monetary Union in 2010–2015 130

Charts

Chart 1: Germany's current account surplus in 2004–2021 (in % of GDP) 44
Chart 2: Current account balances of Germany, France, the United Kingdom, Italy, Ireland, Greece, Spain and Portugal in 1991–2015 (in % of GDP) 44
Chart 3: Growth rates of GDP ***per capita*** in the euro area and the EU in 2004–2021* (in %) 71
Chart 4: Growth rates of GDP ***per capita*** in selected EU Member States in 2009–2021 (in %) 71
Chart 5: Growth rates of GDP ***per capita*** in the Northern European and Central and Eastern European Member States in 2009–2021 (in %) 72
Chart 6: Rates of GDP ***per capita*** growth and contraction in the Southern European and Central and Eastern European Member States of the EU between 2009 and 2021 (in %) 72

Figures

Figure 1: Organisational structure of the Economic and Monetary Union before the euro area debt crisis 30
Figure 2: The organisational structure and the decision-making process in the European Stability Mechanism 91
Figure 3: The organisational structure of the European System of Financial Supervision 100
Figure 4: The organisational structure of the Economic and Monetary Union in 2025 according to the report by Herman Van Rompuy 114
Figure 5: The organisational structure of the Banking Union 120
Figure 6: Single supervisory mechanism 121
Figure 7: Single resolution mechanism 124
Figure 8: The European Deposit Insurance Scheme according to the proposal from the European Commission 161
Figure 9: Roadmap towards the completion of the Economic and Monetary Union by 2025. Stage 1 (the European Commission's concept) 168
Figure 10: Roadmap towards the completion of the Economic and Monetary Union by 2025. Stage 2 (the European Commission's concept) 169
Figure 11: The organisational structure of and the decision-making process in the European Monetary Fund as proposed by the European Commission 177
Figure 12: The powers of the European Monetary Fund as proposed by the European Commission 179
Figure 13: The powers and functions of the European Minister of Economy and Finance as proposed by the European Commission 181
Figure 14: Stabilisation function as proposed by the European Commission 184
Figure 15: Action plan towards completing the Economic and Monetary Union. Stage I: 2017–2018 (Euro Summit design) .. 195
Figure 16: Action plan towards completing the Economic and Monetary Union. Stage II: 2018–2022 (Euro Summit design) 196
Figure 17: Consensus and divergence of views taken by the European Commission and the Euro Summit in 2017–2022 206

Bibliography

1. Documents

A new start for Europe: My agenda for Jobs, Growth, Fairness and Democratic Change, https://ec.europa.eu/commission/presscorner/detail/en/SPEECH_14_546.

Agreement amending the Agreement on the transfer and mutualisation of contributions to the Single Resolution Fund between the Kingdom of Belgium, the Republic of Bulgaria, the Czech Republic, the Kingdom of Denmark, the Federal Republic of Germany, the Republic of Estonia, Ireland, the Hellenic Republic, the Kingdom of Spain, the French Republic, the Republic of Croatia, the Italian Republic, the Republic of Cyprus, the Republic of Latvia, the Republic of Lithuania, the Grand Duchy of Luxembourg, Hungary, the Republic of Malta, the Kingdom of the Netherlands, the Republic of Austria, the Republic of Poland, the Portuguese Republic, the Republic of Slovenia, the Slovak Republic and the Republic of Finland, 27 January 2021, https://www.consilium.europa.eu/, [accessed: 22 July 2022].

Agreement amending the Treaty establishing the European Stability Mechanism between the Kingdom of Belgium, the Federal Republic of Germany, the Republic of Estonia, Ireland, the Hellenic Republic, the Kingdom of Spain, the French Republic, the Italian Republic, the Republic of Cyprus, the Republic of Latvia, the Republic of Lithuania, the Grand Duchy of Luxembourg, the Republic of Malta, the Kingdom of the Netherlands, the Republic of Austria, the Portuguese Republic, the Republic of Slovenia, the Slovak Republic and the Republic of Finland, 27 January 2021, https://www.consilium.europa.eu/, [accessed: 22 July 2022].

Agreement on the transfer and mutualisation of contributions to the Single Resolution Fund between the Kingdom of Belgium, the Republic of Bulgaria, the Czech Republic, the Kingdom of Denmark, the Federal Republic of Germany, the Republic of Estonia, Ireland, the Hellenic Republic, the Kingdom of Spain, the French Republic, the Republic of Croatia, the Italian Republic, the Republic of Cyprus, the Republic of Latvia, the Republic of Lithuania, the Grand Duchy of Luxembourg, Hungary, the Republic of Malta, the Kingdom of the Netherlands, the Republic of Austria, the Republic of Poland, the Portuguese Republic, Romania, the Republic of Slovenia, the Slovak Republic and the Republic of Finland, Brussels, 21 May 2014, EU/SRF.

Bank of Italy. The Eurosystem's asset purchase programmes, https://www.bancaditalia.it/, [accessed: 27 September 2022].

BverfG. 2 BvR 859/15, 2 BvR 1651/15, 2 BvR 2006/15, 2 BvR 980/16. Leitsätze zum Urteil vom 5. Mai 2020, https://www.Bundesverfassungsgericht.de/, [accessed: 25 September 2022].

BVerfG. 2 BvR 859/15, 2 BvR 1651/15, 2 BvR 2006/15, 2 BvR 980/16. Urteil vom 5. Mai 2020, https://www.Bundesverfassungsgericht.de/, [accessed: 25 September 2022].

Central Bank of Ireland. The Public Sector Purchase Programme (PSPP), https://www.ecb.europa.eu/ecb/educational/explainers/show-me/html/app_infographic.en.html, [accessed: 27 September 2022].

Communication from the Commission to the European Parliament, the European Council, the Council, the European Central Bank, the European Economic and Social Committee and the Committee of the Regions of 12 May 2010: Reinforcing economic policy coordination, Brussels, 12.5.2010, COM(2010) 250 final.

Communication from the Commission to the European Parliament, the Council, the European Central Bank, the European Economic and Social Committee and the Committee of the Regions: Enhancing economic policy coordination for stability, growth and jobs – Tools for stronger EU economic governance, Brussels, 30.6.2010, COM (2010) 367 final.

Council Decision (EU, Euratom) 2020/2053 of 14 December 2020 on the system of own resources of the European Union and repealing Decision 2014/335/EU, Euratom, Official Journal of the European Union, L 424, 15.12.2020.

Council Directive 2011/85/EU of 8 November 2011 on requirements for budgetary frameworks of the Member States, Official Journal of the European Union, L 306, 23.11.2011.

Council of the EU, Press release, 30 November 2020, Statement of the Eurogroup in inclusive format on the ESM reform and the early introduction of the backstop to the Single Resolution Fund, https://www.consilium.europa.eu/, [accessed: 22 July 2022].

Council of the EU, Press release, 4 December 2018, Eurogroup report to Leaders on EMU deepening, https://www.consilium.europa.eu/en/, [accessed: 22 July 2022].

Council of the EU. Statement by the Eurogroup President, Paschal Donohoe, on the signature of ESM Treaty and the Single Resolution Fund Amending Agreements, 27 January 2021, https://www.consilium.europa.eu/en/, [accessed: 22 July 2022].

Council of the European Union. Council Conclusions, Brussels, 17 June 2016, https://www.consilium.europa.eu/en/press/press-releases/2016/06/17/conclusions-on-banking-union/, [accessed: 22 July 2022].

Council of the European Union. European Pillar of Social Rights. Press release, Brussels, 17 November 2017, 673/17.

Council of the European Union. Multiannual Financial Framework 2021–2027 and Next Generation EU (commitments, in 2018 prices), https://www.consil ium.europa.eu/en/press/press-releases/2020/12/17/multiannual-financial-framework-for-2021-2027-adopted/, [accessed: 22 July 2022].

Council of the European Union. Press release. Multiannual financial framework for 2021–2027 adopted, Brussels, 17 December 2020, https://www.consilium.europa.eu/en/ infographics/mff2021-2027-ngeu-final/, [accessed: 22 July 2022].

Council Recommendation of 20 September 2016 on the establishment of National Productivity Boards, Official Journal of the European Union, C 349, 24.9.2016.

Council Regulation (EC) No 1055/2005 of 27 June 2005 amending Regulation (EC) No 1466/97 on the strengthening of the surveillance of budgetary positions and the surveillance and coordination of economic policies, Official Journal of the European Union, L 174, 7.7.2005.

Council Regulation (EC) No 1056/2005 of 27 June 2005 amending Regulation (EC) No 1467/97 on speeding up and clarifying the implementation of the excessive deficit procedure, Official Journal of the European Union, L 174, 7.7.2005.

Council Regulation (EC) No 1466/97 of 7 July 1997 on the strengthening of the surveillance of budgetary positions and the surveillance and coordination of economic policies, Official Journal of the European Union, L 209, 2.8.1997.

Council Regulation (EC) No 1467/97 of 7 July 1997 on speeding up and clarifying the implementation of the excessive deficit procedure, Official Journal of the European Union, L 209, 2.8.1997.

Council Regulation (EU) 2020/2094 of 14 December 2020 establishing a European Union Recovery Instrument to support the recovery in the aftermath of the COVID-19 crisis, Official Journal of the European Union, L 433I, 22.12.2020.

Council Regulation (EU) 2020/2094 of 14 December 2020 establishing a European Union Recovery Instrument to support the recovery in the aftermath of the COVID-19 crisis, Official Journal of the European Union, L 433I, 22.12.2020.

Council Regulation (EU) No 1024/2013 of 15 October 2013 conferring specific tasks on the European Central Bank concerning policies relating to the prudential supervision of credit institutions, Official Journal of the European Union, L 287, 29.10.2013.

Council Regulation (EU) No 1096/2010 of 17 November 2010 conferring specific tasks upon the European Central Bank concerning the functioning of the European Systemic Risk Board, Official Journal of the European Union, L 331, 15.12.2010.

Council Regulation (EU) No 1177/2011 of 8 November 2011 amending Regulation (EC) No 1467/97 on speeding up and clarifying the implementation of the excessive deficit procedure, Official Journal of the European Union, L 306, 23.11.2011.

Council Regulation (EU) No 407/2010 of 11 May 2010 establishing a European financial stabilisation mechanism, Official Journal of the European Union, L 118, 12.5.2010.

Council Regulation (EU, Euratom) 2020/2093 of 17 December 2020 laying down the multiannual financial framework for the years 2021 to 2027, Official Journal of the European Union, L 433I, 22.12.2020.

Court of Justice of the European Union. Press release No 192/18, Luxembourg, 11 December 2018, Judgment in Case C-493/17, Heinrich Weiss and Others, https://curia.europa.eu/jcms/, [accessed: 27 September 2022].

CSU-Landesgruppe im Bundestag, Union lehnt gemeinsame europäische Einlagensicherung ab. Regulatorische Sonderbehandlung von Staatsanleihen überprüfen, https://www.csu-landesgruppe.de/, [accessed: 20 July 2020].

Decision (EU) 2015/774 of the European Central Bank of 4 March 2015 on a secondary markets public sector asset purchase programme (ECB/2015/10), Official Journal of the European Union, L 121, 14.5.2015.

Decision (EU) 2015/774 of the European Central Bank, op. cit. pp. 20–24. Decision (EU) 2017/100 of the European Central Bank of 11 January 2017 amending Decision (EU) 2015/774 on a secondary markets public sector asset purchase programme (ECB/2017/1), Official Journal of the European Union, L 16, 20.1.2017.

Decision (EU) 2020/138 of the European Central Bank of 22 January 2020 on the paying-up of the European Central Bank's capital by the national central banks of Member States whose currency is the euro and repealing Decision (EU) 2019/44 (ECB/2020/4), Official Journal of the European Union, L 27I, 1.2.2020.

Decision of the 16 euro area Member States, Luxembourg, 7 June 2010, https://www.consilium.europa.eu/, p. 1 [accessed: 20 July 2022].

Decision of the European Central Bank of 14 May 2010 establishing a securities markets programme, Official Journal of the European Union, L 124, 20.5.2010.

Der Europäische Stabilitätsmechanismus und der Fiskalpakt. Übersicht über den Stand der Ratifikation, Stiftung Wissenschaft und Politik. Deutsches

Institut für Internationale Politik und Sicherheit, http://www.swp-berlin.org/de/, [accessed: 20 July 2022].

Deutscher Bundestag, Verhandlungen des Deutschen Bundestages. Anlagen zu den Stenographischen Berichten (Drucksachen). 18. Wahlperiode. Antrag der Fraktionen der CDU/CSU und SPD zu dem Vorschlag für eine Verordnung des Europäischen Parlaments und des Rates zur Änderung der Verordnung (EU) Nr. 806/2014 im Hinblick auf die Schaffung eines europäischen Einlagensicherungssystems KOM(2015) 586 endg.: Ratsdok. 14649/15, Drucksache 18/7644, 23. February 2016, https://www.bundestag.de/, [accessed: 22 July 2022].

Deutscher Bundestag, Verhandlungen des Deutschen Bundestages. Anlagen zu den Stenographischen Berichten (Drucksachen). 18. Wahlperiode. Antrag der Fraktionen der CDU/CSU und SPD. Zu den Überlegungen der Europäischen Kommission zur Schaffung einer Europäischen Einlagensicherung. Drucksache 18/6548, 4. November 2015, https://www.bundestag.de/, [accessed: 22 July 2022].

Deutscher Bundestag, Verhandlungen des Deutschen Bundestages. Stenographische Berichte. 18. Wahlperiode. 138. Sitzung am 24. November 2015, http://dip21.bundestag.de/, [accessed: 22 July 2022].

Deutscher Bundestag, Verhandlungen des Deutschen Bundestages. Stenographische Berichte. 19. Wahlperiode. 170. Sitzung am 2. Juli 2020, https://www.bundestag.de/, [accessed: 22 July 2022].

Directive (EU) 2017/2399 of the European Parliament and of the Council of 12 December 2017 amending Directive 2014/59/EU as regards the ranking of unsecured debt instruments in insolvency hierarchy, Official Journal of the European Union, L 345, 27.12.2017. European Commission BRRD Transposition status, https://ec.europa.eu/en/, [accessed: 22 July 2022].

Directive (EU) 2019/1023 of the European Parliament and of the Council of 20 June 2019 on preventive restructuring frameworks, on discharge of debt and disqualifications, and on measures to increase the efficiency of procedures concerning restructuring, insolvency and discharge of debt, and amending Directive (EU) 2017/1132 (Directive on restructuring and insolvency), Official Journal of the European Union, L 172, 26.6.2019.

Directive 2013/36/EU of the European Parliament and of the Council of 26 June 2013 on access to the activity of credit institutions and the prudential supervision of credit institutions and investment firms, amending Directive 2002/87/EC and repealing Directives 2006/48/EC and 2006/49/EC, Official Journal of the European Union, L 176, 27.6.2013.

Directive 2014/49/EU of the European Parliament and of the Council of 16 April 2014 on deposit guarantee schemes, Official Journal of the European Union, L 173, 12.6.2014.

Directive 2014/59/EU of the European Parliament and of the Council of 15 May 2014 establishing a framework for the recovery and resolution of credit institutions and investment firms and amending Council Directive 82/891/EEC, and Directives 2001/24/EC, 2002/47/EC, 2004/25/EC, 2005/56/EC, 2007/36/EC, 2011/35/EU, 2012/30/EU and 2013/36/EU, and Regulations (EU) No 1093/2010 and (EU) No 648/2012, of the European Parliament and of the Council, Official Journal of the European Union, L 173, 12.6.2014.

EFSF/ESM. Financial Assistance. Evaluation Report, Luxembourg 2017, https://www.esm.europa.eu/financial-assistance/evaluation-efsfesm-programmes, [accessed: 20 July 2022].

EFSF-ESM. Überblick über die europäischen Finanzhilfen, hrsg. vom Bundesministerium der Finanzen. Stand 31. Dezember 2018, https://www.bundesfi nanzministerium.de/, [accessed: 2 July 2019].

ESM. European Stability Mechanism. Spain: a fast and effective programme, https://www.esm.europa.eu/assistance/spain, [accessed: 20 July 2022].

Euro is irreversible, declares European Central Bank president Mario Draghi. ECB will do 'whatever it takes' to preserve the currency, https://www.theg uardian.com/ business/2012/jul/26/ euro-irreversible-mario-draghi-ecb, p. 1 [accessed: 10 January 2023].

Euro Summit. Statement, Brussels, 14 December 2018, EURO 503/18.

Euro Summit. Statement, Brussels, 21 June 2019, https://www.consilium.europa.eu/, [accessed: 22 July 2022].

Euro Summit. Leaders' Agenda, Brussels, December 2017, www.consilium.eur opa.eu, [accessed: 22 July 2022].

Euro Summit. Leaders' Agenda, Brussels, March 2018, www.consilium.europa.eu, [accessed: 22 July 2022].

Euro Summit. Statement, Brussels, 11 December 2020, EURO 502/20.

Euro Summit. Statement, Brussels, 14 December 2018, EURO 503/18.

Euro Summit. Statement, Brussels, 15 December 2017, https://www.consilium.europa.eu/en/meetings/euro-summit/2017/12/15/, [accessed: 22 July 2022].

Euro Summit. Statement, Brussels, 23 March 2018, www.consilium.europa.eu, [accessed: 22 July 2022].

Euro Summit. Statement, Brussels, 23 March 2018, www.consilium.europa.eu, [accessed: 22 July 2022].

Euro Summit. Statement, Brussels, 24 June 2022, EURO 502/22.

Eurogroup meeting, Brussels, 3 May 2022, https://www.consilium.europa.eu/en/, [accessed: 22 July 2022].

Eurogroup statement on the future of the Banking Union of 16 June 2022, Brussels, 16 June 2022, https://www.consilium.europa.eu/en/, [accessed: 22 July 2022].

European Central Bank. Eurosystem, Asset purchase programmes, https://www.ecb.europa.eu/, [accessed: 27 September 2022].

European Central Bank. Eurosystem, Capital subscription, https://www.ecb.europa.eu/ecb/, [accessed: 27 September 2022].

European Central Bank. Eurosystem, ECB's subscribed capital to remain steady after Bank of England leaves the European System of Central Banks. Press release, 30 January 2020, https://www.ecb.europa.eu/, [accessed: 27 September 2020].

European Commission. A Blueprint for a deep and genuine Economic and Monetary Union: Launching a European debate. Press release, Brussels, 28 November 2012, IP/12/1272.

European Commission. Commission Decision (EU) 2015/1937 of 21 October 2015 establishing an independent advisory European Fiscal Board, Official Journal of the European Union, L 282, 28.10.2015.

European Commission. Communication from the Commission to the European Parliament, the European Council, the Council and the European Central Bank. Deepening Europe's Economic and Monetary Union: Taking stock four years after the Five Presidents' Report. European Commission's contribution to the Euro Summit on 21 June 2019, Brussels, 12 June 2019, COM(2019) 279 final.

European Commission. Communication from the Commission to the European Parliament, the European Council, the Council and the European Central Bank. A European Minister of Economy and Finance, Brussels, 6 December 2017, COM(2017) 823 final.

European Commission. Communication from the Commission to the European Parliament, the European Council, the Council and the European Central Bank. A European Minister of Economy and Finance, Brussels, 6 December 2017, COM(2017) 823 final.

European Commission. Communication from the Commission to the European Parliament, the European Council, the Council and the European Central Bank. New budgetary instruments for a stable euro area within the Union framework, Brussels, 6 December 2017, COM(2017) 822 final.

European Commission. Communication from the Commission to the European Parliament, the European Council, the Council and the European Central

Bank. Further steps towards completing Europe's economic and monetary union: a roadmap, Brussels, 6 December 2017, COM(2017) 821 final.

European Commission. Communication from the Commission to the European Parliament, the Council, the European Central Bank, the European Economic and Social Committee and the Committee of the Regions on completing the Banking Union, Brussels, 11 October 2017, COM (2017) 592 final.

European Commission. Communication from the Commission to the European Parliament, the European Council, the Council and the European Central Bank. Further steps towards completing Europe's economic and monetary union: a roadmap, Brussels, 6 December 2017, COM(2017) 821 final.

European Commission. Communication from the Commission to the European Parliament, the European Council, the Council and the European Central Bank. Further steps towards completing Europe's economic and monetary union: a roadmap, COM(2017) 821 final.

European Commission. Communication from the Commission to the European Parliament, the Council, the European Economic and Social Committee and the Committee of the Regions. The European Pillar of Social Rights Action Plan, Brussels, 4 March 2021, COM(2021) 102 final.

European Commission. Communication from the Commission to the European Parliament, the Council and the European Central Bank. On steps towards Completing Economic and Monetary Union, Brussels, 21 October 2015, COM(2015) 600 final.

European Commission. Communication from the Commission to the European Parliament, the Council and the European Central Bank. A roadmap for moving towards a more consistent external representation of the euro area in international fora, Brussels, 21 October 2015, COM(2015) 602 final.

European Commission. Communication from the Commission to the European Parliament, the Council, the European Central Bank, the European Economic and Social Committee and the Committee of the Regions. "Towards the completion of the Banking Union", Strasbourg, 24 November 2015, COM(2015) 587 final.

European Commission. Communication from the Commission to the European Parliament, the Council, the European Economic and Social Committee and the Committee of the Regions. Action Plan on Building a Capital Markets Union, Brussels, 30 September 2015, COM(2015) 468 final.

European Commission. Communication from the Commission: Europe 2020. A strategy for smart, sustainable and inclusive growth, Brussels, 3 March 2010, COM(2010) 2020 final. European Council Statement by the Heads of State or Government of the Euro area and EU institutions, Brussels, 21 July 2011, http://www.consilium.europa.eu, [accessed: 20 July 2022].

European Commission. Completing Europe's Economic and Monetary Union. Report by: Jean-Claude Juncker in close cooperation with Donald Tusk, Jeroen Dijsselbloem, Mario Draghi and Martin Schulz, Brussels, 22 June 2015.

European Commission. MEMO – Banking union: restoring financial stability in the Eurozone. Updated version of first memo published on 15/04/2014, Brussels, 9 March 2015, MEMO/14/294.

European Commission. President Jean-Claude Juncker. State of the Union Address 2017, Brussels, 13 September 2017, SPEECH/17/3165.

European Commission. President Jean-Claude Juncker's State of the Union Address 2017, Brussels, 13 September 2017, SPEECH/17/3165.

European Commission. Press release. EU Economic governance: a major step forward, Brussels, 31 May 2011, MEMO/11/364.

European Commission. Press release. European Pillar of Social Rights five years on: from principles to concrete action for a strong social Europe, Brussels, 17 November 2022.

European Commission. Press release. Five Presidents' Report sets out plan for strengthening Europe's Economic and Monetary Union as of 1 July 2015, Brussels, 22 June 2015.

European Commission. Proposal for a Council decision laying down measures in view of progressively establishing unified representation of the euro area in the International Monetary Fund, Brussels, 21 October 2015, COM(2015) 603 final.

European Commission. Proposal for a Council Directive laying down provisions for strengthening fiscal responsibility and the medium-term budgetary orientation in the Member States, Brussels, 6 December 2017, COM(2017) 824 final.

European Commission. Proposal for a Council Regulation on the establishment of the European Monetary Fund, Brussels, 6 December 2017, COM(2017) 827 final.

European Commission. Proposal for a Regulation of the European Parliament and of the Council on a governance framework for the budgetary instrument for convergence and competitiveness for the euro area, Brussels, 24 July 2019, COM(2019) 354 final.

European Commission. Proposal for a Regulation of the European Parliament and of the Council on the establishment of the Reform Support Programme, Brussels, 31 May 2018, COM(2018) 391 final.

European Commission. Proposal for a Regulation of the European Parliament and of the Council establishing a Recovery and Resilience Facility, Brussels, 28 May 2020, COM(2020) 408 final.

European Commission. Proposal for a regulation of the European Parliament and of the Council amending Regulation (EU) 806/2014 in order to establish a European Deposit Insurance Scheme, Strasbourg, 24 November 2015, COM(2015) 586 final.

European Commission. Proposal for a Regulation of the European Parliament and of the Council amending Regulation (EU) 2017/825 to increase the financial envelope of the Structural Reform Support Programme and adapt its general objective, Brussels, 6 December 2017, COM(2017) 825 final.

European Commission. Proposal for a Regulation of the European Parliament and of the Council amending Regulation (EU) No 1303/2013 of the European Parliament and of the Council of 17 December 2013 laying down common provisions on the European Regional Development Fund, the European Social Fund, the Cohesion Fund, the European Agricultural Fund for Rural Development and the European Maritime and Fisheries Fund and laying down general provisions on the European Regional Development Fund, the European Social Fund, the Cohesion Fund and the European Maritime and Fisheries Fund and repealing Council Regulation (EC) No 1083/2006 as regards support to structural reforms in Member States, Brussels, 6 December 2017, COM(2017) 826 final.

European Commission. Proposal for a regulation of the European Parliament and of the Council amending Regulation (EU) 806/2014 in order to establish a European Deposit Insurance Scheme, Strasbourg, 24 November 2015, COM(2015) 586 final.

European Commission. Proposal for a Regulation of the European Parliament and of the Council on common provisions for monitoring and assessing draft budgetary plans and ensuring the correction of excessive deficit of the Member States in the euro area, Brussels, 23.11.2011, COM(2011) 821 final.

European Commission. Proposal for a Regulation of the European Parliament and of the Council on the strengthening of economic and budgetary surveillance of Member States experiencing or threatened with serious difficulties with respect to their financial stability in the euro area, Brussels, 23.11.2011, COM(2011) 819 final.

European Commission. Recommendation for a Council Recommendation. On the establishment of National Competitiveness Boards within the Euro Area, Brussels, 21 October 2015, COM(2015) 601 final.

European Commission. Reflection Paper on the deepening of the Economic and Monetary Union, Brussels, 31 May 2017, COM(2017) 291 final.

European Commission. State of the Union Address 2016: Towards a better Europe – a Europe that protects, empowers and defends, Strasbourg, 14 September 2016, Speech/16/3043.

European Commission. State of the Union Address 2017. Roadmap for a more united, stronger and more democratic union, Brussels, 13 September 2017.

European Commission. Statute of the European Monetary Fund. Annex to the Proposal for a Council Regulation on the establishment of the European Monetary Fund, Brussels, 6 December 2017, COM(2017) 827 final.

European Commission. White Paper on the Future of Europe. Reflections and scenarios for the EU27 by 2025, Brussels, 1 March 2017, COM(2017) 2025.

European Council Decision of 25 March 2011 amending Article 136 of the Treaty on the Functioning of the European Union with regard to a stability mechanism for Member States whose currency is the euro, Official Journal of the European Union, L 91, 6.4.2011

European Council meeting (15 October 2015), Conclusions, Brussels, 16 October 2015, EUCO 26/15, p. 6. European Council meeting (15 October 2015), Conclusions, Brussels, 18 December 2015, EUCO 28/15.

European Council meeting (25 and 26 June 2015), Conclusions, Brussels, 26 June 2015, EUCO 22/15.

European Council, 1/2 March 2012, Conclusions, Brussels, 26 April 2012, EUCO 4/2/12, REV 2.

European Council, 13/14 December 2012, Conclusions, Brussels, 14 December 2012, EUCO 205/12.

European Council, 14/15 March 2013, Conclusions, Brussels, 14 March 2013, EUCO 23/13.

European Council, 20/21 March 2014, Conclusions, Brussels, 21 March 2014, EUCO 7/1/14, REV 1.

European Council, 23 October 2011, Conclusions, Brussels, 30 November 2011, EUCO 52/1/11, REV 1.

European Council, 24/25 March 2011, Conclusions, Brussels, 20 April 2011, EUCO 10/1/11/REV 1. Annex I: The Euro Plus Pact. Stronger economic policy coordination for competitiveness and convergence.

European Council, 24/25 March 2011, Conclusions, Brussels, 20 April 2011, EUCO 10/1/11/ REV 1. Annex II: Term Sheet on the ESM.

European Council, 27/28 June 2013, Conclusions, Brussels, 28 June 2013, EUCO 104/2/13, REV 2.

European Council, 28 June 2016, Conclusions, Brussels, 28 June 2016, EUCO 26/16.

European Council. Conclusions of the Heads of State or Government of the Euro area of 11 March 2011, Brussels, 11 March 2011, http://www.consilium.europa.eu/, [accessed: 20 July 2022].

European Council. Council of the European Union. Who does what in the European Semester, https://www.consilium.europa.eu/en/infographics/european-semester/, [accessed: 22 July 2022].

European Council. Leaders' Agenda, Brussels, October 2017, www.consilium.europa.eu, [accessed: 22 July 2022].

European Council. Press release. Remarks by President Van Rompuy at the press conference following the Eurozone Summit, Brussels, 21 July 2011, EUCO 54/11. European Council – 2011. Statement of EU Heads of State or Government, Brussels, 26 October 2011, Publications Office of the European Union, Luxembourg 2012.

European Council. Statement by the Euro area Heads of State or Government, Brussels, 9 December 2011, http://www.consilium.europa.eu, pp. 2–4 [accessed: 20 July 2022].

European Council. The President. Towards a genuine Economic and Monetary Union. [Final report], Brussels, 5 December 2012, http://www.consilium.eur opa.eu/, [accessed: 22 July 2022].

European Council. The President. Towards a genuine Economic and Monetary Union. Interim Report, Brussels, 12 October 2012, http://www.consilium.eur opa.eu/, [accessed: 22 July 2022].

European Parliament. 10 years after "whatever it takes": fragmentation risk in the current context. Compilation of papers. Monetary Dialogue Papers June 2022, Directorate-General for Internal Policies PE 703.367 – June 2022, pp. 1–115, https://www.europarl.europa.eu/RegData/etudes/STUD/2022/703 367/IPOL_STU(2022)703367_EN. pdf, [accessed: 10 January 2023].

European Stability Mechanism. EFSF-ESM, February 2019, https://www.esm.europa.eu/sites/default/files/efsfesmnewinvestorpresentationfebruary2019_0.pdf, [accessed: 2 July 2019].

European Stability Mechanism. EFSF-ESM, February 2019, https://www.esm.europa.eu/sites/default/files/efsfesmnewinvestorpresentationfebruary2019_0.pdf, [accessed: 20 July 2022].

European Systemic Risk Board (ESRB), http://www.esrb.europa.eu, p. 1 [accessed: 20 July 2022].

Europejski Tydzień Parlamentarny [European Parliamentary Week], Ośrodek Informacji i Dokumentacji Europejskiej, https://oide.sejm.gov.pl/oide, [accessed: 28 October 2022].

Eurostat. Government finance and EDP statistics. General government gross debt 2019–2021, Brussels 2022, https://ec.europa.eu/eurostat/en/.

Financial assistance to euro area countries. Financial assistance to Greece, EFSF programme for Greece (expired 30 June 2015), https://www.esm.europa.eu/assistance/greece/efsf-programme-greece-expired, [accessed: 20 July 2022].

Financial assistance to euro area countries. Financial assistance to Ireland, https://economy-finance.ec.europa.eu/eu-financial-assistance/euro-area-countries/financial-assistance-ireland_en, pp. 1–2 [accessed: 20 July 2022].

Financial assistance to euro area countries. Financial assistance to Cyprus. ESM. How Cyprus modernised its economy, https://www.esm.europa.eu/assista nce/cyprus/, [accessed: 20 July 2022].

Financial assistance to euro area countries. Financial assistance to Spain. Summary, https://ec.europa.eu/en, pp. 1–2 [accessed: 20 July 2022].

Financial assistance to euro area countries. Financial assistance to Portugal. Post-Programme surveillance, https://ec.europa.eu/en, [accessed: 20 July 2022].

Informal meeting of the 27 heads of state or government. Bratislava Declaration. Bratislava, 16 September 2016, https://www.informal+meeting+of+the+2 7+heads+of+state+or+government.+Bratislava+, [accessed: 22 July 2022].

Initiative pour l'Europe – Discours d'Emmanuel Macron pour une Europe souveraine, unie, démocratique, Paris, 26 septembre 2017, http://www.elysee.fr/, [accessed: 19 May 2018].

Interinstitutional Agreement of 16 December 2020 between the European Parliament, the Council of the European Union and the European Commission on budgetary discipline, on cooperation in budgetary matters and on sound financial management, as well as on new own resources, including a roadmap towards the introduction of new own resources, Official Journal of the European Union, L 433I, 22.12.2020.

Joint Declaration, 27 January 2021, https://www.consilium.europa.eu/, [accessed: 22 July 2022].

Judgment of the Court (Grand Chamber) of 11 December 2018, Case C-493/17, ECLI:EU:C:2018:1000, https://curia.europa.eu/juris/document/, [accessed: 25 September 2022].

Komisja Nadzoru Finansowego [Polish Financial Supervision Authority]. Europejski System Nadzoru Finansowego [European System of Financial Supervision], http://www.knf.gov.pl/, [accessed: 20 July 2022].

Konferencja Międzyparlamentarna ds. Stabilności, Koordynacji i Zarządzania Gospodarczego w Unii Europejskiej [Interparliamentary Conference on Stability, Economic Coordination and Governance in the European Union], Ośrodek Informacji i Dokumentacji Europejskiej, https://oide.sejm.gov.pl/oide, [accessed: 28 October 2022].

Mayer F. C., Stellungnahme zu dem Bericht „Die Wirtschafts- und Währungsunion Europas vollenden“ (Bericht der fünf Präsidenten) für die öffentliche Anhörung im Deutschen Bundestag, Ausschuss für die Angelegenheiten der Europäischen Union, Montag, 2. November 2015, https://www.bundestag.de/, [accessed: 22 July 2022].

Ministerstwo Gospodarki RP. Semestr europejski. Okres oceny i koordynacji polityki gospodarczej w UE [European Semester. The economic policy assessment and coordination period in the EU], Warszawa 2014.

Ministry of Finance, Finland, Finance ministers from Denmark, Estonia, Finland, Ireland, Latvia, Lithuania, the Netherlands and Sweden underline their shared views and values in the discussion on the architecture of the EMU, https://vm.fi/documents/10623/6305483/Position+EMU+Denmark+Estonia+Finland+Ireland+Latvia+Lithuania+the+Netherlands+and+Sweden.pdf/ [accessed: 22 July 2022].

Monitor konwergencji nominalnej [Nominal Convergence Monitor]. Ministerstwo Finansów [Polish Ministry of Finance]. Departament Polityki Finansowej, Analiz i Statystyki, 2012, no. 4.

Narodowy Bank Polski [National Bank of Poland]. Departament Zagraniczny. Informacja na temat nowych zasad funkcjonowania Europejskiego Instrumentu Stabilności Finansowej oraz przyszłego kształtu Europejskiego Mechanizmu Stabilności [Information on the new principles and rules of the functioning of the European Financial Stability Facility and the future shape of the European Stability Mechanism], http://www.nbp.pl/, [accessed: 20 July 2022].

Narodowy Bank Polski. System finansowy [The financial system], http://www.nbp.pl/ home.aspx?f=/systemfinansowy/esrb.html, [accessed: 20 July 2022].

National transposition measures communicated by the Member States concerning: Directive 2014/49/EU of the European Parliament and of the Council of 16 April 2014 on deposit guarantee schemes (recast). Text with EEA relevance, https://eur-lex.europa.eu/legal-content/, [accessed: 21 October 2022].

Odpowiedź sekretarza stanu w Ministerstwie Finansów [Izabeli Leszczyny] – z upoważnienia prezesa Rady Ministrów – na interpelację nr 30121 w sprawie stanowiska rządu PO-PSL w sprawie unii bankowej [Reply of the Secretary of State at the Ministry of Finance [Izabela Leszczyna] – as authorised by the Prime Minister – to question no. 30121 on the position of the PO-PSL government on the banking union], 3 February 2015, https://www.sejm.gov.pl/sejm7.nsf/InterpelacjaTresc.xsp?key=2117A115, [accessed: 22 July 2022].

OECD.Stat. Growth in GDP per capita, productivity and ULC, https://stats.oecd.org/Index.aspx?DataSetCode=PDB_GR/, [accessed: 22 July 2022].

Pakt fiskalny. Analiza z dnia 26 marca 2012 r. Forum Obywatelskiego Rozwoju, Centrum für Europäische Politik [The Fiscal Compact. Analysis of 26 March 2012. Civil Development Forum, Centrum für Europäische Politik], http://www.for.org.pl/, [accessed: 20 July 2022].

Preparing for Next Steps on Better Economic Governance in the Euro Area', Analytical Note by Jean-Claude Juncker in close cooperation with Donald Tusk, Jeroen Dijsselbloem and Mario Draghi, Informal European Council held on 12 February 2015, https://eur-lex.europa.eu/legal-content/EN/TXT/PDF/?uri=OJ:C: 2016:013: FULL&from=HR, [accessed: 22 July 2022].

Procedure COM(2015) 586.

Procedure COM(2015) 603.

Procedure COM(2017) 824.

Procedure COM(2017) 827.

Procedure COM(2018) 391.

Procedure COM(2019) 354.

Regulation (EU) 2021/241 of the European Parliament and of the Council of 12 February 2021 establishing the Recovery and Resilience Facility, Official Journal of the European Union, L 57, 18.2.202.

Regulation (EU) No 1092/2010 of the European Parliament and of the Council of 24 November 2010 on European Union macro-prudential oversight of the financial system and establishing a European Systemic Risk Board, Official Journal of the European Union, L 331, 15.12.2010.

Regulation (EU) No 1093/2010 of the European Parliament and of the Council of 24 November 2010 establishing a European Supervisory Authority (European Banking Authority), amending Decision No 716/2009/EC and repealing Commission Decision 2009/78/EC, Official Journal of the European Union, L 331, 15.12.2010.

Regulation (EU) No 1094/2010 of the European Parliament and of the Council of 24 November 2010 establishing a European Supervisory Authority (European Insurance and Occupational Pensions Authority), amending Decision No 716/2009/EC and repealing Commission Decision 2009/79/EC, Official Journal of the European Union, L 331, 15.12.2010.

Regulation (EU) No 1095/2010 of the European Parliament and of the Council of 24 November 2010 establishing a European Supervisory Authority (European Securities and Markets Authority), amending Decision No 716/2009/EC and repealing Commission Decision 2009/77/EC, Official Journal of the European Union, L 331, 15.12.2010.

Regulation (EU) No 1173/2011 of the European Parliament and of the Council of 16 November 2011 on the effective enforcement of budgetary surveillance in the euro area, Official Journal of the European Union, L 306, 23.11.2011.

Regulation (EU) No 1174/2011 of the European Parliament and of the Council of 16 November 2011 on enforcement measures to correct excessive macroeconomic imbalances in the euro area, Official Journal of the European Union, 2011, L 306, 23.11.2011.

Regulation (EU) No 1175/2011 of the European Parliament and of the Council of 16 November 2011 amending Council Regulation (EC) No 1466/97 on the strengthening of the surveillance of budgetary positions and the surveillance and coordination of economic policies, Official Journal of the European Union, L 306, 23.11.201.

Regulation (EU) No 1176/2011 of the European Parliament and of the Council of 16 November 2011 on the prevention and correction of macroeconomic imbalances, Official Journal of the European Union, 2011, L 306, 23.11.2011.

Regulation (EU) No 472/2013 of the European Parliament and of the Council of 21 May 2013 on the strengthening of economic and budgetary surveillance of Member States in the euro area experiencing or threatened with serious difficulties with respect to their financial stability, Official Journal of the European Union, L 140, 27.5.2013.

Regulation (EU) No 473/2013 of the European Parliament and of the Council of 21 May 2013 on common provisions for monitoring and assessing draft budgetary plans and ensuring the correction of excessive deficit of the Member States in the euro area, Official Journal of the European Union, L 140, 27.5.2013.

Regulation (EU) No 575/2013 of the European Parliament and of the Council of 26 June 2013 on prudential requirements for credit institutions and investment firms and amending Regulation (EU) No 648/2012, Official Journal of the European Union, L 176, 27.6.2013. Decision (EU) 2015/774 of the European Central Bank, op. cit. pp. 1, 24. For an interpretation of Decision (EU) 2015/774 of the European Central Bank, cf. European Central Bank. Eurosystem, How quantitative easing works, https://www.ecb.europa.eu/ecb/educational/explainers/show-me/html/app_infographic.en.html/, [accessed: 27 September 2022].

Regulation (EU) No 806/2014 of the European Parliament and of the Council of 15 July 2014 establishing uniform rules and a uniform procedure for the resolution of credit institutions and certain investment firms in the framework of a Single Resolution Mechanism and a Single Resolution Fund and amending Regulation (EU) No 1093/2010, Official Journal of the European Union, L 225, 30.7.2014.

Regulation (EU, Euratom) 2020/2092 of the European Parliament and of the Council of 16 December 2020 on a general regime of conditionality for the protection of the Union budget, Official Journal of the European Union, L 433I, 22.12.2020.

Resolution of the European Council on the Stability and Growth Pact, Amsterdam, 17 June 1997, Official Journal of the European Union, C 236, 2.8.1997.

Sejm Rzeczypospolitej Polskiej [Sejm of the Republic of Poland]. VII kadencja. Interpelacje, zapytania, pytania i oświadczenia. Odpowiedź podsekretarza stanu w Ministerstwie Finansów na zapytanie nr 205 w sprawie realizacji priorytetów polskiej prezydencji z obszarów działania Ministerstwa Finansów [Reply of the Under-Secretary of State at the Ministry of Finance to question no. 205 on the implementation of the priorities of the Polish Presidency in the areas of competence of the Ministry of Finance], http://orka2.sejm.gov.pl, [accessed: 20 July 2022].

Semestr Europejski [European Semester], Ministerstwo Gospodarki [Polish Ministry of Economy], http://www.mg.gov.pl, p. 1 [accessed: 20 July 2022].

Semestr europejski. Przebieg cyklu koordynacji na poziomie Unii i Polski (2011–2016) (stan prawny na 30 listopada 2015) [European Semester. The coordination cycle at the Union and Poland's level (legal status as at 30 November 2015)], Ośrodek Informacji i Dokumentacji Europejskiej. Biblioteka Sejmowa, https://oide.sejm.gov.pl/, [accessed: 20 July 2022].

Semestr europejski. Przewodnik po kluczowych dokumentach (stan na 4 czerwca 2012 r.) [European Semester. A guide to key documents (as at 4 June 2012)], Ośrodek Informacji i Dokumentacji Europejskiej Sejmu RP, http://libr.sejm.gov.pl, [accessed: 20 July 2022].

Spotkania Konferencji Międzyparlamentarnej ds. Stabilności, Koordynacji i Zarządzania Gospodarczego w Unii Europejskiej [Meetings of the Interparliamentary Conference on Stability, Economic Coordination and Governance in the European Union], Ośrodek Informacji i Dokumentacji Europejskiej, https://oide.sejm.gov.pl/oide, [accessed: 28 October 2022].

State of play of ESM treaty ratification. Agreement Amending the Treaty Establishing the European Stability Mechanism, https://www.consilium.europa.eu/en/, [accessed: 22 July 2022].

State of play, Agreement amending the Agreement on the transfer and mutualisation of contributions to the Single Resolution Fund, https://www.consilium.europa.eu/en/, [accessed: 22 July 2022].

Statistisches Jahrbuch. Fakten zum deutschen Außenhandel 2013. Außenhandelsergebnisse im Jahre 2013, Statistisches Bundesamt, Berlin 2014.

Structural Reform Support Service, https://ec.europa.eu/en/, [accessed: 20 July 2022].

Szczyt państw strefy euro, Bruksela, 16 grudnia 2021 r. [Euro Summit, Brussels, 16 December 2021], 'Przegląd Spraw Europejskich' December 2021.

The European Pillar of Social Rights in 20 principles, https://commission.europa.eu/strategy-and-policy/priorities-2019-2024/economy-works-people/jobs-growth-and-investment/european-pillar-social-rights/european-pillar-social-rights-20-principles_en, [accessed: 22 July 2022].

The primary objectives of the Eurosystem include the maintenance of price stability and the promotion of financial integration in the euro area, cf. European Central Bank. Eurosystem, Eurosystem mission, https://www.ecb.europa.eu/ecb/, [accessed: 27 September 2022].

Treaty establishing the European Stability Mechanism between the Kingdom of Belgium, the Federal Republic of Germany, the Republic of Estonia, Ireland, the Hellenic Republic, the Kingdom of Spain, the French Republic, the Italian Republic, the Republic of Cyprus, the Grand Duchy of Luxembourg, Malta, the Kingdom of the Netherlands, the Republic of Austria, the Portuguese Republic, the Republic of Slovenia, the Slovak Republic, the Republic of Finland, http://www.european-council.europa.eu/, [accessed: 20 July 2022].

Treaty of Lisbon amending the Treaty on European Union and the Treaty establishing the European Community, signed at Lisbon, 13 December 2007 (consolidated versions), Official Journal of the European Union, C 202, 7.6.2016.

Treaty on Stability, Coordination and Governance in the Economic and Monetary Union between the Kingdom of Belgium, the Republic of Bulgaria, the Kingdom of Denmark, the Federal Republic of Germany, the Republic of Estonia, Ireland, the Hellenic Republic, the Kingdom of Spain, the French Republic, the Italian Republic, the Republic of Cyprus, the Republic of Latvia, the Republic of Lithuania, the Grand Duchy of Luxembourg, Hungary, Malta, the Kingdom of the Netherlands, Republic of Austria, the Republic of Poland, the Portuguese Republic, Romania, the Republic of Slovenia, the Slovak Republic, the Republic of Finland and the Kingdom of Sweden, http://european-council.europa.eu/, [accessed: 22 July 2022].

2. Monographs

50 years of the European treaties: looking back and thinking forward, M. Dougan, S. Currie (eds.), Oxford 2009.

Banking Union for Europe. Risks and Challenges, T. Beck (ed.), London 2012.

Barcz J., Główne kierunki reformy ustrojowej post-lizbońskiej Unii Europejskiej [The main directions of the system reform of the post-Lisbon European Union], Piaseczno 2015.

Barcz J., Unia Europejska na rozstajach. Traktat z Lizbony. Dynamika i główne kierunki reformy ustrojowej [The European Union at a crossroads. The Treaty of Lisbon. The dynamics and main directions of the system reform], Warszawa 2010.

Beck K., Grodzicki M., Konwergencja realna i synchronizacja cykli koniunkturalnych w Unii Europejskiej. Wymiar strukturalny [Real convergence and synchronisation of economic cycles in the European Union. The structural dimension], Warszawa 2014.

Bieber R., Epiney A., Haag M., Die Europäische Union. Europarecht und Politik, Baden-Baden 2005.

Bień A., Optymalny obszar walutowy. Teoria i praktyka [The optimum currency area. Theory and practice], Warszawa 1988.

Chalmers D., A. Tomkins, European Union Public Law, Cambridge 2007.

Chamon M., EU Agencies: Legal and Political Limits to the Transformation of the EU Administration, Oxford 2016.

Christiansen Th., Reh Ch., Constitutionalizing the European Union, Basingstoke 2009.

Cziomer E., Rola Niemiec w kryzysie strefy euro po 2009 r. [The role of Germany in the euro area debt crisis after 2009], Kraków 2013, pp. 70–110.

De Grauwe P., Economics of Monetary Union, Oxford 2018.

Eilmansberger T., Griller S., W. Obwexer (Hrsg.), Rechtsfragen der Implementierung des Vertrages von Lissabon, Wien–New York 2011.

Frenz W., Handbuch Europarecht, Bd. 1–6, Berlin–Heidelberg 2012.

Oppermann T., Europarecht. Ein Studienbuch, München 2009.

Gawlikowska-Hueckel K., Zielińska-Głębocka A., Integracja europejska. Od jednolitego rynku do unii walutowej [European integration. From the single market to Monetary Union], Warszawa 2007.

Götz M., Kryzys i przyszłość strefy euro [The euro area crisis and future], Warszawa 2012. Gruszczyński M., Kryzysy walutowe, bankowe i zadłużeniowe w gospodarce światowej [The currency, banking and debt crises in the world economy], Warszawa 2013.

Gwóźdź-Lasoń M., Miklaszewicz S., Pujer K., Unia Europejska i strefa euro. Doświadczenia i wyzwania ekonomiczne, techniczne, inżynieryjne [The European Union and the euro. Economic, technical and engineering experience and challenges], Warszawa 2017.

Hakenberg W., Nestoruk I. B., Prawo europejskie [European law], Warszawa 2012.

Haratsch A., Koenig Ch., Pechstein M., Europarecht, Tübingen 2006.

Hellmann V., Der Vertrag von Lissabon 2009. Vom Verfassungsvertrag zur Änderung der bestehenden Verträge – Einführung mit Synopse und Übersichten, Berlin 2009.

Kawalec S., Pytlarczyk E., Paradoks euro. Jak wyjść z pułapki wspólnej waluty [The paradox of the euro. How to escape the trap of the common currency], Warszawa 2016.

Lenaerts K., Van Nuffel P., Bray R., Constitutional Law of the European Union, London 2009.

Marciniak S., Makro- i mikroekonomia. Podstawowe problemy współczesności [Macro- and microeconomics. The main problems of modern times, Warszawa 2013.

Narodowy Bank Polski. Kryzys w strefie euro. Przyczyny, przebieg i perspektywy jego rozwiązania [National Bank of Poland. The euro area crisis. The causes, caourse and prospects for resolving it], Warszawa 2013.

Nowak-Far A., Finanse Unii Europejskiej: aspekty instytucjonalne i prawne [The European Union's finance: the institutional and legal aspects], Warszawa 2010.

Nowak-Far A., Pakt Stabilności i Wzrostu. Funkcje, działanie i przyszłość [The Stability and Growth Pact. The functions, functioning and future], Warszawa 2007.

Nowak-Far A., Unia Gospodarcza i Walutowa w Europie [The Economic and Monetary Union in Europe], Warszawa 2001.

Oręziak L., Euro. Nowy pieniądz [The new currency], Warszawa 2004.

Orłowski W.M., Optymalna ścieżka do euro [The optimal path towards the euro], Warszawa 2004.

Prawo Unii Europejskiej. Prawo materialne i polityki [European Union law. Substantive law and policies], J. Barcz (ed.), Warszawa 2006.

Prawo Unii Europejskiej. Zagadnienia systemowe [European Union law. System issues], J. Barcz (ed.), Warszawa 2006.

Principles of European Constitutional Law, A. von Bogdandy, J. Bast (eds.), Oxford 2010. Marchetti A., Demesmay C., Der Vertrag von Lissabon. Analyse und Bewertung, Baden-Baden 2010.

Ruszkowski J., Wojnicz L. (eds.), Multi-Level Governance w Unii Europejskiej [Multi-Level Governance in the European Union], Szczecin-Warszawa 2013.

Scheller H.K., Europejski Bank Centralny. Historia, rola i funkcje [The European Central Bank. The history, role and functions], Warszawa 2006.

Sinn H.-W., The Euro Trap. On Bursting Bubbles, Budgets, and Beliefs, Oxford 2017.

Ślusarczyk B., Ślusarczyk S., Podstawy mikro- i makroekonomii [The basics of micro- and macroeconomics], Lublin 2011.

System ochrony prawnej w Unii Europejskiej [The legal protection system in the European Union], A. Wyrozumska (ed.), Warszawa 2010.

The European Union: Origins – Structure – Acquis, W. Góralski, Sz. Kardaś (eds.), Warszawa 2008.

The Eurozone Crisis: A Consensus View of the Causes and a Few Possible Solutions, R. Baldwin, F. Giavazzi (eds.), London 2015.

Traktat z Lizbony. Główne reformy ustrojowe Unii Europejskiej [The Treaty of Lisbon. The main system reforms of the European Union], J. Barcz (ed.), Warszawa 2008.

Unia Europejska od Traktatów Rzymskich do Traktatu Lizbońskiego [The European Union from the Treaties of Rome to the Treaty of Lisbon], T. Wasilewski (ed.), Toruń 2008.

Ustrój Unii Europejskiej [The system of the European Union], J. Barcz (ed.), Vol. 1–2, Warszawa 2009.

Węc J.J., CDU/CSU wobec polityki niemieckiej Republiki Federalnej Niemiec [CDU/CSU and the policies pursued by the Federal Republic of Germany], Kraków 2000.

Węc J.J., Germany's Position on the System Reform of the European Union in 2002–2016, Berlin-Bern-Bruxelles-New York-Oxford-Warszawa Wien 2018.

Węc J.J., Pierwsza polska prezydencja w Unii Europejskiej. Uwarunkowania – Procesy decyzyjne – Osiągnięcia i niepowodzenia [The first Polish Presidency in the European Union. Conditions – Decision-making – Successes and failures], Kraków 2012.

Węc J.J., Spór o kształt ustrojowy Wspólnot Europejskich i Unii Europejskiej w latach 1950–2010. Między ideą ponadnarodowości a współpracą międzyrządową. Analiza politologiczna [The dispute over the constitutional status of the European Communities and the European Union in 1950–2010. Between the idea of supranationality and international cooperation], Kraków 2012.

Węc J.J., Traktat Lizboński. Polityczne aspekty reformy ustrojowej Unii Europejskiej w latach 2007–2015. Orzecznictwo sądów konstytucyjnych wybranych państw członkowskich UE oraz proces implementacji traktatu lizbońskiego [The political aspects of the system reform of the European Union in 2007–2015. The case-law of the constitutional courts of selected Member States of the EU and the implementation of the Lisbon Treaty], Kraków 2016.

Wouters J., Verhey L., Kiiver P., European Constitutionalism beyond Lisbon, Antwerp 2009.

Zasady ustrojowe Unii Europejskiej [The constitutional principles of the European Union], J. Barcz (ed.), Warszawa 2010.

3. Publications in Scientific Periodicals and Volumes

Adamski D„ Pakt fiskalny a prawo europejskie i polska konstytucja [The Fiscal Compact, European law and the Polish Constitution], 'Europejski Przegląd Sądowy', December 2013.

Afonso A., Huart F., Tovar Jalles J., Stanek P., Assessing the sustainability of external imbalances in the European Union, 'The World Economy', 2019.

Bainczyk M., Czy RFN może współtworzyć państwo europejskie? [Can the FRG co-create a European state?] 'Biuletyn Instytutu Zachodniego' 2022, no. 21.

Bainczyk M., Glosa do wyroku FTK z 5 maja 2020 r. w sprawie obligacji EBC [An opinion on the the BVerfG judgment of 5 May 2020 on ECB bonds], 'Studia Prawnicze: Rozprawy i Materiały' 2020, no. 2.

Beck T. and Peydró J.-L., Five Years of Crisis (Resolution) – Some Lessons, [in:] The Eurozone Crisis: A Consensus View of the Causes and a Few Possible Solutions, R. Baldwin and F. Giavazzi (eds.), London 2015.

Beck K., Why business cycles diverge? Structural evidence from the European Union, 'Journal of Economic Dynamics and Control', December 2021, Vol. 133.

Beck T., Banking union for Europe – risks and challenges, [in:] Banking union for Europe – risks and challenges, T. Beck (ed.), London 2012.

Beck T., Why the rush? Short-term crisis resolution and long-term bank stability, [in:] Banking union for Europe – risks and challenges, T. Beck (ed.), London 2012.

Bénassy-Quéré A., Ragot X., Which Fiscal Union for the euro area?, 'Bruegel Policy Contribution', February 2016.

Borsuk M., Klupa K., Europejski system gwarantowania depozytów (EDIS) jako trzeci filar unii bankowej i jego wpływ na państwa spoza strefy euro – perspektywa Polski [The European Deposit Insurance Scheme (EDIS) as the third pillar of the banking union and its influence on the non-euro area Member States – the perspective of Poland], 'Czasopismo Zarządzanie i Finanse – Journal of Management and Finance' 2017, no. 1.

Buch C.M., Weigert B., Legacy problems in transition to a banking union, [in:] Banking union for Europe – risks and challenges, T. Beck (ed.), London 2012.

Chamon M., The empowerment of agencies under the Meroni doctrine and article 114 TFEU: comment on United Kingdom v. Parliament and Council (short-selling) and the proposed Single Resolution Mechanism, 'European Law Review' 2014, no. 3.

Cichocki M., Europejski Mechanizm Stabilności – główne zasady działania i próba oceny [The European Stability Mechanism – the main principles of functioning and an attempt at assessment], 'International Journal of Management and Economics' 2013, no. 37.

Czekaj J., Kryzys strefy euro. Przyczyny, skutki, drogi wyjścia [The euro area crisis. The causes, consequences, ways out], 'Zarządzanie Publiczne' 2012, no. 3.

De Grauwe P., Design Failures of the Eurozone, [in:] The Eurozone Crisis: A Consensus View of the Causes and a Few Possible Solutions, R. Baldwin and F. Giavazzi (eds.), London 2015.

Europejski Bank Centralny – rozpoczęcie nadzorowania banków strefy euro przez Europejski Bank Centralny [The European Central Bank – The commencement of the supervision of euro area banks by the European Central Bank], 'Przegląd Spraw Europejskich' 2014, no. 11.

Frankel J., Causes of Eurozone Crises, [in:] The Eurozone Crisis: A Consensus View of the Causes and a Few Possible Solutions, R. Baldwin and F. Giavazzi (eds.), London 2015.

Globalizacja i regionalizacja w gospodarce światowej [Globalisation and regionalisation in the world economy], R. Orłowska, K. Żołądkiewicz (eds.), Warszawa 2012.

Górska-Szymczak J., Górski G., Orzeczenia ultra vires Trybunału Sprawiedliwości Unii Europejskiej i ich ocena w orzecznictwie niemieckiego Federalnego Trybunału Konstytucyjnego. Uwagi na marginesie orzeczenia z 5 maja 2020 r. [*Ultra vires* judgments of the Court of Justice of the European Union and their assessments in the case-law of the German Federal Constitutional Court. Remarks on the judgment of 5 May 2020], 'Przegląd Prawa Konstytucyjnego' 2021, no. 3.

Gros D., Busse M., The Macroeconomic Imbalance Procedure and Germany: When is a current account surplus an 'imbalance'? CEPS Policy Brief, 13 November 2013, no. 301, https://www.ceps.eu/ceps-publications/macroeconomic-imbalance-procedure-and-germany-when-current-account-surplus-imbalance/, [accessed: 10 January 2023].

Janoś K., Kubera J., W stronę kompromisu? Stan francusko-niemieckich rozmów o strefie euro [Towards a compromise? The status of Franco–German talks on the euro area], 'Biuletyn Instytutu Zachodniego', 2018, no. 345.

Janus J.. Zmiany struktury instytucjonalnej strefy euro a skuteczność polityki pieniężnej Europejskiego Banku Centralnego [Changes in the institutional structure of the euro area and the effectiveness of the monetary policy of the European Central Bank], [in:] Przyszły instytucjonalny kształt strefy euro [The future institutional shape of the euro area], A. Wojtyna (ed.), Warszawa 2015.

Jurkowska-Zeidler A., Europejski System Gwarantowania Depozytów: trzeci brakujący filar do dokończenia Unii Bankowej [The European Deposit Insurance Scheme: the third missing pillar for completing the Banking Union], 'Annales Universitatis Marie Curie-Sklodowska Lublin – Polonia'. Sectio H, 2016, Vol. L 4.

Jurkowska-Zeidler A., Fundamentalne zmiany regulacji i nadzoru jednolitego rynku finansowego Unii Europejskiej w ramach Unii Bankowej [The fundamental changes to the regulations applicable to and supervision of the single financial market of the European Union within the Banking Union], 'Gdańskie Studia Prawnicze' 2015, Vol. XXXIII.

Kabat-Rudnicka D., Traktat o stabilności, koordynacji i zarządzaniu w Unii Gospodarczej i Walutowej – Analiza krytyczna [The Treaty on Stability, Coordination and Governance in the Economic and Monetary Union – A critical analysis], 'Krakowskie Studia Międzynarodowe' 2012, no. 3.

Kalka P., Czy w strefie euro występuje jeszcze kryzys? [Is the euro area still in crisis?], 'Przegląd Zachodni' 2017, no. 2.

Kawalec M., Wpływ kryzysu finansowego na możliwość wprowadzenia federalizmu fiskalnego w strefie euro [The effects of the financial crisis on the possibility to introduce fiscal federalism in the euro area], 'Zeszyty Naukowe Uniwersytetu Ekonomicznego w Krakowie' 2017, no. 9.

Kirch A.-L., D.Schwarzer D., Die Ratifizierung des Fiskalpakts und des ESM in den Ländern der Eurozone – rechtliche und politische Rahmenbedingungen, Arbeitspapier der Forschungsgruppe 1, 2012, Nr. 2.

Klucznik M., Marczewski K., An EU of convergence or divisions? The European economy 30 years after the Treaty of Maastricht, Polish Economic Institute, Warsaw 2022.

Koczor M., Proces wzmacniania Unii Gospodarczej i Walutowej w kontekście kryzysu w strefie euro [The process of strengthening the Economic and Monetary Union in the context of the euro area crisis], 'Politeja' 2015, no. 5.

Koleśnik J., Europejska unia bankowa – nowy wymiar ryzyka systemowego [The European banking union – a new dimension of systemic risk], 'Problemy Zarządzania' 2013, no. 2.

Komisja Europejska – początek prac nad projektem unii rynków kapitałowych [The European Commission – the start of work on the proposed establishment of a Capital Markets Union], 'Przegląd Spraw Europejskich' 2015, no. 1.

Komisja Europejska – publikacja *Planu działania na rzecz tworzenia unii rynków kapitałowych* [The European Commission – the publication of the *Action Plan on Building a Capital Markets Union*], 'Przegląd Spraw Europejskich' 2015, no. 8–9.

Komisja Europejska – sprawa przeciwko Polsce w związku z niewdrożeniem przepisów unijnych dotyczących systemów gwarancji depozytów [The European Commission – Action against Poland for failure to implement EU provisions on deposit guarantee schemes], 'Przegląd Spraw Europejskich' 2016, no. 5.

Komisja Europejska. Biała Księga dotycząca przyszłości UE [The European Commission. The White Paper on the Future of Europe], 'Przegląd Spraw Europejskich' 2017, no. 3.

Komisja Europejska. Pakiet dokumentów dotyczących pogłębiania unii gospodarczej i walutowej [The European Commission. The package of documents on the deepening of the Economic and Monetary Union], 'Przegląd Spraw Europejskich', grudzień 2017 r. – styczeń 2018 r. [December 2017 – January 2018].

Kozłowska J., Polityka Europejskiego Banku Centralnego w dobie kryzysu finansowego [The policy of the European Central Bank in the days of the financial crisis], 'Zeszyty Naukowe Firma i Rynek' 2015, no. 1.

Kunstein T., W. Wessels W., Die Europäische Union in der Währungskrise. Eckdaten und Schlüsselentscheidungen, 'Integration' 2011, H. 4.

Latoszek E., Sacharski K., Instrumenty zarządzania kryzysem w obszarze polityki budżetowej w unii gospodarczej i walutowej [The crisis management instruments for budgetary policies in the Economic and Monetary Union], 'Studia Europejskie' 2013, no. 3.

Linder I., Stubits M., A Constitutional Treaty for an Enlarged Union. Are there Fundamental Changes for EMU?, 'Proceedings of OeNB Workshops', 5 November 2004, no. 4.

Mik C., Opinia prawna dotycząca orzeczenia Federalnego Trybunału Konstytucyjnego RFN w przedmiocie pierwszeństwa prawa UE [A legal opinion on the judgment by the Germany's Federal Constitutional Court with regard to the primacy of EU law], 'Zeszyty Prawnicze' 2020, no. 3.

Misiak M., Pakt Stabilności i Wzrostu w dobie kryzysu fiskalnego w Unii Europejskiej [The Stability and Growth Pact in the days of the fiscal crisis in the European Union], 'Acta Universitatis Lodziensis' 2010, Folia Oeconomica 238.

Molendowski E., Stanek P., Globalny kryzys finansowo-gospodarczy i strefy euro a sytuacja fiskalna nowych państw członkowskich (UE-10) [The global and euro area financial and economic crisis and the fiscal situations of the new

Member States (EU-10)], 'Acta Universitatis Lodziensis'. Folia Oeconomica, 2012, no. 273.

Moszyński M., Niedopasowania na niemieckim rynku pracy w świetle reform Hartza [Mismatches in the German labour market in the light of the Hartz reforms], [in:] Ekonomiczne problemy funkcjonowania współczesnego świata [Economic issues in the functioning of the modern world], D. Kopycińska (ed.), Szczecin 2009.

Müller-Brandeck-Bocquet G., Deutschland – Europas einizige Führungsmacht?, 'Aus Politik und Zeitgeschichte' 2012, B 10.

Mundell R., A Theory of Optimum Currency Areas, 'The American Economic Review' 1961, no. 4.

Narodowy Bank Polski. Kryzys w strefie euro. Przyczyny, przebieg i perspektywy jego rozwiązania [National Bank of Poland. The crisis in the euro area. The causes, course and prospects for resolving it], Warszawa 2013.

Nicoll W., Salmon T.C., Zrozumieć Unię Europejską, translated by S. Barkowski, Warszawa 2002.

Nowak-Far A., Funkcjonowanie rynku wewnętrznego Unii Europejskiej – wyzwania dla Polski [The functioning of the internal market of the European Union – the challenges facing Poland], [in:] Polska w Unii Europejskiej. Nowe wyzwania [Poland in the European Union. New challenges], J. Barcz, S. Domaradzki, R. Kuligowski, M. Szewczyk, E. Szklarczyk-Amati (eds.), Warszawa 2018.

Nowak-Far A., Narzędzia Unii Europejskiej w przeciwdziałaniu skutkom światowego kryzysu finansowego [The European Union's tools for mitigating the consequences of the global financial crisis], [in:] Unia Europejska wobec kryzysu ekonomicznego [The European Union in the face of the economic crisis], J. Osiński (ed.), Warszawa 2009.

Oręziak L., Finanse publiczne w krajach strefy euro – skuteczność mechanizmów dyscyplinujących politykę budżetową [Public finances of the euro area countries – the effectiveness of mechanisms aimed to discipline fiscal policy], [in:] Euro – ekonomia i polityka [The euro – economics and politics], D. Rosati (ed.), Warszawa 2009.

Oręziak L., Reforma Paktu Stabilności i Wzrostu i jej potencjalne konsekwencje [The reform of the Stability and Growth Pact and its potential consequences], 'Bank i Kredyt', July 2005.

Orłowski W.M., Stabilność finansowa Unii Europejskiej: czy potrzebne są kolejne reformy? [The financial stability of the European Union: are further reforms necessary?], 'Studia BAS' 2021, no. 3.

Pietrzykowski M., Polska na drodze do reformowanej strefy euro [Poland on the way towards the euro area under reform], Poznań 2014.

Pluciński E. M., Euroland: kryzys fiskalny czy fundamentalny. Wybrane aspekty z perspektywy paradygmatu ekonomii integracji oraz kryzysu globalnej gospodarki towarowo-pieniężnej [Euroland: a fiscal crisis or a fundamental crisis. Selected aspects from the perspective of the paradigm of integration economics and the crisis in the global merchandise and monetary economy], [in:] Globalizacja i regionalizacja w gospodarce światowej, Księga jubileuszowa Profesora Jana Rymarczyka [Globalisation and regionalisation in the world economy. Professor Jan Rymarczyk Anniversary Volume], B. Skulska, M. Domiter, W. Michalczyk (eds.), Wrocław 2012.

Płóciennik S., Granice integracji. Niemiecka blokada finalizacji unii bankowej [The limits of integration. Germany's blocking the completion of the banking union], Analizy OSW, 24 June 2022, https://www.osw.waw.pl/, [accessed: 22 July 2022].

Poliński R., Problemy strefy euro [The euro area issues], Nowy Dwór Mazowiecki-Warszawa 2017.

Popławski K., Kształt unii bankowej potwierdza uprzywilejowaną pozycję Berlina w strefie euro [The shape of the banking union confirms Berlin's privileged position in the euro area], Komentarze OSW, 10 January 2014.

Prawda M., Iść wolniej, a w każdym razie inaczej. Jak zbudować opowieść o Unii po pandemii? [Proceeding at a slower pace or, in any event, following a different path. How to build a tale of the Union after the pandemic?], 'Rocznik Integracji Europejskiej' 2021.

Rada Europejska – oświadczenie przywódców państw strefy euro [The European Council – the Euro Summit statement], 'Przegląd Spraw Europejskich' 2014, no. 10.

Rada Unii Europejskiej – Posiedzenie Rady Ecofin 12 lutego 2016 r. Wdrażanie Unii Bankowej [The Council of the European Union – Ecofin Council meeting of 12 February 2016. Implementation of the Banking Union], 'Przegląd Spraw Europejskich' 2016, no. 2.

Rada Unii Europejskiej – Posiedzenie Rady Ecofin 25 maja 2016 r. Postępy we wdrażaniu Unii Bankowej [The Council of the European Union – Ecofin Council meeting of 25 May 2016. Progress on the implementation of the Banking Union], 'Przegląd Spraw Europejskich' 2016, no. 5.

Rada Unii Europejskiej. Posiedzenie Rady Ecofin 6 grudnia 2016 r. Postępy we wdrażaniu Unii Bankowej [The Council of the European Union – Ecofin Council meeting of 6 December 2016. Progress on the implementation of the Banking Union], 'Przegląd Spraw Europejskich' 2016, no. 12.

Rosińska-Bukowska M., Kryzys w strefie euro – wybrane aspekty makro- i mikroekonomiczne [The crisis in the euro area – selected macro- and microeconomic aspects], 'Acta Universitatis Lodziensis'. Folia Oeconomica 2012, no. 273.

Rosińska-Bukowska M., Kryzys w strefie euro – wybrane aspekty makro- i mikroekonomiczne [The euro area crisis – selected macro- and microeconomic aspects], 'Acta Universitatis Lodziensis' 2012, Folia Oeconomica 273.

Rymarczyk J., Antykryzysowe reformy w Europejskiej Unii Gospodarczej i Walutowej [Anti-crisis reforms in the European Economic and Monetary Union], 'Prace Naukowe Uniwersytetu Ekonomicznego we Wrocławiu', 2017, no. 498.

Schoenmaker D. Banking union: Where we're going wrong, [in:] T. Beck (ed.), Banking Union for Europe. Risks and Challenges, Centre for Economic Policy Research, London 2012.

Sporek T., Rozwój strefy euro z perspektywy wybranych państw – wnioski i konsekwencje dla UE [The development of the euro area from the points of view of selected countries – the conclusions and consequences for the EU], 'Studia Europejskie' 2015, no. 2.

Starzyk K., Załamanie międzynarodowej równowagi płatniczej jako przyczyna światowego kryzysu gospodarczego [The collapse of international payment equilibrium as a cause of the global economic crisis], [in:] Globalizacja i regionalizacja w gospodarce światowej, Księga jubileuszowa Profesora Jana Rymarczyka, B. Skulska, M. Domiter, W. Michalczyk (eds.), Wrocław 2012.

Strzałkowski M., Emmanuel Macron przedstawił swój pomysł na UE [Emmanuel Macron has presented his idea to the EU], EURACTIV, 26 September 2017.

Trzcińska A., Europejski Mechanizm Stabilności jako stabilizator w planowanej unii finansowej [The European Stability Mechanism as a stabiliser in the planned financial union], 25 March 2013, https://www.nbp.pl/, [accessed: 20 July 2022].

Waliszewski K., Unia bankowa i unia rynków kapitałowych – analiza porównawcza europejskich projektów integracyjnych w obszarze finansowym [The banking union and the capital markets union – a comparative analysis of European integration proposals for the financial sector], 'Nauki o Finansach. Financial Sciences', 2015, no. 2.

Walkowski M., Europa w kryzysie gospodarczym i finansowym: casus Grecji [Europe in economic and financial crisis: the case of Greece], [in:] Globalizacja i regionalizacja w gospodarce światowej, Księga jubileuszowa Profesora Jana Rymarczyka, B. Skulska, M. Domiter, W. Michalczyk (eds.), Wrocław 2012.

Węc J.J., Debata w Niemczech na temat drugiej reformy ustrojowej Unii Europejskiej (2011–2012). Ewolucja programowa niemieckich partii politycznych w polityce europejskiej [The German debate on the second system reform of the European Union (2011–2012). The programme development of the German political parties in European politics], [in:] Dylematy strategiczne XXI wieku. Księga Jubileuszowa dedykowana Profesorowi Michałowi Chorośnickiemu z okazji czterdziestolecia pracy naukowej [The strategic dilemmas of the 21st century. The Professor Michał Chorośnicki Anniversary Volume honouring 40 years of his research work], B. Szlachta, J.J. Węc (eds.), Kraków 2013.

Węc J.J., Debata w Unii Europejskiej na temat drugiej reformy ustrojowej (2011–2012) [The debate in the European Union on the second system reform (2011–2012)], 'Przegląd Zachodni' 2013, no. 1.

Węc J.J., Die politische Debatte zur zweiten Systemreform der Europäischen Union in Deutschland (2011–2012), 'Zeitschrift des Verbandes Polnischer Germanisten' 2014, H. 2.

Węc J.J., Dynamika reformy ustrojowej strefy euro w latach 2012–2016 [The dynamics of the system reform of the euro area in 2012–2016], 'Politeja' 2016, no. 6.

Węc J.J., Kryzys zadłużeniowy w strefie euro w latach 2010–2018. Geneza, dynamika oraz instrumenty jego przezwyciężenia [The euro area debt crisis in 2010–2018. The origin, dynamics and tools for overcoming it], 'Politeja' 2020, no. 3.

Węc J.J., Niemcy wobec reformy ustrojowej strefy euro [Germany and the system reform of the euro area], 'Roczniki Nauk Społecznych' 2016, no. 3.

Węc J.J., Normatywna działalność Unii Europejskiej w walce z kryzysem zadłużeniowym strefy euro [The normative activities of the European Union in the fight against the euro area debt crisis], [in:] Integracja europejska. Główne obszary badawcze [European integration. The main research areas], K. Wojtaszczyk, J. Tymanowski, P. Stawarz (eds.), Warszawa 2015.

Węc J.J., Nowe zasady sprawowania prezydencji w Radzie Unii Europejskiej. Bilans prezydencji belgijskiej [New rules for presiding the Council of the European Union. Taking stock of the Belgian Presidency], 'Przegląd Zachodni' 2011, no. 3.

Węc J.J., Perspektywy reformy ustrojowej strefy euro do 2025 r. Aspekty instytucjonalno-prawne [Prospects for the system reform of the euro area by 2025. The institutional and legal aspects], [in:] Unia Europejska w turbulentnym świecie: 30 lat Traktatu z Maastricht [The European Union in a turbulent world: 30 years after the Maastricht Treaty], J. M. Fiszer, T. Stępniewski (eds.), Lublin – Warszawa 2022.

Węc J.J., Perspektywy zmian ustrojowych w Unii Europejskiej do 2025 r. Implikacje dla Polski [The prospects for system changes in the European Union by 2025. Implications for Poland], 'Przegląd Zachodni' 2018, no. 1.

Węc J.J., Podstawowe założenia, cele i zasady reformy ustrojowej strefy euro. Implikacje dla Polski [The main assumptions, objectives and principles of the system reform of the euro area. Implications for Poland], 'Krakowskie Studia Międzynarodowe' 2016, no. 1.

Węc J.J., Polityczno-prawne aspekty procesu konstytuowania oraz reformy Unii Gospodarczej i Walutowej. Od planu Wernera do traktatu konstytucyjnego (1970–2004) [The political and legal aspects of the proces of constituting and reforming the Economic and Monetary Union. From the Werner Plan to the Constitutional Treaty], 'Politeja' 2009, no. 12.

Węc J.J., Proces konstytuowania Unii Bankowej. Geneza, podstawy prawne, cele i zasady działania [The process of establishing the Banking Union. The origin, legal bases, objectives and principles of functioning], 'Rocznik Integracji Europejskiej' 2014.

Węc J.J., Prospects for the System Reform of the European Union by 2025: Implications for Poland, 'Przegląd Zachodni' 2019, Special Issue.

Węc J.J., Relacje polsko-niemieckie w Unii Europejskiej i NATO na początku XXI w. Próba bilansu [Poland–Germany relations in the European Union and NATO at the beginning of the 21st century. An attempt at taking stock], 'Prace Komisji Środkowoeuropejskiej PAU', 2015, Vol. XXIII.

Węc J.J., The European Union at a historic turning point. Current challenges and scenarios of overcoming them, [in:] European Integration – Polish Perspective, Z. Czachór, T.G. Grosse, W. Paruch (eds.), Warszawa 2020.

Węc J.J., The European Union Debate on the Second Institutional Reform (2011–2012), 'Przegląd Zachodni' 2014, no. 1.

Węc J.J., Unia Europejska na historycznym zakręcie. Bieżące wyzwania i scenariusze ich przezwyciężenia [The European Union at a historic turning point. Current challenges and scenarios of overcoming them], [in:] Integracja europejska – polska perspektywa [European integration – Poland's perspective], Z. Czachór, T.G. Grosse, W. Paruch (eds.), Warszawa 2018.

Węc J.J., Wpływ rządów Merkel na reformę ustrojową Unii Europejskiej i strefy euro [The influence of Merkel's government on the system reform of the European Union and the euro area], [in:] Interesy – Wartości – Kompromisy. Polityka zagraniczna Niemiec w erze Angeli Merkel [Interests – Values – Compromises. Germany's foreign policy in the era of Angela Merkel], K. Janoś, A. Kałabunowska, J. Kiwerska, T. Morozowski (eds.), Poznań 2022.

Woźnicki T., Współpraca międzyparlamentarna w świetle art. 13. Traktatu o stabilności, koordynacji i zarządzaniu w Unii Gospodarczej i Walutowej [Interparliamentary cooperation in the light of Article 13 of the Treaty on Stability, Coordination and Governance in the Economic and Monetary Union], 'Przegląd Europejski' 2015, no. 3.

Wyplosz Ch., Banking union as a crisis-management tool, [in:] Banking union for Europe – risks and challenges, T. Beck (ed.), London 2012.

Zielińska K., Drogi do unii bankowej – reformy systemu regulacji systemu bankowego [The ways towards the banking union – reforming the regulatory system for the banking system], 'Ekonomia Międzynarodowa' 2013, Issue 4.

Żukrowska K., Globalne następstwa kryzysu – próba oceny i prognozy [The global implications of the crisis – an attempt at assessment and forecast], [in:] Wybrane aspekty z perspektywy paradygmatu ekonomii integracji oraz kryzysu globalnej gospodarki towarowo-pieniężnej, [in:] Globalizacja i regionalizacja w gospodarce światowej, Księga jubileuszowa Profesora Jana Rymarczyka, B. Skulska, M. Domiter, W. Michalczyk (eds.), Wrocław 2012.

4. Internet Publications

Alcidi C., Gros D., Ferrer J.N., Rinaldi D., The Instruments Providing Macro-Financial Support to EU Member States, CEPS. Research Report, 2017, no. 6, March 2017, https://www.ceps.eu/wp-content/uploads/2017/03/RRpt%20No%202017-06%20MacroFinSupport%20to%20MSs_0.pdf, [accessed: 20 July 2022].

Bankowy Fundusz Gwarancyjny, Przymusowa restrukturyzacja w pytaniach i odpowiedziach [Bank Guarantee Fund. Resolution in questions and answers], https://www.bfg.pl/, [accessed: 22 July 2022].

Będkowski-Kozioł M., Status i zadania Europejskiej Agencji Kolejowej – stan obecny i perspektywy w świetle projektu IV pakietu kolejowego UE [The status and tasks of the European Railway Agency – the current state and prospects in the light of the legislative proposals for a fourth railway package], 'internetowy Kwartalnik Antymonopolowy i Regulacyjny', 2014, no. 7, www.ikar.wz.uw.edu.pl, [accessed: 22 July 2022].

Berger R., Czy zmieniać niemiecki model gospodarczy [Should the German economic model be changed], 'Rzeczpospolita', 28 January 2014, p. B11, http://www.rp.pl, [accessed: 22 July 2022].

Bielecki J., Po wyborach w Niemczech reforma strefy euro Macrona jest martwa [Following the federal election in Germany, Macron's reform of the euro area is dead], 25 September 2017, http//:www.rp.pl, [accessed: 22 July 2022].

Bundesministerium der Finanzen. Europäische Finanzhilfen im Überblick (Stand 31. Dezember 2018), Deutscher Gewährleistungsrahmen nach Stabilisierungs mechanismusgesetz, http://www.Bundesfinanzministerium/de/, [accessed: 2 July 2019].

Bundestagswahl 2017. Das Endergebnis und die Ergebnisse in jedem Bundesland, https://www.merkur.de/, [accessed: 18 May 2018].

Bundesverband deutscher Banken, Europäische Einlagensicherung, 25. November 2015, https://bankenverband.de/, [accessed: 18 May 2022].

BVerfG. Pressemitteilung Nr. 38/2021. Erfolglose Vollstreckungsanträge zum Urteil des Zweiten Senats zu dem PSPP-Anleihekaufprogramm der EZB, Karlsruhe, 18. Mai 2021, https://www.bundesverfassungsgericht.de/, [accessed: 22 July 2022].

Der Bundespräsident. Ausfertigung der Gesetze zum 'Euro-Rettungsschirm', Berlin, 13. September 2012, https://www.bundespraesident.de/SharedDocs/Pressemitteilungen/DE/2012/09/120913-Rettungsschirm.html/, [accessed: 20 July 2022].

EFSF-ESM. Überblick über die europäischen Finanzhilfen, hrsg. vom Bundesministerium der Finanzen. Stand 31. Dezember 2018, https://www.bundesfinanzministerium.de/, [accessed: 2 July 2019].

Eksperci: Model ekonomiczny Niemiec nie jest dobry dla całej strefy euro [Experts: the German economic model is not good for the whole euro area], PAP, 24 October 2014, interia.pl, [accessed: 2 July 2019].

ESM und Fiskalpakt: Bundesverfassungsgericht entscheidet über Eilklagen, 'Augsburger Allgemeine', 3. Juli 2012, https://www.augsburger-allgemeine.de/, [accessed: 20 July 2022].

EU riskiert bei Einlagensicherung offenen Streit mit Berlin, Euractiv, 25. November 2015. Schäuble warnt vor "falschen Anreizen" durch EU-Einlagensicherung, 'Handelsblatt', 24. November 2015, https://www.handelsblatt.com/de/, [accessed: 20 July 2022].

Europäische Einlagensicherung. Schäuble will Sparer nicht versichern, 'Die Tageszeitung' 25. November 2015, p. 1, https://taz.de/, [accessed: 20 July 2022].

European Central Bank in the days of the crisis], 2012, https://www.law.muni.cz/sborniky/, [accessed: 21 October 2022].

European Council. Report by President of the European Council Herman Van Rompuy. Towards a genuine Economic and Monetary Union. Press release, Brussels, 26 June 2012, EUCO 120/12,

Ferber M., Verfassungsklagen verzögern den Euro-Rettungsfonds, 'Augsburger Allgemeine', 1. Juli 2012, https://www.augsburger-allgemeine.de/, [accessed: 20 July 2022].

Fischer J., Europa steht in Flammen, 'Süddeutsche Zeitung', 4. Juni 2012, http://www.sueddeutsche.de/, [accessed: 20 July 2022].

Giegerich Th., Ende gut, alles gut? – Europäische Kommission stellt Vertragsverletzungsverfahren gegen Deutschland wegen des Karlsruher PSPP-Urteils ein, 3. Dezember 2021, https://jean-monnet-saar.eu/, [accessed: 30 September 2022].

Grosse T.G., Reformy antykryzysowe czy zmiana kierunku integracji europejskiej? Ocena skutków szczytu UE 8–9 grudnia 2011 r. [Anti-crisis reforms or a reorientation of European integration? An assessment of the results of the EU summit of 8–9 December 2011], Brief programowy Instytutu Kościuszki, https://ik.org.pl/, [accessed: 20 July 2022].

Heiner Flassbeck o tym, dlaczego uczciwość i pracowitość szkodzą [Heiner Flassbeck speaks of why honesty and diligence do harm]. Interview by Żakowski with Flassbeck, 9 July 2013, https://www.polityka.pl/, [accessed: 20 July 2022].

Hollenbeck F., Germany's "Dangerous" Current Account Surplus, 20 November 2013, https://mises.org/library/germanys-dangerous-current-account-surp lus, [accessed: 20 July 2022].

Ifo-Berechnung: Deutschland hat weltweit höchsten Exportüberschuss, Info, 2. Februar 2015, http://www.spiegel.de/, [accessed: 20 July 2022].

Krebs T., Scheffel M., Reforma niemieckiego rynku pracy. Niepopularny sukces [The reform of the German labour market. An unpopular success], 24 September 2013 https://www.obserwatorfinansowy.pl/, [accessed: 20 July 2022].

Kröger M., Europäische Einlagensicherung: Haften deutsche Sparer nun für die Banken der Krisenländer?, 25. November 2015, http://www.spiegel.de/, [accessed: 18 May 2022].

Legrain Ph., Euro-Zone Fiscal Colonialism, 'The New York Times', April 21, 2014, https://www.nytimes.com/2014/04/22/opinion/euro-zone-fiscal-colo nialism.html, [accessed: 20 July 2022].

Matzke M., Nagana dla prymusa. KE gani wysokie nadwyżki eksportowe Niemiec [The top performer reprimanded. The European Commission reproaches Germany for high export surpluses], http://www.dw.de, [accessed: 2 July 2019].

Möbert J., Deutschlands Leistungsbilanz: Das Ende der Kritik, https://www.dbr esearch.de/, [accessed: 2 October 2022].

Mussler W., Währungsunion: Juncker sucht Konflikt mit Schäuble, 15. Dezember 2015, http://www.faz.net/de/, [accessed: 22 July 2022].

Najważniejsze rezultaty prac prezydencji Polski w Radzie Unii Europejskiej. Komunikat prasowy, 22 grudnia 2011 r. [The most important results of the work of the Polish Presidency at the European Council. Press release, 22 December 2011], http://www.pl2011.eu, [accessed: 20 July 2022].

Neuhaus A., Wie die Finanzkrise in Deutschland ankam, 'Handelsblatt', 29. Juli 2017, https://www. handelsblatt.com/finanzen/banken-versicherungen/de/, [accessed: 20 July 2022].

Pakt Euro Plus z Polską [The Euro Plus Pact with Poland], EURACTIV, 28 March 2011, http://www.for.org.pl/, [accessed: 20 July 2022].

Piotrowski J., Strategia Lizbońska. Przyczyny niepowodzenia [The Lisbon Strategy. The causes of failure], Unia Europejska.pl, 2012, no. 1, [accessed: 20 July 2022].

Poliński R., Strefa euro. Kryzys i reformy [The euro area. The crisis and reforms], 2017, www.pte.pl/, [accessed: 22 December 2019].

Polski bank bezkarnie skonfiskował pieniądze klientów [A Polish bank confiscated its customers' money and got away with it], https://rekinfinansow.pl/, [accessed: 20 July 2022].

Schulz S., Kritik der EU-Kommission: Phantomstreit um Deutschlands Exporte, 5. März 2014, http://www.spiegel.de/, [accessed: 20 July 2022].

Sievers M., Verfassungsgericht vor seiner schwersten Entscheidung, 'Frankfurter Rundschau', 10. Juli 2012, p. 1, https://www.fr.de/, [accessed: 20 July 2022].

Singer K.G., Eurozone: Leistungsbilanz-Saldo auf Rekordhoch, http://www.timepatternanalysis.de/, [accessed: 20 July 2022].

Single Resolution Board. Single Resolution Fund, https://www.srb.europa.eu/en/content/single-resolution-fund, [accessed: 28 July 2022].

Single Resolution Mechanism, https://www.consilium.europa.eu/en/, [accessed: 28 July 2022].

Strategia Lizbońska. Droga do sukcesu zjednoczonej Europy [Towards the success of a united Europe], Departament Analiz Ekonomicznych i Społecznych Urzędu Komitetu Integracji Europejskiej [2001], https://www.slaskie.pl/, [accessed: 20 July 2022].

Sudak I., Jest porozumienie na szczycie UE. Wielka Brytania stawia się poza Unią [The EU summit has reached an agreement. The United Kingdom placing itself outside the EU], 'Gazeta Wyborcza', 9 December 2011, https://wyborcza.pl/, [accessed: 20 July 2022].

Zachariasz K., Czechy, Szwecja, Wielka Brytania, Węgry – kto się waha i dlaczego? [The Czech Republic, Sweden, the United Kingdom, Hungary – who is hesitating and why?], 'Gazeta Wyborcza', 9 December 2011, https://wyborcza.pl/, [accessed: 20 July 2022].

Żółciak T., 30 lat traktatu o UE. Różnice rozwojowe między krajami znów zaczęły się pogłębiać [30 years of the Treaty on EU. Development disparities between countries have started to widen again], 7 February 2022, https://www.gazetaprawna.pl/, [accessed: 20 July 2022].

Zürcher B., Exportweltmeister Deutschland mit Rückenwind, 27. März 2012, http://www.oekonomenstimme.org/de/, [accessed: 20 July 2022].

Name Index

Adamski, D. 107
Afonso, A. 95
Alcidi, C. 47–48, 65

Bainczyk, M. 62
Baldwin, R. 14, 18
Barcz, J. 16–19, 82, 85, 87
Barkowski, S. 23
Barroso, J. M. 109
Bast, J. 16–17
Beck, K. 32
Beck, T. 14, 18, 31, 124–125
Będkowski-Kozioł, M. 178
Bénassy-Quéré, A. 18
Berger, R. 41, 43
Bieber, R. 17
Bielecki, J. 187
Bień, A. 32
Borsuk, M. 115, 159–160
Bray, R. 16–17
Buch, C.M. 124
Busse, M. 45

Chalmers, D. 17
Chamon, M. 178
Chorośnicki, M. 66
Christiansen, Th. 17–18
Cichocki, M. 87
Currie, S. 17
Czachór, Z. 46, 171
Czekaj, J. 14, 31
Cziomer, E. 38

De Grauwe, P. 14, 31–32
Demesmay, C. 16–17
Dijsselbloem, J. 141
Domaradzki, S. 19
Domiter, M. 33–34, 50, 52
Donohoe, P. 203–204, 212
Dougan, M. 17
Draghi, M. 56–58, 109, 141

Eilmansberger, T. 17–18
Epiney, A. 17

Ferber, M. 86
Ferrer, J.N. 47–48, 65
Fischer, J. 41–42
Fiszer, J. M. 200
Flassbeck, H. 39–41
Frankel, J. 14, 31
Frenz, W. 16

Gauck, J. 86
Gawlikowska-Hueckel, K. 19
Giavazzi, F. 14, 18
Giegerich, Th. 64
Góralski, W. 17
Górska-Szymczak, J. 62
Górski, G. 62
Götz, M. 31
Griller, S. 17–18
Grodzicki, M. 32
Gros, D. 45, 47–48, 65
Grosse, T.G. 46, 102, 171
Gruszczyński, M. 31
Gwóźdź-Lasoń, M. 32, 147, 183, 185

Haag, M. 17
Hakenberg, W. 16
Haratsch, A. 17
Hartz, P. 40
Hellmann, V. 17–18
Hill, J. 189

Hollande, F. 110
Hollenbeck, F. 43
Huart, F. 95

Janoś, K. 43, 187
Janus, J. 57
Juncker, J. -C. 109, 141, 147–148, 163, 170–171, 186-187, 192-193
Jurkowska-Zeidler, A. 14, 31, 115, 118, 121, 166

Kabat-Rudnicka, D. 107
Kałabunowska, A. 43
Kalka, P. 33, 57
Kardaś, Sz. 17
Kawalec, M. 98
Kawalec, S. 19, 32, 39, 42–43, 184–185
Kenen, P. 31
Kiiver, P. 17–18
Kirch, A.- L. 86
Kiwerska, J. 43
Klucznik, M. 23, 73
Klupa, K. 115, 159–160
Koczor, M. 23–24, 97
Koenig, Ch. 17
Koleśnik, J. 14, 31, 118, 166
Kopycińska, D. 40
Kozłowska, J. 109
Krebs, T. 40
Kröger, M. 189–190
Kubera, J. 187
Kuligowski, R. 19
Kunstein, T. 14, 31

Latoszek, E. 26, 27
Legrain, Ph. 38
Lenaerts, K. 16, 17
Leszczyna, I. 119
Linder, I. 29

Macron, E. 171, 186–187, 192–193
Marchetti, A. 16, 17
Marciniak, S. 31
Marczewski, K. 23, 73
Matzke, M. 45
Mayer, F. C. 188
McKinnon, R. I. 31
Merkel, A. 38–39, 41–43, 102, 110, 187, 193
Michalczyk, W. 33–34, 50, 52
Mik, C. 62
Miklaszewicz, S. 32, 147, 183, 185
Misiak, M. 26–27
Möbert, J. 44–45
Molendowski, E. 69
Monti, M. 56
Morozowski, T. 43
Moszyński, M. 40
Müller-Brandeck-Bocquet, G. 38
Mundell, R. 31, 32
Mussler, W. 190

Nestoruk, I. B. 16
Neuhaus, A. 33
Nicoll, W. 23
Nowak-Far, A. 18, 19, 27, 29

Obwexer, W. (Hrsg.) 17, 18
Oppermann, T. 16
Oręziak, L. 19, 23, 27
Orłowska, R. 23
Orłowski, W.M. 14, 19, 23, 29
Osiński, J. 19

Paruch, W. 46, 171
Pechstein, M. 17
Peydró, J.- L. 14, 31
Pietrzykowski, M. 14, 31
Piotrowski, J. 40
Płóciennik, S. 204
Pluciński, E. M. 33
Poliński, R. 14, 27, 31, 33, 96
Popławski, K. 113
Prawda, M. 200, 204

Pujer, K. 32, 147, 183, 185
Pytlarczyk, E. 19, 32, 39, 42–43, 184–185

Ragot, X. 18
Reh, Ch. 17–18
Reichenbach, H. 49
Reynders, D. 110
Rinaldi, D. 47–48, 65
Rosati, D. 23
Rosińska-Bukowska, M. 14, 31, 33, 51, 53–56
Ruszkowski, J. 178
Rutte, M. 193
Rymarczyk, J. 33–34, 50, 52, 185

Sacharski, K. 26, 27
Salmon, T.C. 23
Samaras, A. 50
Sarkozy, N. 102
Schäuble, W. 110, 188–190
Scheffel, M. 40
Scheller, H.K. 57
Schoenmaker, D. 205
Schröder, G. 39–43
Schulz, M. 141
Schulz, S. 43, 45
Schwarzer, D. 86
Sievers, M. 86
Sikorski, R. 110
Singer, K.G. 41, 43
Sinn, H.- W. 41
Skulska, B. 33–34, 50, 52
Ślusarczyk, B. 31
Ślusarczyk, S. 31
Sporek, T. 34
Stanek, P. 69, 95
Starzyk, K. 34
Stawarz, P. 46
Stępniewski, T. 200
Strzałkowski, M. 186
Stubits, M. 29
Sudak, I. 102
Szewczyk, M. 19
Szklarczyk-Amati, E. 19
Szlachta, B. 66

Tomkins, A. 17
Tovar Jalles, J. 95
Trichet, J. -C. 56
Trzcińska, A. 91, 122, 183
Tsipras, A. 51
Tusk, D. 141, 192–194
Tymanowski, J. 46

Van Nuffel, P. 16–17
Van Rompuy, H. 45, 84, 108–112, 114, 118, 141, 143
Verhey, L. 17, 18
von Bogdandy, A. 16–17

Waliszewski, K. 205
Walkowski, M. 50
Wasilewski, T. 17
Węc, J.J. 17–18, 21–22, 24–25, 29, 31, 35, 38–39, 43, 45–46, 65–66, 77, 83, 83–84, 88, 100, 103, 110–111, 113–114, 116, 119, 141, 166, 171, 178, 200, 204
Weidmann, J. 189
Weigert, B. 124
Weiss, H. 60
Wessels, W. 14, 31
Wojnicz, L. 178
Wojtaszczyk, K. 46
Wojtyna, A. 57
Wouters, J. 17–18
Woźnicki, T. 81
Wyplosz, Ch. 124
Wyrozumska, A. 17

Zachariasz, K. 102
Zielińska-Głębocka, A. 19
Zielińska, K. 124

Żołądkiewicz, K. 23
Żółciak, T. 73
Żukrowska, K. 33
Zürcher, B. 41

Studies in European Integration, State and Society

Edited by Magdalena Góra, Zdzisław Mach and Katarzyna Zielińska

Vol. 1 Józef Niżnik: Democracy versus Solidarity in the EU Discourse. 2012.

Vol. 2 Grzegorz Żuk: Europe in Polish Public Discourse. 2013.

Vol. 3 Zdzisław Mach (ed.): Local Community, Power and European Integration. 2017.

Vol. 4 Janusz Józef Węc: Germany's Position on the System Reform of the European Union in 2002–2016. 2018.

Vol. 5 Krzysztof Kowalski / Łucja Piekarska-Duraj / Barbara Törnquist-Plewa (eds.): Narrating Otherness in Poland and Sweden. European Heritage as a Discourse of Inclusion and Exclusion. 2019.

Vol. 6 Marek Aleksander Cichocki / Tomasz Grzegorz Grosse (eds.): The Many Faces of Crisis. An Analysis of Crisis Management from an Economic and Political Perspective. 2019.

Vol. 7 Marek Aleksander Cichocki (ed.): Contemporary States and the Crisis of the Western Order. 2019.

Vol. 8 Marta Kołodziejczyk: The Use of Technology for the Regulation of the European Union Immigration and Asylum Policy. 2020.

Vol. 9 Paweł Kubicki / Bożena Gierat-Bieroń / Joanna Orzechowska-Wacławska: The European Capital of Culture 2016 Effect. How the ECOC Competition Changed Polish Cities. 2020.

Vol. 10 Łucja Piekarska-Duraj: The Invisible Hand of Europe. The Museum as a Civilizing Tool. 2020.

Vol. 11 Milan Bufon / Tove H. Malloy / Colin H. Williams (eds.): Societies and Spaces in Contact. Between Convergence and Divergence. 2021.

Vol. 12 Elżbieta M. Mach / Grzegorz Pożarlik / Joanna Sondel-Cedarmas (eds.): Post-totalitarian Societes in Transformation. From Systemic Change into European Integration. 2022.

Edited by Zdzisław Mach and Bożena Gierat-Bieroń

Vol. 13 Emilia Moddelmog-Anweiler / Zdzisław Mach (eds.): Religion in the Public Sphere in Central and Eastern Europe. 2022.

Vol. 14 Janusz Józef Węc: The System Reform of the Economic and Monetary Union (2010-2022). Dynamics-Successes-Failures 2023.

www.peterlang.com

www.ingramcontent.com/pod-product-compliance
Ingram Content Group UK Ltd.
Pitfield, Milton Keynes, MK11 3LW, UK
UKHW041827100926
8556IPUK00002B/55

9 783631 896198